CHEAT SHEET

D1205107

☑ Progres[s]

Unit 1: Taking It from the Top

❏ Lesson 1-1: How Much Computer Do You Need?

❏ Lesson 1-2: How Much Software Do You Need?

❏ Lesson 1-3: How Much HTML Do You Really Need to Know?

Unit 2: Basic Design Considerations

❏ Lesson 2-1: Plain Old Text

❏ Lesson 2-2: The Graphical Web

❏ Lesson 2-3: The Lowdown on Links

❏ Lesson 2-4: Beyond the Basics

❏ Lesson 2-5: Other Design Considerations

Unit 3: HTML Basics

❏ Lesson 3-1: The Nuts and Bolts of HTML

❏ Lesson 3-2: Preserving Your Efforts

❏ Lesson 3-3: Check, Please!

Unit 4: HTML To Go

❏ Lesson 4-1: Getting a Better Title in Lieu of a Salary Increase

❏ Lesson 4-2: Giving Your Page Some Body (Text)

❏ Lesson 4-3: Getting Attention at the Head of the Class

❏ Lesson 4-4: Making the Link

Unit 5: Your Picture-Perfect Web Page

❏ Lesson 5-1: It's All in the Format

❏ Lesson 5-2: The Hunt for Good Art

❏ Lesson 5-3: Putting an Image on the Page

❏ Lesson 5-4: The Graphical Link

❏ Lesson 5-5: Cool GIF Tricks: Animations and Transparencies

❏ Lesson 5-6: The Lowdown on Backgrounds

Unit 6: Advanced HTML

❏ Lesson 6-1: A World Outside the Web

❏ Lesson 6-2: The Well-Formed Form

❏ Lesson 6-3: Laying the Data on a Table

❏ Lesson 6-4: You've Been Framed

❏ Lesson 6-5: Getting There with Image Maps

Web Page Software Comparison

Product	WYSIWYG	Tables	Captions	Image Maps	Site Management	Extra Tools
PageMill	Y	Y	Y	Y	N	Y
Home Page	Y	Y	N	Y	N	N
FrontPage	Y	Y	Y	Y	Y	Y
Web.Graphics Suite	Y	Y	N	Y	N	Y
HotDog Pro	N	Y	Y	P	N	N
MyInternetBusinessPage	Y	N	N	N	N	N
Fusion	Y	Y	N	Y	Y	N
Composer	Y	Y	Y	N	N	N
FrontPad (beta)	Y	P	P	P	N	N

Key: Y = full support, P = partial support, N = no support

The Kim Komando Dos and Don'ts of Web Page Design

DO make navigation of your site easy, easy, easy.

DO check your HTML code, and check your Web page with more than one type of browser.

DO add your page to all the different search engines.

DO put your e-mail address on your Web page.

DON'T use large images, which take a long time to download.

DO make sure your colors match, and make sure your background image and background color match.

DO keep your pages fresh by updating information often.

DON'T take yourself or your Web page too seriously.

Unit 7: The Pages are Alive with Multimedia

❏ Lesson 7-1: Why Multimedia? Why Not?
❏ Lesson 7-2: Let's Add Some Sound
❏ Lesson 7-3: Time for Some Action
❏ Lesson 7-4: Creating an Online Slide Show

Unit 8: Taking the Easy Way Out

❏ Lesson 8-1: What the Heck is this Lesson (WTHITL)?
❏ Lesson 8-2: Adobe PageMill
❏ Lesson 8-3: Claris Home Page
❏ Lesson 8-4: Microsoft FrontPage
❏ Lesson 8-5: Corel Web.Graphics Suite
❏ Lesson 8-6: Sausage Software HotDog Pro
❏ Lesson 8-7: MySoftware MyInternet-BusinessPage
❏ Lesson 8-8: NetObjects Fusion
❏ Lesson 8-9: Netscape Composer
❏ Lesson 8-10: Microsoft FrontPad
❏ Lesson 8-11: Getting by with a Little Help from Your Word Processor

Unit 9: Publishing with Online Services

❏ Lesson 9-1: Web Publishing with America Online
❏ Lesson 9-2: Web Publishing with CompuServe
❏ Lesson 9-3: Web Publishing with Prodigy
❏ Lesson 9-4: Web Publishing with The Microsoft Network

Unit 10: Getting Space on a Web Server

❏ Lesson 10-1: Exactly What is a Server, Anyway?
❏ Lesson 10-2: What's in a Domain Name?
❏ Lesson 10-3: What to Look for in an ISP

Unit 11: Exposing Your Site to the World (And Having People Browse It)

❏ Lesson 11-1: Putting FTP to Work
❏ Lesson 11-2: Making the Final Check
❏ Lesson 11-3: Doing Your Follow-Up Work

Basic HTML

HTML Tag	Function
<A HREF="filename.html"> </A>	Internal link
<A HREF="http://www.webpage.com"> </A>	External link
<A NAME="anchor"> </A>	Anchor
<B> </B>	Bold type
<BODY> </BODY>	Text
 	Line break
<HEAD> <TITLE> </TITLE> </HEAD>	Title bar
<HR>	Horizontal line
<I> </I>	Italic type
<P> </P>	Paragraph breaks

File Extensions

Extension	File type
.aif (for Windows)/ .aiffl (for Mac)	Audio Interchange files
.au	Web sound file
.avi	Windows AVI movies
.dcr	Shockwave multimedia
.gif	GIF images
.htm/.htm	HTML files
.jpg	JPEG images
.mov	QuickTime movies
.mpg/.mpeg	MPEG movies
.txt	Plain text file
.wav	WAVE sound files

Copyright © 1997 IDG Books Worldwide, Inc. All rights reserved. Cheat Sheet $2.95 value. Item 0163-1 For more information on IDG Books, call 1-800-762-2974

®

...FOR DUMMIES

COMPUTER BOOK SERIES FROM IDG

References for the Rest of Us! ®

Are you intimidated and confused by computers? Do you find that traditional manuals are overloaded with technical details you'll never use? Do your friends and family always call you to fix simple problems on their PCs? Then the *...For Dummies*® computer book series from IDG Books Worldwide is for you.

...For Dummies books are written for those frustrated computer users who know they aren't really dumb but find that PC hardware, software, and indeed the unique vocabulary of computing make them feel helpless. *...For Dummies* books use a lighthearted approach, a down-to-earth style, and even cartoons and humorous icons to diffuse computer novices' fears and build their confidence. Lighthearted but not lightweight, these books are a perfect survival guide for anyone forced to use a computer.

> *"I like my copy so much I told friends; now they bought copies."*
>
> **Irene C., Orwell, Ohio**

> *"Quick, concise, nontechnical, and humorous."*
>
> **Jay A., Elburn, Illinois**

> *"Thanks, I needed this book. Now I can sleep at night."*
>
> **Robin F., British Columbia, Canada**

Already, millions of satisfied readers agree. They have made *...For Dummies* books the #1 introductory level computer book series and have written asking for more. So, if you're looking for the most fun and easy way to learn about computers, look to *...For Dummies* books to give you a helping hand.

™

IDG BOOKS WORLDWIDE

5/97

DUMMIES 101®: CREATING WEB PAGES

by Kim Komando

Foreword by Barry Young

IDG Books Worldwide, Inc.
An International Data Group Company

Foster City, CA ✦ Chicago, IL ✦ Indianapolis, IN ✦ Southlake, TX

Dummies 101®: Creating Web Pages

Published by
IDG Books Worldwide, Inc.
An International Data Group Company
919 E. Hillsdale Blvd.
Suite 400
Foster City, CA 94404
http://www.idgbooks.com (IDG Books Worldwide Web site)
http://www.dummies.com (Dummies Press Web site)

Copyright © 1997 IDG Books Worldwide, Inc. All rights reserved. No part of this book, including interior design, cover design, and icons, may be reproduced or transmitted in any form, by any means (electronic, photocopying, recording, or otherwise) without the prior written permission of the publisher.

Library of Congress Catalog Card No.: 97-72421

ISBN: 0-7645-0163-1

Printed in the United States of America

10 9 8 7 6 5 4 3 2 1

1M/SW/QW/ZX/IN

Distributed in the United States by IDG Books Worldwide, Inc.

Distributed by Macmillan Canada for Canada; by Transworld Publishers Limited in the United Kingdom; by IDG Norge Books for Norway; by IDG Sweden Books for Sweden; by Woodslane Pty. Ltd. for Australia; by Woodslane Enterprises Ltd. for New Zealand; by Longman Singapore Publishers Ltd. for Singapore, Malaysia, Thailand, and Indonesia; by Simron Pty. Ltd. for South Africa; by Toppan Company Ltd. for Japan; by Distribuidora Cuspide for Argentina; by Livraria Cultura for Brazil; by Ediciencia S.A. for Ecuador; by Addison-Wesley Publishing Company for Korea; by Ediciones ZETA S.C.R. Ltda. for Peru; by WS Computer Publishing Corporation, Inc., for the Philippines; by Unalis Corporation for Taiwan; by Contemporanea de Ediciones for Venezuela; by Computer Book & Magazine Store for Puerto Rico; by Express Computer Distributors for the Caribbean and West Indies. Authorized Sales Agent: Anthony Rudkin Associates for the Middle East and North Africa.

For general information on IDG Books Worldwide's books in the U.S., please call our Consumer Customer Service department at 800-762-2974. For reseller information, including discounts and premium sales, please call our Reseller Customer Service department at 800-434-3422.

For information on where to purchase IDG Books Worldwide's books outside the U.S., please contact our International Sales department at 415-655-3200 or fax 415-655-3295.

For information on foreign language translations, please contact our Foreign & Subsidiary Rights department at 415-655-3021 or fax 415-655-3281.

For sales inquiries and special prices for bulk quantities, please contact our Sales department at 415-655-3200 or write to the address above.

For information on using IDG Books Worldwide's books in the classroom or for ordering examination copies, please contact our Educational Sales department at 800-434-2086 or fax 817-251-8174.

For press review copies, author interviews, or other publicity information, please contact our Public Relations department at 415-655-3000 or fax 415-655-3299.

For authorization to photocopy items for corporate, personal, or educational use, please contact Copyright Clearance Center, 222 Rosewood Drive, Danvers, MA 01923, or fax 508-750-4470.

LIMIT OF LIABILITY/DISCLAIMER OF WARRANTY: AUTHOR AND PUBLISHER HAVE USED THEIR BEST EFFORTS IN PREPARING THIS BOOK. IDG BOOKS WORLDWIDE, INC., AND AUTHOR MAKE NO REPRESENTATIONS OR WARRANTIES WITH RESPECT TO THE ACCURACY OR COMPLETENESS OF THE CONTENTS OF THIS BOOK AND SPECIFICALLY DISCLAIM ANY IMPLIED WARRANTIES OF MERCHANTABILITY OR FITNESS FOR A PARTICULAR PURPOSE. THERE ARE NO WARRANTIES WHICH EXTEND BEYOND THE DESCRIPTIONS CONTAINED IN THIS PARAGRAPH. NO WARRANTY MAY BE CREATED OR EXTENDED BY SALES REPRESENTATIVES OR WRITTEN SALES MATERIALS. THE ACCURACY AND COMPLETENESS OF THE INFORMATION PROVIDED HEREIN AND THE OPINIONS STATED HEREIN ARE NOT GUARANTEED OR WARRANTED TO PRODUCE ANY PARTICULAR RESULTS, AND THE ADVICE AND STRATEGIES CONTAINED HEREIN MAY NOT BE SUITABLE FOR EVERY INDIVIDUAL. NEITHER IDG BOOKS WORLDWIDE, INC., NOR AUTHOR SHALL BE LIABLE FOR ANY LOSS OF PROFIT OR ANY OTHER COMMERCIAL DAMAGES, INCLUDING BUT NOT LIMITED TO SPECIAL, INCIDENTAL, CONSEQUENTIAL, OR OTHER DAMAGES.

Trademarks: All brand names and product names used in this book are trade names, service marks, trademarks, or registered trademarks of their respective owners. IDG Books Worldwide is not associated with any product or vendor mentioned in this book.

 is a trademark under exclusive license to IDG Books Worldwide, Inc., from International Data Group, Inc.

About the Author

Computer technology is nothing new to Kim Komando. She was nine years old when she first sat at a computer; now *Information Week* calls her a "one-person PC industry." After earning a Bachelor of Science degree in Computer Systems from Arizona State University in 1985, a degree she financed by providing computer hardware and software training classes, Kim secured a position as a Marketing Representative with IBM. She then became a large business systems Account Manager at AT&T, where she received various awards for her sales achievements, and then moved to Unisys Corporation, where she single-handedly closed what was then the company's largest commercial deal — an $11 million sale to a Fortune 500 company in 1991.

Kim began writing her weekly syndicated newspaper computer column and hosting radio and television programs during her Unisys career. Her initial media success gave birth to The Komando Corporation, which now has worldwide ventures in the computer, media, and publishing industries through its divisions, Peak Interactive, Inc., and Komando Radio, the network radio and audio production company.

Today, you can visit Kim Komando's Komputer Klinic on America Online (keyword KOMANDO) or the Komputer Klinic on the Internet (`http://www.komando.com`). Maybe you read her weekly *Los Angeles Times* syndicated newspaper computer column or her regular editorial magazine features in *Computer Life, Continental Profiles, TWA Ambassador, Office Systems,* and *America West Airlines Magazine,* to name a few. It could be that you have referred to one of Kim's books — *401 Great Letters; 101 Komando Internet Tips, Tricks and Secrets; 1,001 Komputer Answers,* and her previous most recent book for IDG Books Worldwide, Inc., *CyberBuck$: Marketing Your Business and Products Online.*

On the weekends, Kim takes your calls on her top-rated syndicated network talk radio show heard on more than 160 talk radio stations throughout the U.S., Canada, and Australia. Turn on your TV and you can see Kim on FOX television as a computer expert correspondent. Shop at CompUSA, Egghead Software, Montgomery Ward's, Staples, or other notable chains and you can buy Komando Corporation software programs, CD-ROMs, audio tapes, or video tapes. On America Online, Kim and her staff are the service's "Personal Shopper," holding consumers' hands as they recommend products members buy and select to purchase on the service.

Kim was elected the most successful A.S.U. graduate (out of nearly 10,000 persons) for her graduating year and is listed in several issues of the prestigious Marquis *Who's Who* directory. Her expert opinion is frequently sought on air and in print, and she has been cited or interviewed by ABC, *The New York Times,* The *Chicago Tribune,* The New York *Daily News, The Washington Times, The Orlando Sentinel, Parade* magazine, *FamilyPC, Electronic Retailing, Mobile Office Computing, Home Office Computing, Entrepreneur, PC Computing, PC World,* and other national publications. She was also the official host of the television broadcast of COMDEX.

ABOUT IDG BOOKS WORLDWIDE

Welcome to the world of IDG Books Worldwide.

IDG Books Worldwide, Inc., is a subsidiary of International Data Group, the world's largest publisher of computer-related information and the leading global provider of information services on information technology. IDG was founded more than 25 years ago and now employs more than 8,500 people worldwide. IDG publishes more than 275 computer publications in over 75 countries (see listing below). More than 60 million people read one or more IDG publications each month.

Launched in 1990, IDG Books Worldwide is today the #1 publisher of best-selling computer books in the United States. We are proud to have received eight awards from the Computer Press Association in recognition of editorial excellence and three from *Computer Currents'* First Annual Readers' Choice Awards. Our best-selling *...For Dummies®* series has more than 30 million copies in print with translations in 30 languages. IDG Books Worldwide, through a joint venture with IDG's Hi-Tech Beijing, became the first U.S. publisher to publish a computer book in the People's Republic of China. In record time, IDG Books Worldwide has become the first choice for millions of readers around the world who want to learn how to better manage their businesses.

Our mission is simple: Every one of our books is designed to bring extra value and skill-building instructions to the reader. Our books are written by experts who understand and care about our readers. The knowledge base of our editorial staff comes from years of experience in publishing, education, and journalism — experience we use to produce books for the '90s. In short, we care about books, so we attract the best people. We devote special attention to details such as audience, interior design, use of icons, and illustrations. And because we use an efficient process of authoring, editing, and desktop publishing our books electronically, we can spend more time ensuring superior content and spend less time on the technicalities of making books.

You can count on our commitment to deliver high-quality books at competitive prices on topics you want to read about. At IDG Books Worldwide, we continue in the IDG tradition of delivering quality for more than 25 years. You'll find no better book on a subject than one from IDG Books Worldwide.

John Kilcullen
CEO
IDG Books Worldwide, Inc.

Steven Berkowitz
President and Publisher
IDG Books Worldwide, Inc.

Eighth Annual
Computer Press
Awards ≥1992

WINNER
Ninth Annual
Computer Press
Awards ≥1993

WINNER
Tenth Annual
Computer Press
Awards ≥1994

Eleventh Annual
Computer Press
Awards ≥1995

IDG Books Worldwide, Inc., is a subsidiary of International Data Group, the world's largest publisher of computer-related information and the leading global provider of information services on information technology. International Data Group publishes over 275 computer publications in over 75 countries. Sixty million people read one or more International Data Group publications each month. International Data Group's publications include: **ARGENTINA:** Buyer's Guide, Computerworld Argentina, PC World Argentina; **AUSTRALIA:** Australian Macworld, Australian PC World, Australian Reseller News, Computerworld, IT Casebook, Network World, Publish, Webmaster; **AUSTRIA:** Computerwelt Osterreich, Networks Austria, PC Tip Austria; **BANGLADESH:** PC World Bangladesh; **BELARUS:** PC World Belarus; **BELGIUM:** Data News; **BRAZIL:** Annuário de Informática, Computerworld, Connections, Macworld, PC Player, PC World, Publish, Reseller News, Supergamepower; **BULGARIA:** Computerworld Bulgaria, Network World Bulgaria, PC & MacWorld Bulgaria; **CANADA:** CIO Canada, Client/Server World, ComputerWorld Canada, InfoWorld Canada, NetworkWorld Canada, WebWorld; **CHILE:** Computerworld Chile, PC World Chile; **COLOMBIA:** Computerworld Colombia, PC World Colombia; **COSTA RICA:** PC World Centro America; **THE CZECH AND SLOVAK REPUBLICS:** Computerworld Czechoslovakia, Macworld Czech Republic, PC World Czechoslovakia; **DENMARK:** Communications World Danmark, Computerworld Danmark, Macworld Danmark, PC World Danmark, Techworld Denmark; **DOMINICAN REPUBLIC:** PC World Republica Dominicana; **ECUADOR:** PC World Ecuador; **EGYPT:** Computerworld Middle East, PC World Middle East; **EL SALVADOR:** PC World Centro America; **FINLAND:** MikroPC, Tietoverkko, Tietoviikko; **FRANCE:** Distributique, Hebdo, Info PC, Le Monde Informatique, Macworld, Reseaux & Telecoms, WebMaster France; **GERMANY:** Computer Partner, Computerwoche, Computerwoche Extra, Computerwoche FOCUS, Global Online, Macwelt, PC Welt; **GREECE:** Amiga Computing, GamePro Greece, Multimedia World; **GUATEMALA:** PC World Centro America; **HONDURAS:** PC World Centro America; **HONG KONG:** Computerworld Hong Kong, PC World Hong Kong, Publish in Asia; **HUNGARY:** ABCD CD-ROM, Computerworld Szamitastechnika, Internetto online Magazine, PC World Hungary, PC-X Magazin Hungary; **ICELAND:** Tolvuheimur PC World Island; **INDIA:** Information Communications World, Information Systems Computerworld, PC World India, Publish in Asia; **INDONESIA:** InfoKomputer PC World, Komputek Computerworld, Publish in Asia; **IRELAND:** ComputerScope, PC Live!; **ISRAEL:** Macworld Israel, People & Computers/Computerworld; **ITALY:** Computerworld Italia, Macworld Italia, Networking Italia, PC World Italia; **JAPAN:** DTP World, Macworld Japan, Nikkei Personal Computing, OS/2 World Japan, SunWorld Japan, Windows NT World, Windows World Japan; **KENYA:** PC World East African; **KOREA:** Hi-Tech Information, Macworld Korea, PC World Korea; **MACEDONIA:** PC World Macedonia; **MALAYSIA:** Computerworld Malaysia, PC World Malaysia, Publish in Asia; **MALTA:** PC World Malta; **MEXICO:** Computerworld Mexico, PC World Mexico; **MYANMAR:** PC World Myanmar; **NETHERLANDS:** Computer! Totaal, LAN Internetworking Magazine, LAN World Buyers Guide, Macworld Netherlands, Net, WebWereld; **NEW ZEALAND:** Absolute Beginners Guide and Plain & Simple Series, Computer Buyer, Computer Industry Directory, Computerworld New Zealand, MTB, Network World, PC World New Zealand; **NICARAGUA:** PC World Centro America; **NORWAY:** Computerworld Norge, CW Rapport, Datamagasinet, Financial Rapport, Kursguide Norge, Macworld Norge, Multimediaworld Norge, PC World Ekspress Norge, PC World Nettverk, PC World Norge, PC World ProduktGuide Norge; **PAKISTAN:** Computerworld Pakistan; **PANAMA:** PC World Panama; **PEOPLE'S REPUBLIC OF CHINA:** China Computer Users, China Computerworld, China InfoWorld, China Telecom World Weekly, Computer & Communication, Electronic Design China, Electronics Today, Electronics Weekly, Game Software, PC World China, Popular Computer Week, Software Weekly, Software World, Telecom World; **PERU:** Computerworld Peru, PC World Profesional Peru, PC World SoHo Peru; **PHILIPPINES:** Click!, Computerworld Philippines, PC World Philippines, Publish in Asia; **POLAND:** Computerworld Poland, Computerworld Special Report Poland, Cyber, Macworld Poland, Networld Poland, PC World Komputer; **PORTUGAL:** Cerebro/PC World, Computerworld/Correio Informático, Dealer World Portugal, Mac*In/PC*In Portugal, Multimedia World; **PUERTO RICO:** PC World Puerto Rico; **ROMANIA:** Computerworld Romania, PC World Romania, Telecom Romania; **RUSSIA:** Computerworld Russia, Mir PK, Publish, Seti; **SINGAPORE:** Computerworld Singapore, PC World Singapore, Publish in Asia; **SLOVENIA:** Monitor; **SOUTH AFRICA:** Computing SA, Network World SA, Software World SA; **SPAIN:** Communicaciones World España, Computerworld España, Dealer World España, Macworld España, PC World España; **SRI LANKA:** Infolink PC World; **SWEDEN:** CAP&Design, Computer Sweden, Corporate Computing Sweden, Internetworld Sweden, it.branschen, Macworld Sweden, MaxiData Sweden, MikroDatorn, Nätverk & Kommunikation, PC World Sweden, PCaktiv, Windows World Sweden; **SWITZERLAND:** Computerworld Schweiz, Macworld Schweiz, PCtip; **TAIWAN:** Computerworld Taiwan, Macworld Taiwan, NEW ViSiON/Publish, PC World Taiwan, Windows World Taiwan; **THAILAND:** Publish in Asia, Thai Computerworld; **TURKEY:** Computerworld Turkiye, Macworld Turkiye, Network World Turkiye, PC World Turkiye; **UKRAINE:** Computerworld Kiev, Multimedia World Ukraine, PC World Ukraine; **UNITED KINGDOM:** Acorn User UK, Amiga Action UK, Amiga Computing UK, Apple Talk UK, Computing, Macworld, Parents and Computers UK, PC Advisor, PC Home, PSX Pro, The WEB; **UNITED STATES:** Cable in the Classroom, CIO Magazine, Computerworld, DOS World, Federal Computer Week, GamePro Magazine, InfoWorld, I-Way, Macworld, Network World, PC Games, PC World, Publish, Video Event, THE WEB Magazine, and WebMaster; online webzines: JavaWorld, NetscapeWorld, and SunWorld Online; **URUGUAY:** InfoWorld Uruguay; **VENEZUELA:** Computerworld Venezuela, PC World Venezuela; and **VIETNAM:** PC World Vietnam.   3/24/97

Dedication

To Mom and Dad. Because of them, I'm not a dummy.

Author's Acknowledgments

Here's the place I get to thank all the people that made this book possible. (Doing so is one of those book-publishing rituals, like just when you finally figure out how to use Microsoft Word's revision features, you've typed your last page.)

First, I'd like to thank Radical Rev "them up" Mengle for his masterful editing that left most of my sick, but very funny, humor in this book and for understanding when it was a bad day to talk about rewrites. Patricia "Pounce on the author" Pan worked her magic editing the text, while Killer Kevin Spencer worked his magic on the CD. Jumping Joyce Pepple and Marvelous Mary Bednarek are cool chicks (is that politically correct?) who saw through the legal and tedious details. Slews of other people at IDG also helped with this book. Their names are forever endeared and remembered on the next page.

Oh, but wait, more people are behind this great tome. Helping me out was Joanne "Get it Done" Robb, John "Got it done" San Filippo, Dino "Funny Man" Londis, and my staff, family, and friends who dealt with me when I was on deadline while running two corporations, hosting a national talk radio show, doing deals, writing a handful of feature magazine articles, and trying to remodel my home simultaneously.

And special personal thanks go to my mom and dear friend Barry Young. Now, go get me a drink with a little umbrella in it.

Publisher's Acknowledgments

We're proud of this book; please send us your comments about it by using the IDG Books Worldwide Registration Card at the back of the book or by e-mailing us at feedback/dummies@idgbooks.com. Some of the people who helped bring this book to market include the following:

Acquisitions, Development, and Editorial

Project Editor: Rev Mengle

Acquisitions Editor: Gareth Hancock

Product Development Director: Mary Bednarek

Media Development Manager: Joyce Pepple

Associate Permissions Editor: Heather H. Dismore

Copy Editor: Patricia Pan

Technical Editor: David Medinets

Editorial Manager: Seta K. Frantz

Editorial Assistant: Chris H. Collins

Production

Associate Project Coordinator: E. Shawn Aylsworth

Layout and Graphics: Cameron Booker, Linda Boyer, Angela F. Hunckler, Drew R. Moore, Mark C. Owens, Brent Savage

Proofreaders: Laura L. Bowman, Christine Berman, Joel K. Draper, Robert Springer, Karen York

Indexer: Sherry Massey

Special Help: Access Technology, CD-ROM Interface and Design; Kevin Spencer, Associate Technical Editor; Stephanie Koutek, Proof Editor; Diane Giangrossi, Associate Editor/Quality Control

---

General and Administrative

IDG Books Worldwide, Inc.: John Kilcullen, CEO; Steven Berkowitz, President and Publisher

IDG Books Technology Publishing: Brenda McLaughlin, Senior Vice President and Group Publisher

Dummies Technology Press and Dummies Editorial: Diane Graves Steele, Vice President and Associate Publisher; Judith A. Taylor, Product Marketing Manager; Kristin A. Cocks, Editorial Director

Dummies Trade Press: Kathleen A. Welton, Vice President and Publisher

IDG Books Production for Dummies Press: Beth Jenkins, Production Director; Cindy L. Phipps, Supervisor of Project Coordination, Production Proofreading, and Indexing; Kathie S. Schutte, Supervisor of Page Layout; Shelley Lea, Supervisor of Graphics and Design; Debbie J. Gates, Production Systems Specialist; Tony Augsburger, Supervisor of Reprints and Bluelines; Leslie Popplewell, Media Archive Coordinator

Dummies Packaging and Book Design: Patti Sandez, Packaging Specialist; Lance Kayser, Packaging Assistant; Kavish + Kavish, Cover Design

♦

The publisher would like to give special thanks to Patrick J. McGovern, without whom this book would not have been possible.

♦

Contents
ABC 123 **at a Glance**

Introduction 1

Part I: And Then There Was Light... 11
Unit 1: Taking It from the Top 13
Unit 2: Basic Design Considerations 21

Part II: Creating Your Page 37
Unit 3: HTML Basics 39
Unit 4: HTML To Go 49

Part III: Getting Fancy 75
Unit 5: Your Picture-Perfect Web Page 77
Unit 6: Advanced HTML 93
Unit 7: The Pages are Alive with Multimedia 121

Part IV: So Advanced, It's Simple! 139
Unit 8: (Got a Good Reason for) Taking the Easy Way Out 141
Unit 9: Web Publishing with Online Services 175

Part V: The Big Payoff: Getting Your Page Online 197
Unit 10: Getting Space on a Web Server 199
Unit 11: Exposing Your Site to the World (And Having People Browse It) 217

Part VI: Appendixes 239
Appendix A: A Sampling of ISP Prices 241
Appendix B: Answers 245
Appendix C: About the CD 249

Index 259

Licensing Agreement 270

Installation Instructions 272

IDG Books Worldwide Registration Card ....Back of Book

Files at a Glance

The files on the CD can be grouped into three categories: a Webstuff folder of example files and files you can use with the lessons in this book; a Webimgs folder of background samples that you can use on your Web page; and various individual programs, which get installed into their own folders, depending on your computer. Here's a listing of all of the files on the CD, and where in the book they are first mentioned. For installation instructions, see Appendix C.

Lesson 3-1: The Nuts and Bolts of HTML .... BBEdit, HotDog

Lesson 4-1: Getting a Better Title in Lieu of a Salary Increase .... RGB Color Box

Lesson 4-2: Giving Your Page Some Body (Text).......................... Breaks.htm, Text.htm, Type.htm, Lists.htm

Lesson 4-3: Getting Attention at the Head of the Class .... Headings.htm, Horzrule.htm, Info.htm, Index.htm, Links.htm, Download.htm

Lesson 5-1: It's All in the Format .... Paint Shop Pro, GraphicConverter

Lesson 5-3: Putting an Image on the Page .... Image.gif, Image.htm

Lesson 5-4: The Graphical Link Image2.htm, Page2.htm

Lesson 5-5: Cool GIF Tricks: Animations and Transparencies .... GIFWeb

Lesson 5-6: The Lowdown on Backgrounds .... Webimgs folder, Backgrnd.htm

Lesson 6-1: A World Outside the Web.. Email.htm, FTP.htm, Gopher.htm, Newsgrp.htm

Lesson 6-2: The Well-Formed Form .... Form.htm

Lesson 6-3: Laying the Data on a Table .... Tables.htm

Lesson 6-4: You've Been Framed .... Index.htm, Test1.htm, Test2.htm

Lesson 6-5: Getting There with Image Maps .... LiveImage, ImageMapper

Lesson 7-2: Let's Add Some Sound.. Sound.wav

Lesson 7-3: Time for Some Action.. Qt.mov, Quiktime.htm

Lesson 7-4: Creating an Online Slide Show................................... Slide1.htm, Slide1.gif, Slide2.htm, Slide2.gif, Slide 3.htm, Slide3.gif, Slide.wav

Lesson 9-3: Web Publishing with Prodigy .... WS_FTP, Anarchie

Table of Contents

Introduction 1

Part I: And Then There Was Light... 11
  Unit 1: Taking It from the Top 13
    Lesson 1-1: How Much Computer Do You Need? 14
      How much computer is too much? 14
      Making the connection 15
    Lesson 1-2: How Much Software Do You Need? 17
    Lesson 1-3: How Much HTML Do You Really Need to Know? 19
    Unit 1 Quiz 19
    Unit 1 Exercise 20
  Unit 2: Basic Design Considerations 21
    Lesson 2-1: Plain Old Text 22
    Lesson 2-2: The Graphical Web 24
      Designing with graphics 24
      Rules for rules 25
      Click here 25
    Lesson 2-3: The Lowdown on Links 26
    Lesson 2-4: Beyond the Basics 26
      Frames, forms, and tables 26
      Plugging in 28
    Lesson 2-5: Other Design Considerations 29
      Content essentials 29
      Looking good 30
      The darker side of the Web 31
    Unit 2 Quiz 31
    Unit 2 Exercise 32
    Part I Review 33
    Part I Test 34
    Lab Assignment 36
      Step 1. Review your Web page outline 36
      Step 2: Compare with an existing Web page Compare with an existing Web page 36
      Step 3: Improve your Web page outline 36

Part II: Creating Your Page **37**

  Unit 3: HTML Basics **39**

    Lesson 3-1: The Nuts and Bolts of HTML 40
      Tag — you're it! 40
      Your first HTML code 41
      Checking up on your neighbor 41
    Lesson 3-2: Preserving Your Efforts 42
      The right format is everything 42
      Naming your files 43
    Lesson 3-3: Check, Please! 45
    Unit 3 Quiz 47
    Unit 3 Exercise 48

  Unit 4: HTML To Go **49**

    Lesson 4-1: Getting a Better Title in Lieu of a Salary Increase 50
      Playing the title role with the <TITLE> tag 50
      Coloring your text and life 51
    Lesson 4-2: Giving Your Page Some Body (Text) 53
      Line breaks 54
      Paragraph breaks 55
      Bold (but not necessarily courageous) type 56
      Italic type 56
      Blinking type 57
      Monospaced type 57
      Indents 58
      Lists 58
    Lesson 4-3: Getting Attention at the Head of the Class 60
      Headings 60
      Horizontal line (the shortest distance to my point) 62
    Lesson 4-4: Making the Link 63
      Internal links 64
      External links 66
      Missing links 66
      Anchors aweigh! 67
      Downloadable files 68
    Unit 4 Quiz 69
    Unit 4 Exercise 70
    Part II Review 71
    Part II Test 72
    Part II Lab Assignment 74
      Step 1: Find a good Web page 74
      Step 2: Look for coded elements 74
      Step 3: Try to figure out the HTML code behind those elements 74
      Step 4: Look at the actual code used 74

Part III: Getting Fancy **75**

  Unit 5: Your Picture-Perfect Web Page **77**

    Lesson 5-1: It's All in the Format 77
    Lesson 5-2: The Hunt for Good Art 79
      The do-it-yourself approach 79
      In search of graphics 81
    Lesson 5-3: Putting an Image on the Page 82
    Lesson 5-4: The Graphical Link 85
    Lesson 5-5: Cool GIF Tricks: Animations and Transparencies 87

Lesson 5-6: The Lowdown on Backgrounds 88
Unit 5 Quiz 90
Unit 5 Exercises 92
Unit 6: Advanced HTML **93**
Lesson 6-1: A World Outside the Web 94
Automatic e-mail 94
Files galore (or a James Bond girl who never was) 96
Looking for Gopher holes 98
All the news that's fit to report and lots of stuff you wouldn't care to read 100
Lesson 6-2: The Well-Formed Form 101
The FORM tag 102
Creating a form 102
Lesson 6-3: Laying the Data on the Table 107
Creating a basic table 107
Simple table formatting 109
Simple cell formatting 111
Lesson 6-4: You've Been Framed 113
Frame attributes 115
Frames and links 116
Lesson 6-5: Getting There with Image Maps 117
Unit 6 Quiz 118
Unit 6 Exercise 120
Unit 7: The Pages are Alive with Multimedia **121**
Lesson 7-1: Why Multimedia? Why Not? 122
Playing devil's advocate 122
I scream for multimedia 124
Lesson 7-2: Let's Add Some Sound 125
The simple linked sound 125
How about some mood music? 126
Lesson 7-3: Time for Some Action 127
Lesson 7-4: Creating an Online Slide Show 130
Unit 7 Quiz 133
Unit 7 Exercise 134
Part III Review 135
Part III Test 136
Part III Lab Assignment 138
Step 1: Return to that good-looking Web page 138
Step 2: Identify more coded elements 138
Step 3: Try to re-create that HTML code 138
Step 4: Grade yourself 138
Part IV: So Advanced, It's Simple! **139**
Unit 8: (Got a Good Reason for) Taking the Easy Way Out **141**
Lesson 8-1: What the Heck Is in This Lesson? (WTHIITL) 142
Lesson 8-2: Adobe PageMill 144
PageMill: What's hot and what's not 144
PageMill: The sample page 146
Lesson 8-3: Claris Home Page 148
Home Page: What's hot and what's not 149
Home Page: The sample page 149
Lesson 8-4: Microsoft FrontPage 151
FrontPage: What's hot and what's not 151
FrontPage: The sample page 152

Lesson 8-5: Corel Web.Graphics Suite 154
  Web.Graphics Suite: What's hot and what's not 154
  Web.Graphics Suite: The sample page 155
Lesson 8-6: Sausage Software HotDog Pro 158
  HotDog Pro: What's hot dog and what's not 158
  HotDog Pro: The sample page 158
Lesson 8-7: MySoftware MyInternetBusinessPage 160
  MyInternetBusinessPage: What's hot and what's not 160
  MyInternetBusinessPage: The sample page 161
Lesson 8-8: NetObjects Fusion 163
  Fusion: What's hot and what's not 163
  Fusion: The sample page 163
Lesson 8-9: Netscape Composer 165
  Composer: What's hot and what's not 166
  Composer: The sample page 166
Lesson 8-10: Microsoft FrontPad 167
  FrontPad: What's hot and what's not 168
  FrontPad: The sample page 168
Lesson 8-11: Getting by with a Little Help from Your Word Processor 170
  WordPerfect version 7 170
  Microsoft Word 97 170
Unit 8 Quiz 171
Unit 8 Exercise 172

Unit 9: Web Publishing with Online Services **173**
Lesson 9-1: Web Publishing with America Online 176
  Easy Web publishing with Personal Publisher 176
  Other AOL Web publishing options 179
Lesson 9-2: Web Publishing with CompuServe 181
Lesson 9-3: Web Publishing with Prodigy 185
Lesson 9-4: Web Publishing on The Microsoft Network 187
Lesson 9-5: One More Online Tool — from Me 188
Unit 9 Quiz 190
Unit 9 Exercise 191
Part IV Review 193
Part IV Test 194
Part IV Lab Assignment 196
  Step 1: Use the program to go through the Unit 8 steps 196
  Step 2: Sit back and contemplate your work 196
  Step 1: Open your standard Lab Assignment Web page 196
  Step 2: Use the online tools to design that same exact page 196

Part V: The Big Payoff: Getting Your Page Online **197**
Unit 10: Getting Space on a Web Server **199**
Lesson 10-1: Exactly What Is a Server, Anyway? 200
  Phone line fun 200
  Battling traffic jams 201
  You and your server 202
Lesson 10-2: What's in a Domain Name? 203
  So what? 203
  Just in the InterNIC of time 204
  Using your domain name 208

Lesson 10-3: What to Look for in an ISP 209

Serving up your Web site 210

Pricing and terms 212

The extras 213

Unit 10 Quiz 214

Unit 10 Exercise 216

Unit 11: Exposing Your Site to the World (And Having People Browse It) **217**

Lesson 11-1: Putting FTP to Work 218

Lesson 11-2: Making the Final Check 222

When I enter my Web address, all I see is a list of files 223

The Web page loads, but the graphics don't load 223

My skin's become pale, I recoil at sunlight, and I don't know what day it is 223

My Web browser can't locate the page that a link is supposed to lead to 224

And the triple check 225

Lesson 11-3: Doing Your Follow-Up Work 226

Unit 11 Quiz 232

Unit 11 Exercise 234

Part V Review 235

Part V Test 237

Part V Lab Assignment 238

Step 1: Look for mistakes on Web pages 238

Step 2: Check your site for mistakes 238

Part VI: Appendixes **239**

Appendix A: A Sampling of ISP Prices **241**

Appendix B: Answers **245**

Appendix C: About the CD **249**

System Requirements 249

Putting the CD Files on Your Hard Drive 250

Installing the exercise files in Windows 250

Installing the exercise files on a Mac OS computer 252

Removing the exercise files 252

Removing CD icons from Windows 253

Installing the Windows programs from the CD 254

Removing Windows programs from your PC 254

Installing and removing Mac OS programs 255

Extra Stuff 256

If You've Got Problems (Of the CD Kind) 257

Index **259**

Licensing Agreement **270**

Installation Instructions **272**

IDG Books Worldwide Registration Card .... **Back of Book**

Foreword

I admit it. I've reached the point where I am not only on the Internet every day but have come to completely depend on my computer for communicating, writing, keeping my checkbook balanced, and generally keeping tabs on just about everything.

Unfortunately, I am a "tinkerer." I am constantly "tweaking" my computer to get it to work better and faster. The problem is that on some occasions, my simple desire to make the darn thing faster ends up causing

A. a system crash

B. a PC that will not boot up

C. mass panic and mild hysteria in my office

D. all of the above

More often than not, following a few hours of begging and pouting from me, Kim Komando has come to my office and, within minutes, resuscitated my machine through some secret ritual known only to her and a few guys who wear pocket protectors and their pants one inch too short.

So I wasn't really surprised when I was asked to write this foreword. It is the least I could do to repay Kim for coming to my rescue time after time. In recent months, however, Kim has urged me (in the strongest of language) to stop tinkering so much, as her schedule would not allow her to drop by so often just to "fix" things.

As a result, I have come to rely on Kim's books. In fact, I believe that many of her books were written primarily for my benefit. Kim's books prove that she has great insight on many of the problems that hit your computer like a bolt of lightning from out of the blue. As you can see, I believe in avoiding clichés like the plague.

Each week during her live, nationally syndicated radio talk show, I marvel at the depth of Kim's knowledge about the technical aspects of computers, the Internet, the incomprehensible number of software offerings available, and the general state and future of the computer industry itself. As a result of her radio program, e-mail arrives at our office from all over the country. People trust Kim to help them, to guide them along the way to better understanding and enjoying the use of their PCs.

In this book (as in all her others), you'll find clear, concise answers, explanations, shortcuts, and reminders. In short order, you too can design and create Web pages that will attract and entertain millions.

And if you don't believe me, just take a look at Kim's Web pages (http://www.komando.com) and see for yourself. It's no wonder that Information Week called Kim Komando "a one-person PC industry" and her fans refer to her as the "Digital Goddess."

Barry Young

Barry Young is founder and president of WestStar TalkRadio Network. He has produced a number of nationally syndicated radio programs, including The Kim Komando Show (now heard live via satellite on over 165 stations across the USA, Canada, and Australia). Mr. Young has been in the broadcasting industry over for 30 years and lives in Scottsdale, Arizona. He has a Web page, too. It's http://www.weststar.com.

Introduction

Welcome to *Dummies 101: Creating Web Pages*, and warm greetings from the World Wide Web.

Just by virtue of the fact that you're reading this book and you were smart enough to buy it (if you are reading this book now in the store, just buy it! But if you don't, try not to bend the spine), I have to assume that you know a little something about the Internet and the World Wide Web. The only problem is that I don't know exactly how much you know. So, just to make sure that everybody starts on the same page (pun clearly intended), I'm going to take a few minutes of your time in this Introduction to tell you about some basic Internet stuff. If you know this already, click here. (Sorry, force of habit. You can't link in a book.)

Even if you think you know it all, you may want to hang in there and read the Introduction because I'll give you some tips on how the book is structured. And, hey, I may even have a few tips up my sleeve that you didn't know about that can change your life.

What is the Internet?

The history part is where all Internet-related books seem to begin, so I can't let you skip the subject. But I promise I won't bore you to death. I don't think you really need to know every historical fact about the Internet just to create a Web page. If you're really interested in that sort of thing, plenty of other books fill the bill quite nicely. (Of course, if you buy a book just to learn the history of the Internet, you're wasting your money. Everything you could possibly want to know about the 'Net is available online, so you can be bored to death for free!)

So just what do you need to know about the Internet to be a successful Web publisher? Basically, you need to know what the Internet is today. I'm going to do this in one breath.

Stated in the simplest terms, the Internet is just a giant network of millions of interconnected computers. But the Internet is very different from the *local area network* (LAN) you may be used to at work. In a small network like a LAN, all the computers depend on each other somewhat for various things (kind of like kids are dependent on parents, the government is dependent on our tax money, and bosses are dependent on their staff to make them look good). One of the key ideas behind the Internet is that the computers aren't really dependent on each other — all the millions of computers are linked together just to exchange information.

All types of computers are connected to the Internet. Most major colleges and universities, as well as many large companies, have connections right into what's called the Internet *backbone*, the worldwide series of major junction points that ties the whole thing together. The computers of people like you and me are connected to the Internet through an *Internet Service Provider* (ISP). Your ISP may be connected to another, bigger ISP, or possibly directly to the backbone. And finally, millions of people have Internet access through commercial online services such as America Online or CompuServe.

This all adds up to millions and millions of people communicating over the Internet day in and day out. The Internet is populated by scholars and con artists, intellectuals and idiots, lovers and fighters — in short, it's full of the same people you're likely to meet walking down a busy city street on any given day, although that would be one heck of a street.

Whew, I did it.

What is a Web Page?

"Oh, what a tangled Web page we weave."

—William Shakespage

Believe it or not, the Internet and its early ancestors crept along for more than 30 years based only on textual information. The Internet had *e-mail* for sending text-based information to specific individuals. The Internet had *Gopher* for creating openly available archives of text-based data. The Internet had text-based *FTP* (File Transfer Protocol) programs for uploading and downloading program files. But not a single graphic could be found on the Internet.

Then along came the World Wide Web. The Web — as it's fondly referred to by people in the know, which you now are — is based on a rather old concept called *hypertext*. You've probably never thought about it, but when you buy a book, you're pretty much forced to extract the information in the book in a linear manner. You begin at the beginning and end at the end. Sure, maybe you're more creative — you do some jumping around or you read the last page first to make sure the bad guy gets it in the end (that's what happens in this book). Or maybe the book includes cross-references, so you're flipping pages back and forth. But in general, the physical design of a book, any book, makes it more suited for a linear read.

On the other hand, a computer doesn't force you to put information in any particular order. The idea behind hypertext is that you can arrange information in a nonlinear way so that you have access to the information you need the moment you need it. For example, if you're reading a biography on Abraham Lincoln, perhaps you'll want to take a quick detour to the Lincoln Memorial. If you are reading a book, chances are you'll have to go find another book to find what you want. But a hypertext document on your computer may offer a direct *link* to another hypertext document that discusses the Lincoln Memorial. When you've read all you want about the related subject on the Web, you can pop right back to where you started.

The World Wide Web basically brings the concept of hypertext to the Internet, allowing mouse-clickable links from any one document to any other document on the entire Web. This is incredible stuff, like being able to have the fat sucked out of your thighs rather then exercising it off. I'm sure there are hundreds of Web sites devoted to that. Anyway, the Web brings one more important element to the Internet: graphics. For the first time ever, the Web lets people on the Internet present information in a graphical format. (That way folks can see your before and after pictures.)

These capabilities are all made possible through a set of special codes collectively known as the *Hypertext Markup Language*, or *HTML*. Using HTML codes, you can "mark up" plain text files to give them different display attributes when you view them through a *Web browser* like Netscape Navigator or Microsoft Internet Explorer. For example, you can add HTML codes that tell your Web browser to center a particular line of text, like a title, on your computer screen. I can hear those sirens going off in your head. They're warning you: "Wait a minute — that sounds like programming." Well, don't turn tail and flee yet. I admit it: HTML *is* programming, but HTML is easy. I promise. And with a lot of the programs I talk about later in the book, you don't even have to bother with programming HTML at all.

In the early stages of the Web, graphics were limited to simple, still pictures. But as more people flocked to the Web, some brilliant programmers around the world figured out ways to incorporate sound, animation, video, and all sorts of other goodies. With all that action added, the Web became what it is today — a true multimedia experience.

Ah, but the original question was: What is a Web *page*? A Web page is a single World Wide Web document. You can create a Web page that contains just about anything you want and that will be your own little corner of the Internet. When you place your Web page on a *server* (a computer designed to hold and allow access to Web pages) the entire world can see the fruit of your Web efforts. So make sure the fruit of your Web efforts isn't a lemon. If you have more information than will practically fit on a Web page, you can organize a collection of Web pages into a Web *site*, with appropriate hypertext links that let your site visitors navigate from page to page.

Anatomy of a Web Address

Before we move on, let me take a moment to dissect a Web address so that you understand all the different parts. The technical name for a Web address is *Uniform Resource Locator,* or URL. (You pronounce it by saying each letter by itself, not all squished together like *earl.*) Here's what a URL looks like.

```
http://www.komando.com/abtkk/staff
```

No, it's not alphabet soup. There's actually a method to all this. Here's how the Web address breaks down.

- **http://**: The *http* stands for HyperText Transfer Protocol, which is the standard method used to transport Web documents over the Internet. Virtually all Web addresses start with this. Note that the slashes are regular slashes, not the backslashes you may be familiar with from your DOS days.

- **www.komando.com**: This part of the address is called the domain name. You can pay to have your own domain name registered with the Internet powers-that-be, just like I did. Or if you don't pay, this particular part of your own Web address includes your ISP's domain name.

- **/abtkk**: This indicates a subdirectory or subfolder, on the Web server. In this case, it's the file on my server that is about my Komputer Klinic. Remember that your little piece of Web space is just a spot on your ISP's hard drive. From there, you can create subdirectories just as you would on your own computer.

- **/staff**: This is the name of the actual HTML file to which this Web address points. (Sometimes you see these files with the *.htm* or *.html* extension.) The terms *HTML file* and *Web page* are almost interchangeable. When you talk about it as a file sitting on a computer system somewhere, *HTML file* and *HTML document* are more commonly used. However, when you talk about it as page of information displayed through a Web browser, it's more common to call this beast a Web page.

Why Would You Want Your Own Web Page?

Because you can! Because it's there! This really is the million-dollar question. I could say, "You tell me!" You'd probably think I was being rude, but really, the question isn't far from the mark. When you get right down to it, there are as many reasons that exist for creating a Web page as there are Web pages. Each person's motivation is a little different.

The Web is all about publishing information, which is all about making some sort of contact with other people. There's no point in putting out information if you don't think anyone will read it. Why bother? So the first thing you should think about is exactly who you want to reach with your Web page, and why you want to reach them.

I have to believe that, because you're reading this book, you already have some little inkling of an idea of what you want on your Web page. No, no, don't tell me. First, start firming up your plans. For the most part, your Web page should fit into one of the three basic categories I'm about to describe.

Let's get personal

The World Wide Web allows anyone on the planet to be an exhibitionist of sorts. No, I don't mean you have to show the world all the wrinkles and rolls on your body — though no one would stop you if you wanted to post a picture of yourself on your Web site. What I mean is that the Web lets you showcase what's going on inside your head.

A personal Web page can tell absolutely anything about you that you don't mind the whole world knowing. Do you have a strong opinion on a particular topic? Post it on your Web page. Do you want to create an online family photo album so your relatives in Timbuktu can stay up to date? Post your photos on your Web page. Do you want to show off your pit bull to the whole world? Post the pooch's picture on your Web site.

I think you get the idea. You can make your personal Web page into anything you want. At first, this may seem like an odd undertaking, but if you do a little Web exploration, you'll discover that there are some pretty interesting (and of course, some really bizarre) personal Web pages out there. Why not add yours?

A common bond

I guess a hobby-related page can technically be considered a personal page, but hey, I'm the author here and I want to discuss hobby pages separately. So there!

The main difference that distinguishes hobby/theme/special interest pages (hereafter referred to simply as hobby pages) from other personal pages is focus. Instead of telling the whole world details about your personal life, a hobby page explores one specific interest that you have.

No matter what your hobby is, chances are somebody has created a Web page dedicated to that topic already. In fact, more likely than not, several somebodies have done so. Does that mean you shouldn't bother with your hobby page? Quite the contrary.

Your Web page should be a reflection of your take on the topic at hand. As you explore the Web and find other Web pages dedicated to the same interests, you can make new cyberfriends and create hypertext links from your page to theirs and back again. You can create a little virtual community dedicated to one particular interest.

Show me the money!

I know what you're thinking. Yeah, yeah, Komando, who really cares about a Web site dedicated to Elvis Presley and Richard Nixon postage stamps? I want to make some cold, hard cash.

To that, I say, ".com down." You really can make money on the Web. Many people are doing it right now, and many more will do so in the years to come.

From fine wines to hot pepper sauce, from works of art to amateur films, and from CDs to CDs (compact discs to certificates of deposit, that is), companies large and small are staking their claims on the wide-open cyberfrontier.

Telling you exactly how to make money online is beyond the scope of this book. If you feel you need a little guidance in the area of online commerce, I know of a great book called *CyberBuck$: Making Money Online* (IDG Books Worldwide, Inc.). I know the book is great because I wrote it. So let's leave it at this: If you've got a business and you want people to know about what you do, you aren't going to find any bigger market than the millions of people who inhabit the Web.

A Quick Checklist for Creating a Web Page

- Get the idea for your Web page.
- Talk about it with your friends until they say, "Do it already."
- Talk about it some more.
- Lie awake in bed imagining all the things your page will do.
- Buy *Dummies 101: Creating Web Pages*. (Oh, you did that!)
- Get started.

Do You Really Want to Do This Yourself?

If the answer to this question is no, I suppose you wouldn't be reading this book, right? Nevertheless, I still have to ask it. And it's a question you should give some serious thought.

Creating a basic Web page is pretty simple stuff. But, depending on what you want to do with your page (especially if you want to use it to sell stuff), things can get complicated in a hurry. Perhaps you'll want to use what's called a *shopping cart application*, which allows shoppers to select items from different pages on your site and then have them all tallied for fast "checkout" when they're through. Maybe you'll want to add interactive *Java* elements to your Web page. (Java is a special programming language that lets multimedia applications run in the Web.) Fill-in-the-blank online forms can come in handy for all sorts of things, too.

I'm not trying to scare you off. But you do need to be aware that some of the more advanced Web page elements can be pretty tricky if you're not sure what you're doing. If you just want to get started with a basic Web page, then you've come to the right place. This book is for you.

Where do I turn for help?

Exactly what kind of help you may need in creating your Web page depends on your own skills and the amount of time you have to invest. Maybe you're a real whiz at Web page design and won't need any help at all in creating a highly sophisticated and advanced Web site that takes advantage of all the latest technology — but I doubt it.

Depending on where your own skills leave off, any of the following may come in handy:

- **Graphic artist:** If you're like me, you're capable of producing some amazing works of art — in your own head. Getting your ideas committed to the computer screen is another story. If your artistic ability is, shall we say, less than spectacular, a good (and reasonably priced) graphic artist can be a life saver.
- **HTML/Java programmer:** Plenty of people specialize in making easy work of the more complicated aspects of Web design. Many of these are high-priced consultants. But just as many, if not more, are students and other "amateurs" who are willing to do a first-rate job for a price that won't break the bank.

Finally, no matter who creates your Web page, you're going to need a place to put it. For most people, that means an ISP or commercial online service. Everything you could possibly want to know about getting your page online (and then some) is covered in Part V of this book. Which brings me to . . .

How This Book Is Organized

This book is basically a workbook. It presents information, quizzes you on what you've learned, and then takes you through exercises that help you put your new knowledge to use. In other words, the idea behind this book is to teach you to create your own Web page by actually having you do it.

This book is divided into five main parts:

Part I: And Then There Was Light and It Wasn't a Train

This section covers all of the basic information you need to know to get started creating a Web page. Is your computer adequate? What do you need in terms of software and software knowledge? This part closes with tips and advice on how to put together a Web page that not only contains all the information you want, but just as important, how to present that information as effectively as possible.

Part II: Creating Your Page, or The Legend Lives

Every Web page had a beginning. Part II is where your Web page goes from a few organized thoughts into something that you can see on your Web browser. You start with some basics of HTML, like how to create, save, and test an HTML file. Then I show you how to work with text in Web pages, including how to create bold, italic, and blinking text. The part also addresses one of the most important points of all — how to create hypertext links to other documents.

Part III: Getting Fancy

I don't know if a picture is really worth a thousand words, but I can tell you that a Web page with a thousand words and no pictures is pretty darn boring. This section touches on all the important considerations of using graphics on your Web page including appropriate file formats, download time considerations, tips for creating your own pictures, where to find pictures that other people will let you use royalty-free, how to add moving pictures (emotionally and otherwise), using pictures for links, and more.

But wait! There's more! Today only, and I mean *today*, I've also thrown in, for all our loyal readers who have come to know us as a reliable source, informative tips on creating fill-in-the-blank forms on your Web page; on setting up tables; on using frames; and using image maps. No, this won't cost you anything and you can use these for weeks (or years, if you're a slow learner) in your own home or office. Take them, they're yours.

Part IV: So Advanced, It's Simple!

The great thing about HTML is that all you need to create a Web page is a text editor or word processor. Oh, a little patience doesn't hurt either. All of the HTML codes are simply combinations of text characters. The downside is that to create a Web page with just a text editor or word processor, you need to know plenty of HTML code.

If you're into that sort of thing, fine. But if you're the kind of person who'd rather take a shortcut as long as the results aren't compromised, plenty of software tools are available to help you in the Web page creation process. That's what this section is all about.

I'll tell you about some of the shareware and freeware tools that are available, as well as the tools offered by the commercial online services should you decide to publish your Web page through them. I also tell you how to use *my* very own Web page creation software, which purchasers of this book can use free for a trial period. Finally, this section provides extensive coverage of the now-many commercial programs that are available to help you create Web pages.

Part V: The Big Payoff: Getting Your Page Online

By the time you get to this section, you'll have created one of the most wonderful and astounding Web pages. The only problem is that the Web page is still just sitting there on your computer, waiting for the world to see it and drop its collective jaw in amazement.

This section tells you exactly how to get your Web page from your computer to someplace where millions of people can access it at will, 24 hours a day, seven days a week. This section also offers sound advice on what to do with your Web page *after* it's online.

Part VI: Appendixes

I include some bonus items that I think you'll appreciate. No Ginsu knives, but I do have an appendix with a sampling of ISP prices, so you get an idea of what kind of financial commitment you're looking at with a Web page.

Then you find the appendix with all of the part quiz answers. That's the part of the book I haven't told you about, because I didn't want to scare you off. At the end of each part, you'll find a little quiz. Now remember, I won't be hanging over your shoulder to see if you get every question right. That's not the point of these quizzes. The point is that you should know if you have a firm grasp of all the material in each part. If you do, *Bravo!* You're ready to go on to the next part. If you don't, you may want to review so you'll be fully up to the task of creating the best Web page you can. Appendix B helps out by giving you the correct answers and an idea of where to review.

Finally, you'll find an appendix that gives you more information about the CD-ROM attached to the inside of this book's back cover.

About the CD-ROM

Remember the CD-ROM I was just telling you about? It has all sorts of good stuff on it, including files that you can use to follow along with the lessons in the book; handy software that you can use for the lessons and beyond; and more than 200 custom backgrounds that you can use on your Web page. To install the CD-ROM files, see Appendix C.

Icons used in this book

Every so often I want to give special emphasis to something in the book, and I use icons in the margins to point these parts out. Here are the icons I use and what they say about the text they're next to:

on the test

Remember, the quizzes at the end of each unit are your friends. To reinforce that concept, I use this icon to point out things that maybe, just maybe you should keep in mind while you look over the quizzes. Is that enough of a hint?

on the CD

This icon lets you know when I talk about one of the programs or files included with this book's CD.

extra credit

I use this icon to point out information that's not absolutely necessary, but that you may find handy.

heads up

Pay special attention to this icon. I use it to highlight things that can ruin your day while you're creating your Web page and ways to avoid them.

Other conventions

A book about Web pages for computers includes, naturally, some instructions on how to use some computer programs. Occasionally you may see something like this in the steps in this book:

File⇨Save As

This tells you to point your mouse cursor on the File menu of the program, click the left mouse button, and then click again on the Save As option in the menu that appears. Easy breezy.

Where to Go from Here

The best advice I can give you: Have fun and just jump in. If you start at the beginning, I'll walk you through all the steps you need to build your basic Web page. Sure, you can jump around a little, but this book is organized in a logical order that'll help you make sense of the Web. So have fun. The world is just waiting for new and creative Web sites like the ones you're going to post. Good luck!

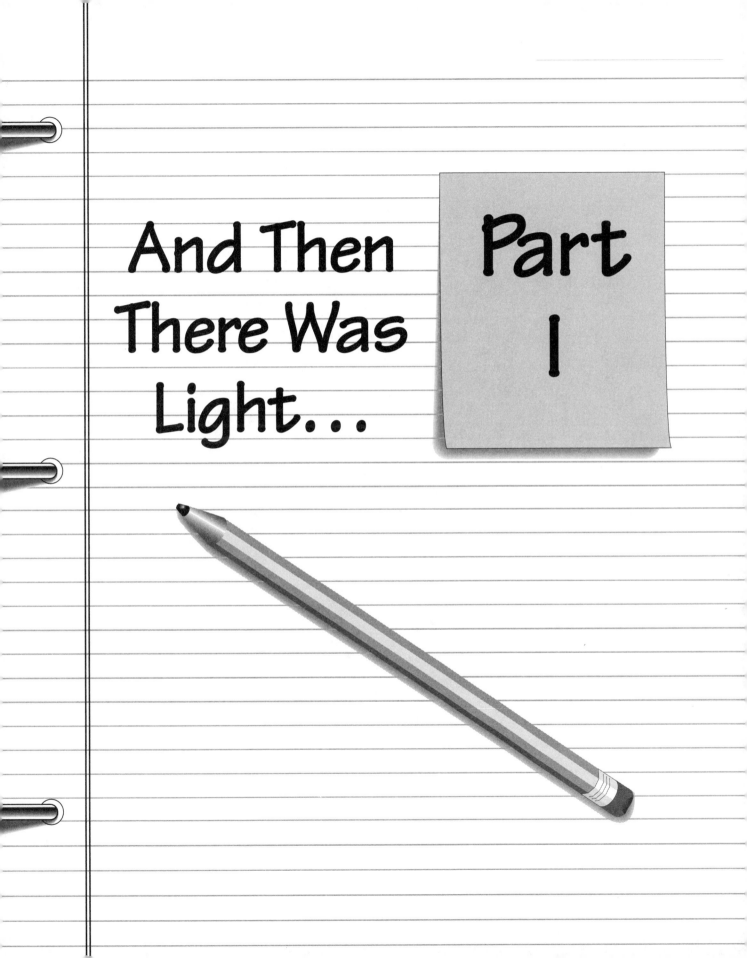

In this part . . .

Remember how your mom always made you eat your string beans before you got dessert? Well, in this part you get a little background information that comes in handy when you design your Web page. First, I tell you about the chips and salsa of Web page design. (Chips and salsa is the '90s way to say "hardware and software." Can you guess what I mean by chips? Yes, that's right. Hardware! You get a gold star.) After you learn about the hardware and software tools that make your Web-creation project run smoothly, I show you some fundamental design rules to help your Web page look good.

You'll find out why text is so important in a Web page. You'll read about the basics of using graphics and figure out which file formats are appropriate for certain types of images. You'll discover some super tricks of the design trade for formatting a page properly. You'll also read about some of the elements that you shouldn't apply when you design a Web page — the missteps that make someone a one-time visitor to your site.

You know you're at a desperate site when you see . . .

"You are Visitor 0000001."

"Please, don't hit the back button yet!"

"Bookmark this page, you idiot!"

I know. You're bursting with excitement to just put your page up on the Web. But slow down for a few minutes to read through this part. You'll get clear direction on how to make your page the best it can be. If some brilliant ideas pop into your head as you read, jot down some notes or draw a little sketch in the margins! That's why the margins are there in the first place, in case you wondered.

Taking It from the Top

Prerequisites
♦ Turning on your computer
♦ Finding and installing the CD that comes with this book (Appendix C)
♦ The will, the desire, and an "I can do this" attitude

Objectives for This Unit

✓ Gathering all the software, hardware, and other goodies you need to make Web publishing work for you

✓ Assessing how much programming language training you need

As easy as I try to make Web publishing for you in this book, I still have to take a short station-identification break to be sure you're familiar with some basic concepts and facts. That's what this unit is all about.

I know you're anxious to get started. But stop and think about it for a minute. How well can you drive if you get behind the wheel of a car without any training or background information? Or, what if everywhere you go in your car, you always get behind a slowpoke? Well, cruising the Information Superhighway is no different.

Put on your seat belt and rev your engine. Vrooom! Let's get going! Oh, don't forget to crank up the radio too. Who knows? The worldwide Kim Komando Computer Talk Radio Show may be on the air this very moment! Talk about sensory stimulation — or would that be overload?

Lesson 1-1

How Much Computer Do You Need?

Notes:

If you publish anything on the World Wide Web, you need more than just this book; you need a computer on which to create your cybermasterpiece. Your computer is like a big chunk of stone from which you carve a work of art.

You also need some software — the virtual hammer and chisel that serve as your tools as you undertake this endeavor. You also need a way to get the finished product from your computer to its eventual home on the Web, much like a truck carries a 2-ton sculpture to a museum.

How much computer is too much?

One of the main concerns that may scare you from Web publishing is the notion that you need a whiz-bang, pricey 200 MHz Pentium system with MMX just to get anything done. Well, that belief may or may not be true, but that equipment is a sure way to win *my* heart. Equipment requirements really depend on exactly what you want to do and how efficiently you want to do it.

You see, there are two ways you can use your computer for Web publishing. The first is creating Web pages. HTML (HyperText Markup Language — the "programming" language of the Web) is entirely a text-based programming language. (Don't panic — remember, I use the term *programming language* rather loosely here. HTML is more a publishing language.) That means that if you're an HTML expert, you can probably produce prolific numbers of Web pages on an old 286 system running some DOS-based version word processor. After all, for sheer speed, Microsoft Word 4.0 for DOS is about the fastest word processor I've ever seen. Sure, Word 4.0 can't do a fraction of what today's Microsoft Word can do because it lacks bells and whistles, but Word 4.0 is *fast*. Of course, fast is a relative term, much like fishermen describing the size of their last catch.

While that old 286 may be fine for whipping out HTML pages, you may run into a problem when you want to view the fruits of your labor. To view a Web page, you need a Web browser, which is the special software you use to — duh — browse the Web. I cover this more in a moment. My point is that both of the major Web browsers, Netscape Navigator and Microsoft Internet Explorer, offer versions that cover operating systems back to Windows 3.1, but no further.

on the test

Sure, I suppose that technically you can run Windows 3.1 on a 286-based system. You can walk from Omaha to Los Angeles just to see a Dodgers game, too, and I guess that way, you get to see every restroom along the way up close and personal. However, if you're interested in doing anything productive in this lifetime, I don't recommend either. To view the pages you create, you need a system that can run at least Windows 3.1 without blowing a gasket. On the Mac side, you can't get by with anything less than a Quadra-level (68040-based) system. Again, you can probably crawl along with an older system, but you may regret it.

PC users need a system that can run at least Windows 3.1

Mac users need at least a Quadra-level machine

Four ways to know that your computer is too slow:

▶ You clip your nails more than once in a sitting while you are waiting for your computer to boot-up

▶ That little hourglass burns an image into your screen

▶ Your spouse leaves you because of "that damn computer"

▶ The Internet is obsolete

The more up-to-date your system, the better off you are. As time goes by, support for Windows 3.1 will undoubtedly fade, and future developments are almost guaranteed to target the Windows 95/Windows NT and beyond market. The question of how much computer to buy is one that I practically hear in my sleep nowadays. My bottom-line answer is always the same: Buy as much computer as you can reasonably afford. What more can anyone ask of you? What more can you possibly ask of yourself?

Remember that I said there are two levels of involvement when it comes to Web publishing? The first is creating the Web page, and the second level is serving up Web documents. When you transfer your completed Web pages to your Internet Service Provider (all of which you learn about in Unit 10), your ISP keeps your files on a special computer called a Web server. This server connects directly to the Internet via one or more high-speed telephone lines and runs specific software that lets people around the world browse your Web pages.

Most of the Web servers on the Internet run under the UNIX operating system, although Windows NT also makes a strong showing. Web server software that runs on off-the-shelf PCs and Macs is also available. However, such software often performs at a less than stellar level. If you get your system working well, you still end up spending several hundreds, maybe even thousands, of dollars just for monthly phone service. The bottom line: You don't need your computer to double as a Web server. Just get a regular ol' PC (or Mac, of course).

Making the connection

No matter what kind of computer you decide on, you need a way to connect to the Internet and get your Web page from your computer to the Web server. For most of you, that means using a *modem*, your computer's equivalent of a telephone.

plug your computer into a telephone line via a modem

You can get connected in other ways besides using a garden-variety modem. One that you've probably heard of is ISDN, which stands for Integrated Services Digital Network. Don't bother. ISDN equipment is expensive, service is expensive, and it's still a hassle to get it set up.

Nope. Get a regular old modem, but make sure you get a fast one. Remember, modem speeds are a lot like a car's speedometer. As the number goes up, the faster the information is transferred over regular phone lines when connecting to a commercial online service or the Internet. For the past year or so, 28.8K V.34 modems were the consumer's choice, offering high-speed access and reliable connections.

get the fastest
modem you can
afford, but make
sure the modem
uses a true
industry standard

☑ **Progress Check**

If you can do the following, you've mastered this lesson:

❑ Differentiate between acceptable and non-acceptable computers for Web page design.

❑ Explain the role of a modem and differentiate between acceptable and non-acceptable modems for connecting to the Web.

When a new crop of 33.6K modems hit the streets, no one really cared. A 4.8K speed increase isn't enough to make an earth-shattering difference when you are talking about online connection speeds. But if you have a 28.8K modem, go ahead, upgrade it to 33.6K. Many 28.8K modems can be upgraded to the 33.6K speed with a free software upgrade (called firmware) or a $25 ROM chip upgrade.

As I write this, 56K modems are beginning to appear big-time on the market. However, don't rush to be the first in line for one of these puppies. Here's why: A standards war is going on in the modem industry between the US Robotics x2 technology and Lucent Technologies, which is banking on the Rockwell K56flex technology. The international standard winner has not been announced at the time of this writing, but already modem manufacturers are dangling the faster-connection carrot to speed hungry online users. I've been using a 56K US Robotics modem for the past month and the increased speed does make a difference, assuming you are able to connect at the higher speed.

heads up

Making the 56K connection is not perfect. For starters, your commercial online service or Internet provider must accept higher speed connections. Unfortunately, 56K access is limited. So even if you have a 56K modem, depending on where you live, you presently may not be able to use all the speed.

As I write this, America Online customers located in San Francisco; Washington, D.C.; Chicago; New York; and Skokie, Illinois, can dial a local access number to connect at 56K. If you're not lucky enough to live in one of these cities, you can use a toll-free number to connect at 56K. This toll-free number does cost you, though. Currently, America Online has a surcharge of 10 cents per minute, or $6 per hour, for the entire time you are connected using this number (even during your free trial period). By the time you read this paragraph, America Online will have more cities offering 56K local access. Besides the modem and the dial-up access number, you'll also need to download a special release of the service's software available in the x2 forum (keyword **x2**).

CompuServe currently offers 56K connections only through a toll-free number surcharge scenario like America Online's. Prodigy users have to call White Plains, N.Y., to get online at 56K. More than 400 Internet Service Providers offer 56K access.

Once you do get online at 56K, my experience has been that the actual connection speeds range anywhere from 32K to 53K. The US Robotics x2 modems theoretically can download information at 56K. However, current FCC regulations limit the download speed to 53K over regular phone lines in the United States.

You can send information up to 33.6K, but I rarely see that number in my connection status screen. Like any modem, though, factors such as line noise, local telephone switches, and even the phone line wiring in your home play an integral part in determining the x2 speeds you will achieve. If you live in an area with poor-quality phone lines, you may find that a 56K modem performs more like a 28.8K modem.

If you don't want to take any risks about which 56K-modem standard is going to come out on top, you're probably best off with a 33.6K modem. That's the fastest garden-variety modem you can get, and it should do the job just fine. Wait until the technology matures and the prices drop before making the high-speed connection with a 56K modem.

Recess

Speed is good . . .

- ◆ for a modem
- ◆ while flying
- ◆ when reading

Speed is *not* good . . .

- ◆ while sleeping
- ◆ when you are daydreaming
- ◆ while on a romantic walk on the beach

Notes:

How Much Software Do You Need?   Lesson 1-2

In Part IV (that's Part 4 for all you non-Romans out there), you find out about all sorts of *optional* software programs that can make your life as a Web creator a whole lot easier. The key point to remember is that all those programs really are optional; you actually only need a couple of pieces of software.

The first is a text editor or word processor. The Windows Wordpad or even Notepad can fill the bill here, if necessary. On the Mac side, you can make it all happen by using a program as simple as SimpleText. The only real problem with these kinds of programs is efficiency; the free editors that come with your computer typically lack the extra automation features — I'm talking about features such as spell checking, sophisticated search and replace functions . . . that sort of thing — that help you become a truly prolific Web creator.

My recommendation is that you at least use a recent version of a reasonably good word processor. Of course, the first one that comes to mind is Microsoft Word, followed by WordPerfect, but others out there can serve you just as well.

After you decide on a program to help you create your Web pages, you need another program to help you view your finished product (and everything else on the World Wide Web, for that matter). The program I'm talking about is the aforementioned Web browser.

Just as with most types of software, the browser arena has two major contenders: Netscape Navigator-Communicator, which holds the lion's share of the market, and Microsoft Internet Explorer, which continues to make steady gains. Internet Explorer's progress is due in no small part to the fact that the browser is 100 percent free to the entire world and that you have to shell out money for Netscape's product.

if you don't want to buy a software program to help with Web page creation, just use your favorite word processor

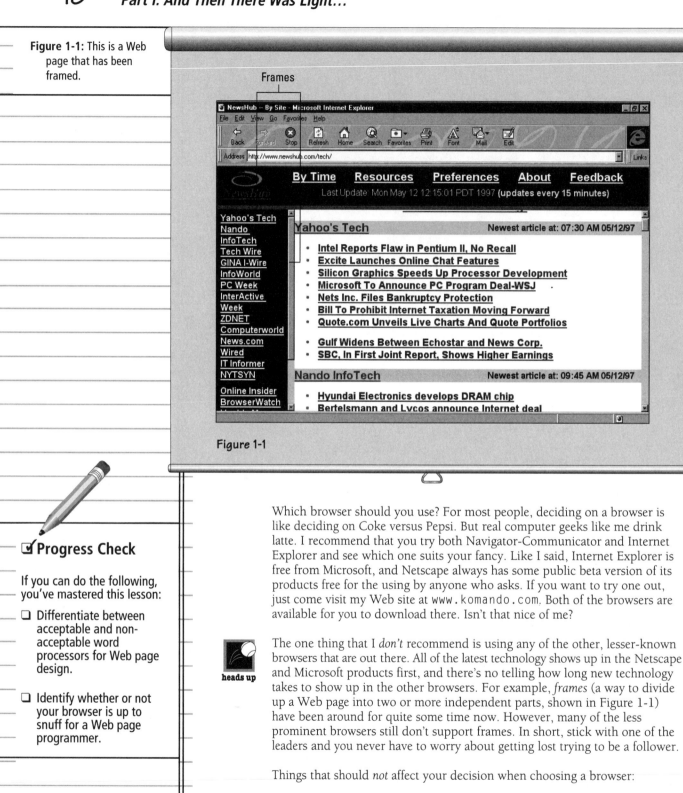

Figure 1-1: This is a Web page that has been framed.

Figure 1-1

☑ **Progress Check**

If you can do the following, you've mastered this lesson:

❑ Differentiate between acceptable and non-acceptable word processors for Web page design.

❑ Identify whether or not your browser is up to snuff for a Web page programmer.

Which browser should you use? For most people, deciding on a browser is like deciding on Coke versus Pepsi. But real computer geeks like me drink latte. I recommend that you try both Navigator-Communicator and Internet Explorer and see which one suits your fancy. Like I said, Internet Explorer is free from Microsoft, and Netscape always has some public beta version of its products free for the using by anyone who asks. If you want to try one out, just come visit my Web site at www.komando.com. Both of the browsers are available for you to download there. Isn't that nice of me?

The one thing that I *don't* recommend is using any of the other, lesser-known browsers that are out there. All of the latest technology shows up in the Netscape and Microsoft products first, and there's no telling how long new technology takes to show up in the other browsers. For example, *frames* (a way to divide up a Web page into two or more independent parts, shown in Figure 1-1) have been around for quite some time now. However, many of the less prominent browsers still don't support frames. In short, stick with one of the leaders and you never have to worry about getting lost trying to be a follower.

Things that should *not* affect your decision when choosing a browser:

▶ Peer pressure

▶ Believing that choosing one will "send a message" to Bill Gates

▶ Searching for a sense of belonging

♦ Sympathy

♦ Fear

How Much HTML Do You Really Need to Know?

on the test

You already know that HTML is the "programming" language of the World Wide Web. This book covers the basics of HTML, enough for you to put together a basic Web page. But is that enough HTML for you? That question has a different answer for every Web page creator. To find your answer, ask yourself the following questions:

♦ How complex do I want my Web page to be? I cover Web page design in the very next unit.

♦ What tools am I going to use to create my Web page?

♦ Am I willing to pay somebody else to do any complex work that I may not be able to do by myself?

♦ Can I do this on my boss's time without his knowing?

on the test

At one extreme, you may be the do-it-yourself type who wants to create your whole page with just a simple text editor. More power to you. If so, you need to know plenty of HTML, and you also may want to consider investing in *HTML For Dummies*, 3rd Edition, by Ed Tittel and Steve James (IDG Books Worldwide, Inc.). The book is a good companion to this one.

At the other end of the spectrum, perhaps you're going to spend a few dollars to buy a program like Adobe's PageMill (which I cover in Unit 8). With a program like PageMill, you can create very attractive and robust Web pages without knowing a single speck of HTML code. How? PageMill uses a WYSIWYG (what you see is what you get) approach to Web page creation. You concentrate on making the page *look* the way you want it to look, and the program generates the necessary HTML code to make it so.

My suggestion, though, is that even if you use one of these WYSIWYG programs, be sure you're familiar with the HTML basics — in short, all of the HTML coding I cover in this book. You just never know when you may need to make some adjustment to your Web page without benefit of your favorite Web creation program.

even if you buy a program that fills in all the HTML code for you, it's a good idea to know the basics

☑ Progress Check

If you can do the following, you've mastered this lesson:

❑ Identify what your Web page goals are and whether you need to do all your own programming from scratch.

❑ Plan to learn enough HTML code to meet those needs.

Unit 1 Quiz

Circle the letter of the correct answer or answers to each of the following questions. Some questions may have more than one correct answer.

Notes:

1. **The best kind of computer to use for creating Web pages**

    A. Runs at least Windows 3.1

    B. Probably runs Windows 95

    C. Is the old computer that your mom wanted to donate to the Salvation Army

    D. Is a 486

2. **Why do you need a browser?**

    A. To see better

    B. To access the information that's available on the Web

    C. To view your Web pages as you're creating them

    D. Because it's better than a looker

3. **What's the best kind of modem you can use to connect to the Web?**

    A. Whatever you can afford

    B. The modem that came with your computer

    C. A 33.6K or faster modem

    D. An ISDN modem

4. **HTML is short for...**

    A. Hot tamales made low-in-fat

    B. Hard to master language

    C. Hyper toddlers must lie down

    D. HyperText Markup Language

5. **What kind of software can you use to make a Web page?**

    A. A program that balances your checkbook

    B. A program that predicts lottery numbers

    C. A program that teaches you about spiders

    D. A simple text editor

Unit 1 Exercise

1. Double-check to be sure that you have all the right hardware and software to create a Web page.

2. Make sure your modem is working properly.

3. Figure out where on the complexity scale you should rank your initial Web page plans.

Basic Design Considerations

Objectives for This Unit

- ✓ Learning about the role of text in your Web page
- ✓ Figuring where graphics fit into the picture
- ✓ Debating the pros and cons of multimedia
- ✓ Considering general design issues before you go too far

Prerequisites

- ▶ Checking to make sure that you've got adequate hardware (Lesson 1-1)
- ▶ Checking to make sure that you've got adequate software (Lesson 1-2)
- ▶ Some idea as to what you want to do with your Web page (independent study)

Remember when you were learning to read back in elementary school, and your teacher would point at different letters on a big wall chart and have the entire class say things like, "A, ahhh," and "J, juh" together? What the teacher was teaching you were the basic elements of the language. You had to learn those elements individually before you could learn to put them all together into words.

on the test

Well, that's sort of what I do in this unit. No, don't worry, you won't be doing any group phonetics, so you don't have to worry that you forgot your blankie for nap time. We're going to talk about the basic elements of Web pages, which are illustrated in Figure 2-1, including:

- ▶ **Text.** For the sake of this discussion, the words on your page that are not in graphics and do not serve as links.

- ▶ **Graphics.** Pictures, drawings, and other elements that don't fit into the text category.

Figure 2-1: Common Web
page elements.

Notes:

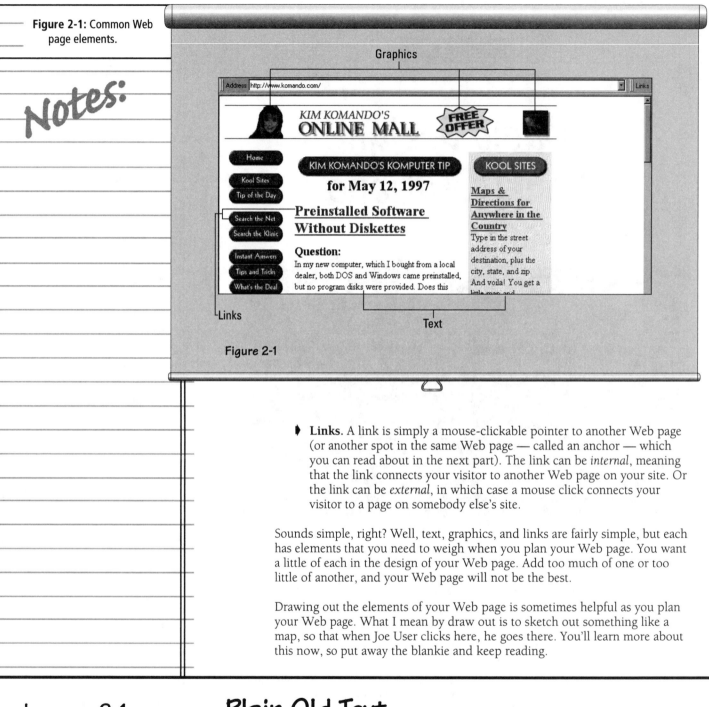

Figure 2-1

♦ **Links.** A link is simply a mouse-clickable pointer to another Web page
(or another spot in the same Web page — called an anchor — which
you can read about in the next part). The link can be *internal*, meaning
that the link connects your visitor to another Web page on your site. Or
the link can be *external*, in which case a mouse click connects your
visitor to a page on somebody else's site.

Sounds simple, right? Well, text, graphics, and links are fairly simple, but each
has elements that you need to weigh when you plan your Web page. You want
a little of each in the design of your Web page. Add too much of one or too
little of another, and your Web page will not be the best.

Drawing out the elements of your Web page is sometimes helpful as you plan
your Web page. What I mean by draw out is to sketch out something like a
map, so that when Joe User clicks here, he goes there. You'll learn more about
this now, so put away the blankie and keep reading.

Lesson 2-1   Plain Old Text

Despite all the snazzy graphical elements the World Wide Web has to offer,
text is still the main medium for getting your message across to your Web-
browsing audience.

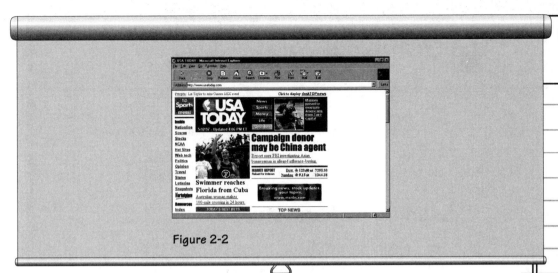

Figure 2-2

Why? Text is easy to generate and easy to read. And text is clearly the most efficient way to present information on a computer. Whoa, hold on a second. I'm sure some of you are wondering what other way information can be presented on a computer. Let me clarify exactly what I mean when I use the term *text*.

heads up

Text is anything you type in, can come back to and change later, and that somebody browsing your page can copy and paste into a word processing document (provided that it isn't a copyright violation). What I'm *not* talking about is text that's incorporated into any sort of graphic image. For the sake of this discussion, I consider text that appears in a graphic image as a graphic.

Why use text instead of graphics? The real issue is a matter of download time. Most of the people who connect to your Web page do so by modem, and the speed of their modems determines how quickly they can load your Web page. You can do your potential visitors a big favor by not filling your Web page with tons of stuff that takes forever to download.

Text downloads are much faster than graphic downloads. Well, technically, that's not true — it's like saying a pound of nails is heavier than a pound of feathers. Really, everything downloads at pretty much the same speed. However, graphics files are much bigger, so they take longer for viewers to see on their computer screen. The bottom line? Text is much faster, so present the bulk of your information as text.

text files, being smaller, download quicker than graphics files

heads up

The most effective Web pages that I've seen take what I call the *USA Today* approach, as shown in Figure 2-2. Such Web pages present small, concise bites of information up front, with the option for more detail.

heads up

The key to making such a document less burdensome for visitors is to provide a summary of your main Web page, and a hypertext link to another Web page that contains the entire document. People who want to read the document have instant access, and people who don't aren't troubled by an unnecessary download. Such a Web page makes everybody happy. People will throw feathers instead of nails at you.

☑ Progress Check

If you can do the following, you've mastered this lesson:

❑ Figure out the difference between text and a graphic on a Web page.

❑ Determine the most efficient approach to present information to users.

Lesson 2-2   # The Graphical Web

Notes:

I'll be perfectly frank. Although text is the most efficient way to present online information, a Web page that contains no graphical elements is unattractive. Unless you're hoping to win the Boring Site of the Year award, include at least a few well-placed graphics on your Web page. Of course, if you do add graphics, you need to think through some considerations.

Designing with graphics

The first thing you need to decide about graphics is exactly how they fit into the overall design of your Web page. The elements and needs vary from person to person, page to page.

For example, if you're an artist, you may want to include images of your work as primary elements of your Web page so you can showcase your work. On the other hand, if the purpose of your Web page is to promote your consulting business, the graphics may be merely ornamental. You need to show the guts of your business.

heads up

No matter what the exact purpose of your graphics, remember one golden rule: Don't overdo it!

on the test

You already know the first reason. Graphics generally take a long time to download. People exploring the Web often simply abandon a Web page in mid-download just because the site is taking too long. You certainly don't want your Web page to fall into that catagory.

The other reason to avoid graphical overkill is that a Web page with too many graphics can be even uglier than a page with no graphics at all. When desktop publishing first became popular, people started using 20 different fonts in the same document just because they could. The result was millions of amateurish-looking (and often moronic) documents that made your eyes hurt. The same seems true today of graphics and the Web. People put stuff in their Web pages because they *can*, never stopping to think of whether they really *should*. Yes, you should use graphics in your Web page, but no, you shouldn't go graphics-crazy.

Recess

Time to take a breather! Five entities that would benefit from a slow download:

- The CIA
- Swiss banks
- The Warren Commission page
- The Coca-Cola Secret Formula page
- The Department of Motor Vehicles

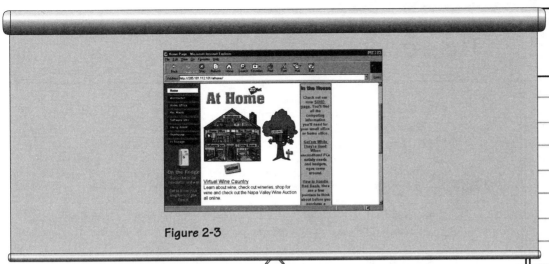

Figure 2-3

Figure 2-3: Where you click in the house determines what you get.

Rules for rules

You can create one and only one type of graphic from HTML code, and that's a simple horizontal rule — you know, a line that runs horizontally across your Web page. The reason I mention it here is that even though HTML code defines the horizontal rule, the rule is subject to all the same concerns associated with graphics, such as download time. Also, I want to make you aware now that if you need a horizontal rule, you don't have to create one in a graphics program. And although a horizontal rule is a graphical element, it really behaves more like text. For all intents and purposes, you can think of a horizontal rule as one big text character.

Click here

Up until now, when I've discussed hypertext links, I've addressed only text-based links — that is, text you can click your mouse on to access some other Web page. The truth is, hypertext links (or some words on your Web page that take the user to another area of your site) don't have to consist of any text at all. A graphic can serve as a clickable link just as easily as text can. You can create links from graphics in two ways.

The first is to create a simple graphic that serves as a clickable button. You know: Click your mouse on the button and something happens. Nothing mysterious there. You dive into the "how-tos" in Unit 5.

The other way to use graphics as hypertext links is through what's called an *image map*. This is one single graphic that serves as a link to several other Web pages. Exactly which page you get depends on where you click on the graphic. Take a look at Figure 2-3 to see what I mean.

Image maps are a little tricky to create, but they can also be very effective from a visual standpoint. You'll learn more about image maps in Lesson 6-5. For more on links, read the next lesson.

☑ Progress Check

If you can do the following, you've mastered this lesson:

❏ Identify how many graphics on a Web page is too many.

❏ Know what an image map is.

❏ Identify a horizontal rule.

Lesson 2-3

The Lowdown on Links

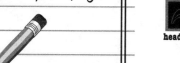

internal and external links help visitors navigate your page

☑ **Progress Check**

If you can do the following, you've mastered this lesson:

❑ Determine what a link is on a Web page.

❑ Know the difference between internal and external links.

❑ Know that a diamond bracelet is the best link to a woman's heart.

This is a short lesson, but an important one. So far, I've made several references to hypertext links, or just links, for short. However, it's a good time to go into a little detail about exactly what I mean.

heads up

Remember, links can be either internal (connects the visitor to another Web page on your site) or external (connects to a page on someone else's site).

Internal links are easy to deal with. After all, you know what's on your site and it shouldn't be hard to help people get from one page to another.

External links are another matter. You start by locating other pages that you want to link to, which, depending on the purpose and topic of your Web page, may or may not be an easy task. If your page has to do with some popular computer-related topic, you'll probably find plenty of external Web pages to link to. On the other hand, if your Web page focuses on the mating habits of the nearly extinct Asian elephants, it may take you awhile to find some appropriate links.

Also, you have to keep in mind that the World Wide Web is constantly changing. Web pages come and Web pages go. That means that if you link to somebody else's Web page today, there's no guarantee that the same page will even exist tomorrow. Much like the Asian elephants. If your page includes external links, make a habit of checking to make sure those links are still valid. Depending on how many external links your Web page includes, this can eat up quite a bit of your time. As you discover in Unit 5, programs exist that can help you out in this area, but whether you do it or your software does it, continual checking is essential.

Lesson 2-4

Beyond the Basics

Text and graphics. Those words probably describe more than 90 percent of the Web pages you're likely to come across. However, you can do plenty more on a Web page. You can create some of the bells and whistles right within HTML; other special stuff, like multimedia, is a little more complicated.

Frames, forms, and tables

Sounds like a shopping list from the office supply store, doesn't it? Actually, frames, forms, and tables are three unique element types you can create with HTML, each with a very specific use.

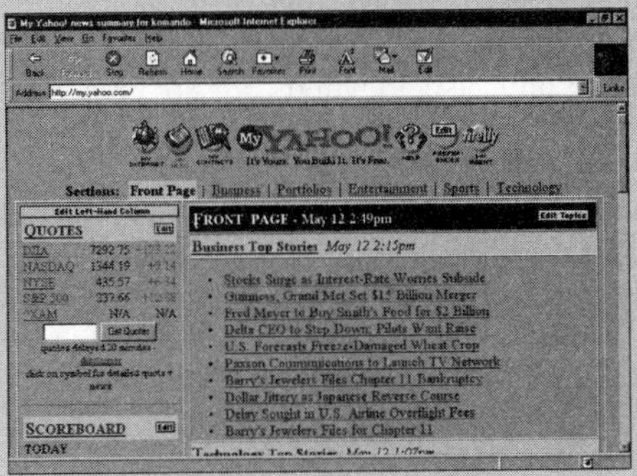

Figure 2-4: This Web page is divided into two frames.

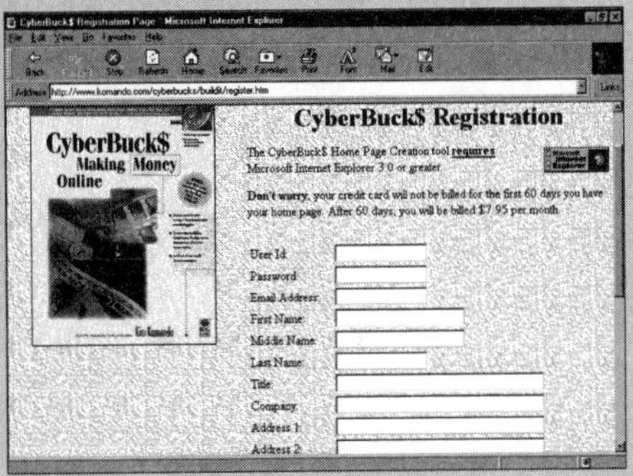

Figure 2-5: Your visitors just fill in the blanks.

Figure 2-4

Figure 2-5

Notes:

Frames refer to a feature that the current versions of all the major Web browsers support. This feature enables you to section off your Web page into individual segments called — you guessed it — frames. Technically, you can have as many frames on a single page as you want. However, most Web pages that use frames use only two of them, although I've seen some Web pages that get by with three. Any more than that would be overkill. Figure 2-4 shows an example of a page that uses frames.

Like the Web page in Figure 2-4, the most common use of frames is to create one smaller frame that holds a navigational aid — an image map, for example — and one larger frame that contains the Web main contents of the page. When a Web user clicks on a link in the smaller frame, the contents of the new frame appear in the larger frame. This way, your navigational aid is always available to your visitors.

A *form* is an online, fill-in-the-blank document that you can use to gather information from your visitors. This way you can fill in the blanks about *them*. You can use forms to collect survey results, take orders from customers, provide customer feedback, and so on. One such form appears in Figure 2-5.

heads up

You need to be aware of one important aspect of forms. Although you can create your form in HTML, an external program called a *CGI program,* or *script,* must process the data that the form collects. CGI stands for Common Gateway Interface, and such programs provide a "gateway" that enables data from Web forms to migrate to non-Web applications.

For example, a simple CGI script may take the results of some form input and send them directly to you via e-mail or even fax. Another, more complex CGI script may initiate credit card verification and take other steps to process an order one of your customers submitted online.

The reason I mention CGI is that CGI programming is real programming and typically requires the skills of a qualified programmer. Your Internet Service Provider may offer some built-in CGI scripts — maybe one that e-mails form data to you. If you want anything special in terms of CGI scripts, you may have to shell out a few bucks to your favorite programmer — who may become your not-so-favorite programmer when you get her bill.

One of the drawbacks of the early days of the World Wide Web was that the Web couldn't display tabular data — that is, neat little rows and columns of information. That all changed a couple of years ago when codes to create *tables* made their debut.

A table on your Web page is just like a table in your favorite spreadsheet or word processor. HTML tables enable you to create rows, columns, and captions — you get the idea. The HTML coding that you need to create a table is a little complex, but the results are quite nice.

Plugging in

Plug-ins are programs that extend the capability of your off-the-shelf Web browser so that your browser can support new and different file formats. What makes the Web and all the Web browsers so versatile is that all the major Web browsers support plug-ins. Don't misunderstand me — every browser doesn't necessarily support the exact same plug-ins. The people that make these plug-ins have to produce different versions for different browsers, but that's another story.

heads up

The important thing to know now is that these plug-ins enable you to view previously unsupported file formats. That's how multimedia came to life on the Web. No browser offers direct multimedia support, but by adding the right plug-ins, you can take advantage of all the multimedia the Web has to offer.

This may sound pretty exciting, and to some extent it is. However, before you go rushing off to plan your Web-based multimedia extravaganza, consider a few critical points.

on the test

First, when you add a sound, animation, a movie, or whatever to your Web page, you're automatically assuming that people who visit your Web page have the appropriate plug-in already installed on their browser. Think again. As much fun as plug-ins are when you're viewing, they can be a real hassle to install.

You can get almost all plug-ins as freeware, meaning you can legally pass copies around at will. So if you want, you can have the appropriate plug-ins available for download directly from your Web page. The downside is that plug-ins create extra steps for your viewer. Your Web visitor has to download the plug-in, install it, and restart the browser — just to look at your page. A certain percentage of your visitors won't be willing to go the extra mile just to get a look at your handiwork.

Multimedia elements don't grow on trees. Sure, you may be able to find some freeware multimedia on the Internet, but the quality probably won't be very good. For a modest investment, you may be able to pick up some better quality stuff on CD-ROM. If you want anything original, you have to create it yourself. Often, this is neither cheap nor easy.

Take Macromedia's Shockwave plug-in, for example. If you've ever experienced a Shockwave-enabled page, you already know that you can create some pretty incredible Web-based multimedia. What you may not have realized is that the multimedia content that Shockwave makes possible is created in another Macromedia program called Director. This is a high-end multimedia-authoring tool that costs several hundred dollars and requires a lot of time and

plug-ins add nifty functionality to your page, but can make it difficult for visitors to download your page

☑ **Progress Check**

If you can do the following, you've mastered this lesson:

❑ Determine what frames are and how they're helpful in Web page navigation.

❑ Explain how forms work, why they're useful, and why they are difficult to add to a page on your own.

❑ Identify the pros and cons of using plug-ins.

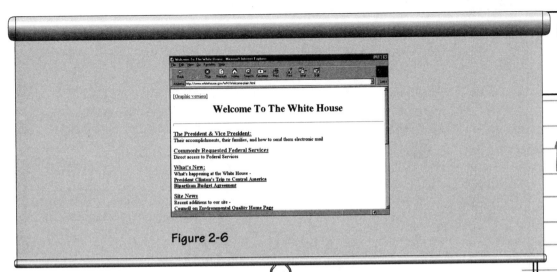

Figure 2-6

Figure 2-6: The White House links are available even without the image map.

Notes:

commitment to learn. After you create your multimedia content in Director, you convert it to Shockwave format using another Macromedia program called Afterburner. This is all about as clear as mud, right? Let me put it to you this way: Unless you have the big bucks, you may not be able to justify the up-front cost and time needed to make complicated animations on your page.

Of course, you can always call in the pros. You can save yourself some time, but you'll spend it on overtime at your job paying for professional services. I'm not really trying to steer you away from multimedia. I think it's great. But I want to be sure you understand everything that's involved if you decide you want to put multimedia on your Web page.

Other Design Considerations

Lesson 2-5

heads up

If an ounce of prevention is worth a pound of cure, an ounce of planning ahead is worth about a ton of going back to tweak things later — especially when it comes to Web page design. Before you type your first character of HTML code you should already be aware of the two most important aspects of your Web page: what it will say and how it will look. As far as content goes, I think every Web site should include certain things. As for design, there are plenty of essentials, as well as plenty of things to avoid.

I'm going to cover the basic dos and don'ts of Web page design in this lesson. Don't worry that you don't know exactly *how* to do these things right now. That comes later. Just make sure you consider all of these as you plan your page.

Content essentials

I've mentioned several times the need for graphics, and in Lesson 2-2 you found out about using graphics for your hypertext links. However, one thing you need to be aware of is that some people don't like to see any graphics at

an ounce of prevention is worth a pound of cure: plan your Web page before you start creating it

Notes:

all. Most browsers let you turn off automatic graphic loading, and some Web users opt for that choice. This creates a problem if you use graphical links.

The answer to this problem is a set of text-based links that correspond to your buttons and image maps. Many Web pages provide users the option to view Web pages with or without the graphics. See Figure 2-6 for an example of what I mean. These text-based alternative links don't need to be extremely prominent, but you should have them somewhere, nevertheless.

heads up

Here's something else to consider when you're thinking about your page. One easy way to lure people into your Web site (or your store or your bank or your taco shop or your whatever) is to give people something for nothing. It's an age-old marketing concept: The dollar value of what you're giving away isn't nearly as important as the fact that you're giving it away for free.

The easiest thing to give away is information. Do you have some unique computer tips (or tips for whatever the topic of your Web page is)? If you're an expert on a particular topic, you may want to consider publishing an electronic newsletter that you distribute through your Web page.

on the test

Another thought: If you want to put a Web page out there for the whole world to see, use proper Internet etiquette, or *netiquette*, to get input from the people who view your page. The easiest way to do this is to include a *mailto* link. Instead of bringing up a new Web page, clicking on this type of link pops up an e-mail message window with the message already pre-addressed to you. A mailto link makes it easy for people to contact you by e-mail without having to copy your e-mail address.

If you're running an online business, don't stop at mailto links. Remember to include your real address and your phone number. Now and then, I need a phone number for some company, and I find it easier to locate the company's Web page for the number. I am amazed that so many companies fail to put this basic contact information on their Web pages.

heads up

The last thing about content concerns quality control. Nothing makes a good site look really bad more than blatant typographical errors. Use your spell checker, but don't stop there. A spell checker is a great tool, but spell checkers cant sea awl you're miss steaks. Get my point? Read your pages over and over before you put them online. If you can, let somebody else proofread them, too.

Looking good

A truckload of costume jewelry or garish clothing can make even the most attractive person look cheap. The same goes for graphics and Web sites. Overload your Web site with even the best-looking individual graphics and you'll have a very hard time avoiding that cheesy costume jewelry look.

The same holds true for colors. As you learn in Units 4 and 5, you have complete control over the colors of text, backgrounds, and borders. First of all, make sure your colors match. If you're not sure, ask somebody. (Make sure he's not color-blind.) Even if your colors match, don't use too many different ones.

Maybe it's happened to you. You find this great-looking Web site and spot a link to some other page on the site that sounds too good to be true. Anxiously, you click on the link and wait a moment to see if your dreams will come true. An instant later, you see a goofy beaver in a hard hat, along with the words, "This page is currently under construction."

heads up

This is what I call "under constructionitis." Believe me, this is one disease you don't want to catch. If you want to include a statement on your Web page that says, "I'm working on another page that will include such-and-such," fine. That line lets people know what you're up to. Don't build their expectations and then disappoint them by dragging them all the way to another page just to have them find out that you haven't finished the page yet. It's a real turn-off.

The darker side of the Web

Sex. Now that I have your attention, I suppose I should take a moment to address the issue of pornography and the Web. It may be sad, but it's true. The porno sites are among the most popular on the Web. If you want to put up a porno site, I guess that's up to you. But there's much more positive stuff on the Web than all the news reports of online porno would have some people believe. Pornography just gives the Web a bad name for those people who haven't been exposed (no pun intended) to all the great content that's available.

Online pornography can be a risky proposition, too. As I write this, the Federal Communications Commission recently shut down some Web sites that promised people absolutely free porno images as long as they downloaded special viewing software to access the site. What those Web site operators didn't tell you is that the "free" software automatically disconnected you from your own ISP and re-established your Internet connection through a phone number in the former Soviet Union. The people running these sites made some big bucks by collecting a share of the international phone charges incurred by unsuspecting porno seekers.

As a Web page developer, maybe you're tempted to take advantage of the interest in online porno and include an innocent little "Bikini Girl of the Week" picture just to bring people into your site. I'd be lying if I said that approach hasn't worked for some sites that otherwise have nothing to do with pornography. In my humble opinion, it's just a cheap trick. On this one, I say you're better off on the moral high road.

☑ Progress Check

If you can do the following, you've mastered this lesson:

❑ List a few important tips to consider and implement when creating a Web page.

❑ Explain when you've gone overboard with graphics, colors, and fonts.

❑ Identify features that are rude to your potential Web visitors.

Unit 2 Quiz

Circle the letter of the correct answer or answers to each of the following questions. Some questions may have more than one correct answer, so take your time.

1. **The basic elements for Web pages include**

   A. Earth, wind, water, and fire

   B. Text, graphics, and links

   C. Your dossier and photo

   D. There aren't any

2. **An attractive, easy to read Web page has**

   A. Interesting text

   B. Some eye-catching graphics

   C. A tasteful mix of colors and fonts

   D. All of the above

3. **Adding multimedia to your Web page**

   A. Can be a drain on your resources

   B. Is really easy

   C. Sometimes requires visitors to your site to download and use plug-ins

   D. Requires that you hire a programmer

4. **If you're following good netiquette**

   A. You send people to a site that's under construction or that no longer exists

   B. You give people only a little bit of information at the top of your page so they can click if they want more and skip it if they don't

   C. You carefully proofread your page for typos and other mistakes

   D. You solicit feedback from your visitors

Unit 2 Exercise

1. Draft a table of contents that you can use as an outline of your page.

2. Do a sketch of your page. Be sure that you don't put too much information at the top of your page.

3. Cull through the graphic images and photographs you want to use and pick out only the most important ones.

Part I Review

Unit 1 Summary

- **Hardware you need:** You don't necessarily need a top-of-the-line computer to build a decent Web page. If you're a PC user, you'll need a system that can at least run Windows 3.1. If you're a Mac user, you'll need at least a Quadra-level machine. You'll also need the fastest type of modem you can afford.

- **Software you need:** You can use programs to help you build your Web page, but if you want just the basics, you can use a text editor or word processor. You'll also need a browser — either Netscape Navigator or Microsoft Explorer — to view your work.

- **HTML you need:** Products on the market will do HTML programming for you, so, technically, you don't need to know how to do any HTML programming. However, knowing the basics is important for an understanding of how your page works.

Unit 2 Summary

- **Text and your Web page:** Text on a Web page is important for several reasons. First, text is the best way to communicate information to your cybervisitors. Second, text downloads faster than any other file type. When designing text on your page, be sure to organize it in small, readable chunks.

- **Graphics and your Web page:** Graphics are important to dress up your Web page, but they're also slow to download. Be careful not to overdo them.

- **Links and your Web page:** Hypertext links enable people to jump around the Web. You can build links so people can jump from place to place on your Web page, or they can go to other sites altogether. Even graphics can act as links.

- **Other elements:** In addition to text, graphics, and links, your page can include frames, forms, tables, and multimedia. Often, multimedia on the Web requires your visitors to use plug-ins to view it.

- **Other design considerations:** Here are a few extra touches you may consider in order to insure that people will visit your Web page again: offer free stuff; always provide a way for visitors to give feedback or comment; be sure you check your page for errors; don't overdo it on fonts and colors; and keep it clean.

Part I Test

The questions on this test cover all the material presented in Part I (Units 1 and 2).

True False

T   F   1. You need to have a 200 MHz Pentium with MMX to build a Web page.

T   F   2. An Internet Service Provider keeps Web page files on a special computer called a Web server.

T   F   3. It's smart to buy a 56K modem.

T   F   4. Different factors — like line noise — can slow your modem connection.

T   F   5. You can design a whole Web page in Windows Wordpad or Notepad.

T   F   6. HTML coding is really just for super techie-nerds.

T   F   7. Everyone will always view all the graphics you put on your Web page.

T   F   8. Frames divide your Web page into several separate viewable areas.

Multiple Choice

For each of the following questions, circle the correct answer or answers. Some questions may have more than one right answer, so read all the answers carefully.

9. Why is it probably not a good idea to buy a 56K modem?

A. It will cost too much

B. Faster connections may soon be available

C. There are two competing standards for 56K modems, so if you buy now, your hardware may soon be obsolete

D. All ISPs and online services don't provide 56K dial-in access

10. A Web browser helps you

A. View all the content of the Internet

B. View your Web page as you design it

C. View all the cobwebs that have accumulated in your house as you've read this book

D. Check out all of today's hottest new fashions

11. How much HTML you need to know depends on several factors. These include

A. How complex you want your Web page to be

B. The tools you are going to use to design your Web page

C. Whether or not your brother's best friend — who is a programmer — offered to help you

D. How much money you plan to spend on your page

12. The *USA Today* approach of Web page design means

A. You read the newspaper and then type everything you've read into your new page

B. You present small bits of information up front and give visitors the option for more detail if they want it

C. You put up a page that competes with the *New York Times*

D. You offer concise bits of information

Part I Test

13. On a Web page, rules are

    A.   All the dos and don'ts in this book

    B.   A horizontal line across your Web page

    C.   The only type of graphic you can create using only HTML code

    D.   The stuff your dad used to remind you of when you were acting out

14. CGI scripts are

    A.   Necessary to process forms on a Web page

    B.   The Clear Graphical Interface that your Web page needs

    C.   Easy to design yourself

    D.   What Shakespearean actors memorize to put on a good performance

Matching

15. Match the following acronyms with the words that they stand for:

A. HTML	1. Internet Service Provider
B. CGI	2. What You See is What You Get
C. ISP	3. Common Gateway Interface
D. WYSIWYG	4. HyperText Markup Language

16. Match the following Web page extras with their purpose:

A. Frames	1. Allows visitors to give feedback
B. Forms	2. Allows you to present information in columns
C. Tables	3. Makes your page more entertaining
D. Multimedia	4. Allows you to split the page into separate sections for easier navigation

Lab Assignment

This exercise will help you see the subtle differences in Web page elements.

Step 1. Review your Web page outline

Take the Web page outline you drew up at the end of Unit 2, with the text, graphics, and links you want on your page.

Step 2: Compare with an existing Web page Compare with an existing Web page

Find a simple Web page you admire and draw up a similar outline, making sure to point out which text and graphics also serve as links.

Step 3: Improve your Web page outline

Now go back and look at your own Web page outline and make any revisions based on your new-found knowledge.

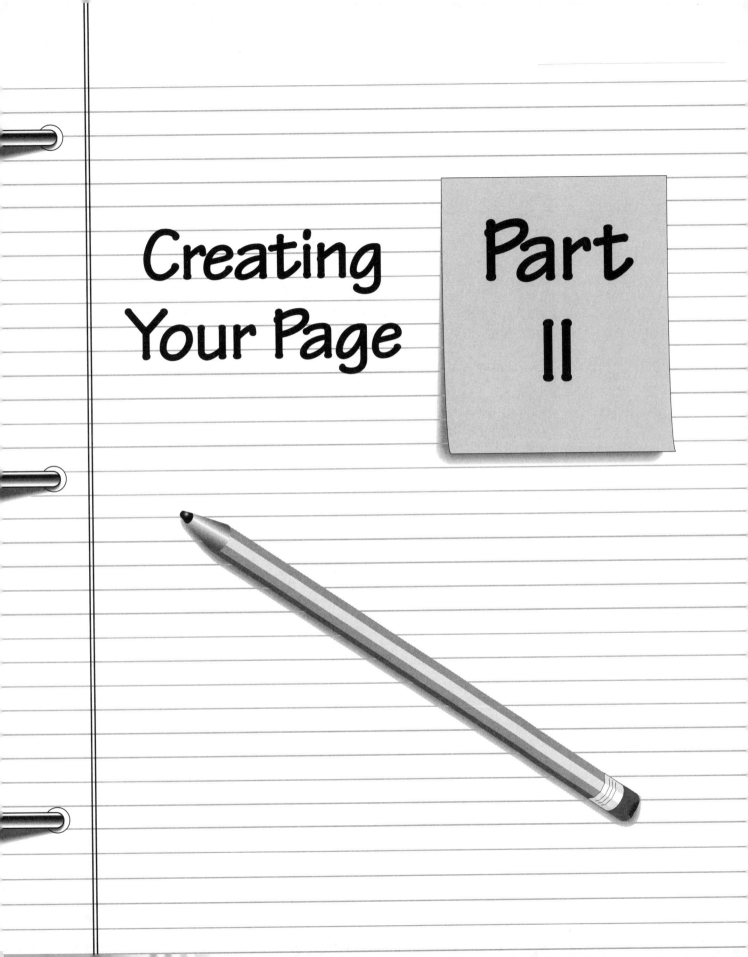

Creating Your Page

Part II

In this part...

Thinking back on my childhood, one of my fondest memories was helping my mother bake cookies. At the time, it seemed like my mom knew how to bake about a million different kinds of cookies. Some of them were as simply wonderful as she is. Some were much more elaborate. But the one thing that always amazed me was that they all started out with the same basic ingredient: flour. No matter what the recipe, it was always flour and some other stuff — nuts, vanilla, raisins, chocolate chips, whatever. And that other stuff turned that flour into some pretty incredible cookies. (Okay, my mother never baked cookies, but she can microwave one mean frozen dinner. Stick with me here. You'll see how the cookie analogy works in a moment.)

Now I don't mean to sound like Forrest Gump here, but in a way, creating Web pages is a lot like baking cookies. Every Web page starts out with one basic ingredient: words. Then you add some combination of other ingredients — in this case, HTML code — to turn those words into a unique online creation. You can mix and match these ingredients any way you want. Sometimes you end up with a winner; other times, if you're not careful, you end up with something the dog won't eat, which is really bad if you have to eat your words.

No, this part isn't going to teach you how to bake some killer chocolate chip cookies. But this part will teach you about some of the basic ingredients — HTML code — that you need to create solid, super-duper Web pages. By the time you finish this part, you'll be able to create complete — although not extremely complex — HTML code that's suitable for viewing on the World Wide Web. You'll be truly amazed at your newfound talent for presenting yourself to the world on the Internet.

Unit 3
• • • • • • • • • • •

HTML Basics

Objectives for This Unit

✓ Understanding what HTML code is and how to create a new HTML document.

✓ Figuring out how to save your work no matter what program you use

✓ Understanding file extensions

✓ Checking your work

Prerequisites

▶ A computer and a modem

▶ A working knowledge of the different parts that comprise a Web page — text, graphics, and links (Lessons 2-1 through 2-3)

▶ A stick-with-it attitude that should be easy to muster not only because I write so well . . . this is a relatively short unit

on the CD

▶ BBEdit Lite (Macs)

▶ Hotdog (Windows)

I am sure that it's happened to you at some point. There you are working on your PC at two in the morning. CNN is the only channel worth watching, unless you consider reruns of *I Dream of Jeannie* stimulating. You're on your third pot of coffee when suddenly and without warning, your PC decides it's going to sleep with or without you. The hourglass hangs on your screen like a bad haircut. And you hadn't saved your work before the deep freeze. Although you've read *Winning through Intimidation* by Robert Ringer, he knew nothing about trying to salvage lost work from a bunch of electronics. So you do what most adults do: swear and then cry.

This is a short but very important unit about creating and saving HTML Documents. It makes sense. You want to use your HTML talents as soon as you develop them. And you always want save your work early and often. Think of it this way: No matter what work you do on your computer, you must save it so you can use it later or show it off to your friends or e-mail it to your mom.

When it comes to Web pages, how you save your files is just as important as the fact that you save them at all. Web browsers expect certain things from the Web pages that they display. Browsers aren't really very smart: If a Web browser comes across something that it doesn't recognize, the browser won't know what to do with it. And if the browser doesn't know what to do with it, it won't show that item on your Web page. Basically, you've got to talk browser talk — and to save things so browsers can understand them. You're going to figure out how to talk the talk and walk the walk in this unit.

heads up

A lot of what I cover in this unit depends on exactly which program you use to create your Web pages. For example, if you use one of the programs designed just for creating Web pages (check out Unit 8 to see which programs do that work for you), the program takes care of lots of the details for you. This unit addresses the lowest common denominator — those of you who don't want to invest in the quick and easy software programs, but want to do it yourself with your word processor.

Lesson 3-1

The Nuts and Bolts of HTML

There ain't no bolts, but there are many nuts on the Internet. HTML, the "programming" language of the World Wide Web, stands for HyperText Markup Language. Don't get hyper on me. HTML is hyper easy.

Tag — you're it!

Each individual piece of HTML code is an HTML *tag*. Each tag performs a function, and comprises simple text characters enclosed by angle brackets.

on the test

Some HTML tags — those that indicate a specific action — have only one part. For example, if you want to add a *line break* (which is the equivalent of pressing the return key when you're using your word processor), you simply type in the tag *
*.

On the other hand, you probably need an HTML tag that has two parts if you format text. One part (the open tag) tells where the formatting starts, and the other part (the close tag) tells where the formatting ends. For example, suppose you want to put the words "My Home Page" in italics. The HTML for this is *<I>My Home Page</I>*. Note that the close tag has a forward slash. Any Web browser that views this coding knows to turn italics on when it gets to the beginning of this portion of text, and then turn italics off at the end.

I get into more HTML coding specifics in the next unit, so you don't have to worry too much about remembering the specific code for italics. At this point, I just want to make sure you have the right idea. Two other things not to worry about:

 ♦ Your weight
 ♦ Your age

After all, Elvis didn't. Speaking of nuts on the Internet, did you know that Elvis has his very own Web page that the Web page creator says he reportedly visits too? But I digress.

on the test

In a nutshell: As your Web browser reads a Web page, the browser looks for anything between angle brackets, like in the previous examples. The Web browser assumes that anything inside those brackets is some sort of HTML instruction. If the Web browser recognizes the instruction, the browser does whatever it's supposed to do. If the Web browser doesn't recognize the instruction, the browser simply ignores it. For example, if the instruction is a new HTML tag that the browser doesn't know, or if you entered the text incorrectly, the browser ignores the text the way you ignored your mom when she told you to come home from the prom early. She should have been in brackets.

Your first HTML code

Now it's time to get to the meat of the matter. You're about to enter the world of HTML programming and change your life forever. Is programming gonna be hard? Not really — it's pretty easy. Programming is fun, too, so enjoy it.

Here's how you create an HTML document. Really.

on the CD

1 **Create a new document in your word processor.**

As I told you in Unit 1, any word processor will do. Call me old-fashioned, but I like to use NotePad or a text editor. Now type the desired HTML code. Mac users may want to use BBEdit Lite, which I include on this book's CD. If you have Windows, you can use the appropriate HotDog Web editor program from the CD. The HotDog programs are a little more complex, as you can read in Unit 8, but you can use them to enter HTML code as well.

2 **For the purpose of this exercise, start at the top and type:**

```
<HTML>
<HEAD>
<TITLE>This proves Web page programming is easy!</
          TITLE>
</HEAD>
```

3 **Call your mother and tell her you are a programmer.**

Actually, you still have a couple of critical steps before you are a full-fledged programmer — saving and testing your code, which I cover later in this unit. But before I get to those topics, let me show you how to get some code ideas from other Web pages.

Checking up on your neighbor

heads up

One way to get a good idea of what HTML looks like and how HTML works is to go out on the Web and find a page that interests you and then get a close look at the HTML code on that page. This is a great trick, so pay attention.

1 **Find a slick page on the Web.**

2 **Call up the source code for that page.**

If you are using the Microsoft Internet Explorer, choose <u>V</u>iew⇨<u>S</u>ource; Netscape Navigator folks should choose View⇨Document Source.

You end up with a separate window that has the raw HTML code for that page, as shown in the example in Figure 3-1. Incredible.

☑ Progress Check

If you can do the following, you've mastered this lesson:

❑ Understand what symbols a Web browser needs to see for it to know that it's reading a line of HTML code.

❑ Create a new document on your word processor that you can type HTML code into.

❑ Check the source code on Web pages you admire.

❑ Stop hyperventilating about programming long enough to read the next lesson.

Figure 3-1: A page viewed in HTML code.

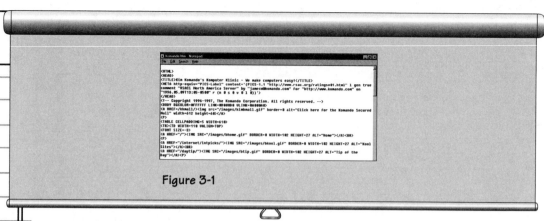

Figure 3-1

on the test

viewing the source
is a quick way to
see the coding
that makes a Web
page all that it is

The <u>View</u>⇨Sour<u>c</u>e option in your Web browser is not only a valuable learning tool, you can use it as a development tool, too. Every once in a while, you're likely to come across a page that makes you say, "How'd they do that?" Well, if you choose <u>View</u>⇨Sour<u>c</u>e, you can find out exactly how they did it. Because HTML is out there for everyone to use with virtually no restriction, nothing prevents you from imitating that code in your own Web page. The technical term for this is stealing — ahem, I mean *borrowing*.

Lesson 3-2   Preserving Your Efforts

Every Web page you create has two important components: the file format and the filename extension. The easier of these to screw up is the file format.

The right format is everything

on the test

saving information
for your Web page
isn't quite as easy
as saving stuff in
your word processor

Formatting is like real estate — what counts most is location, location, location. When it comes to file formats, there's really only one rule that you need to remember: HTML is all text-based. All HTML code consists of characters you create by pressing any of the standard "typewriter" keys on your keyboard. Taking that idea one step further, it stands to reason that a Web browser, which is designed to interpret HTML code, can't recognize anything but HTML code.

What's the point here? Suppose that you create your Web page by using WordPerfect as a text editor. If you save your Web page and leave the document in WordPerfect's proprietary file format, you have saved all your work — but in a format that your Web browser can't understand. Try to open that file with your Web browser, and all you see is a bunch of gobbledygook, perhaps interspersed with the text you intended to present, unless your site is called *http\\www.gobblydygook.com*. That may be fine if you want the world to know about your kid's first words, but it's not much help for the rest of us.

heads up

The key to successfully saving your Web page documents is to save them as *plain text*. Now, that doesn't mean your work is *plain. Your* taste is extraordinary. How do I know? You bought this book, didn't you? Anyway, virtually all

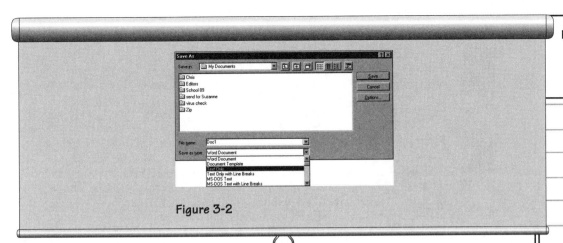

Figure 3-2

Figure 3-2: Microsoft Word lets you save your documents in a number of different formats.

save your Web pages as text only to avoid problems

Notes:

word processors have a "save as" option, and — if you're working in a plain ol' word processor — this is what you need to use to save your Web pages. Figure 3-2 shows the Save As dialog box from Microsoft Word.

When you do a "save as," the exact format options vary according to the program you use. The correct option for your Web pages may be *Plain Text, Text Only, Text, ASCII Text,* or something similar. You may also see options such as *MS-DOS Text, UNIX Text,* or *Mac Text.* If your program provides multiple text options, which one do you choose? My rule of thumb is that you use the simplest option, plain text.

Here's how to save a file as a text file. Come on boys and girls, let's do it together:

1 Open your favorite word-processing program.

2 Type some text.

Any old text will do. But if you have already been using your word processing program to do the steps in this lesson, no gold star for you yet!

3 From the menu bar, choose File⇨Save As.

This brings up a dialog box with a place to give the file a name and a pull-down menu of different file options.

4 Click in the file name box and type in a name.

5 Click on the down-arrow to access the file options pull-down menu, choose Text as the format option, and then click on OK.

That's it. Now you get the gold star!

Naming your files

You can name your files "Frank" or "Elena," but if you do, such names are likely useless. Come with me. Your Web browser relies exclusively on file extensions to figure out what type of files it is receiving. Your HTML code may be flawless, but if you save your Web page with the wrong file extension there's no way that your Web browser knows what to make of it.

on the test

Lucky for you, the secret solution is really easy. You need to speak the language that your Web browser can understand. Therefore, every Web page you create must end with either *.htm* (if you use Microsoft Windows system) or *.html* (if you use a UNIX or Macintosh system). Either of these two file extensions lets the Web browser know that the file it's about to display really is a Web page.

heads up

Now, I just told you about saving your file as plain text, and that still holds. However, saving files as plain text has to do with file formatting; the file gets stripped of any *extended formatting*. Basically, you can't have any fancy fonts or use the Tab key to make paragraphs or anything like that. Saving a file as plain text doesn't have to do with the file extension that your Web browser understands. However, here's the catch: Sometimes when you save your file as plain text, your word processor adds an extension of its own. In Word documents, for example, your file adds a *.txt* extension when you save it as Plain Text. So even though the actual file is in a format that HTML understands, the browser can't make sense of the extension. The problem is easy to fix, though. All you do is manually change the extension to *.htm* or *.html* so your browser can read it.

every Web page you create must end with either .htm (if you use a Microsoft Windows system) or .html (if you use a UNIX or Macintosh system)

extra credit

Other file extensions

As you create more and more complex Web pages, you may run into other file extensions beyond those used for actual Web pages. Also, as you discover later in this book, every graphic format and multimedia format has its own file extension. Unit 5 introduces you to two common graphics extensions, *.gif* for GIF files and *.jpg* for JPEG files. Other common extensions include *.wav* for WAVE sound files, *.avi* for Windows AVI movies (as in "A vi movie for us to see."), and *.mov* for QuickTime movies created on either Mac or Windows systems. Another really common file format that you may run into is the *.txt* file I was just talking about. If you have a text file to display and *it requires no special HTML codes*, you can post a file that uses the *.txt* extension. You may use the *.txt* file extension when you test out your HTML code later in this unit. It usually works without a hitch.

heads up

Although the file extension is perhaps the most important part of the filename, you need to think about other naming conventions when you name your Web pages. For starters, keep in mind that filenames on the Internet in general, and therefore Web page file names in particular, are case-sensitive. This means that *resources.html* and *Resources.html* represent two different files, just by virtue of the fact that one has an uppercase R and the other one doesn't. Here's a tip: Stick with all lowercase letters for your filenames. That way you never have to try to remember whether you used uppercase when you named the file. Lower Case closed.

keep your filenames standard and use only lowercase characters in the filenames

Web filenames generally can be as long as you want, but because a wide variety of computers are out there, stick with eight-charater names plus the extension. The filename can't contain any spaces or most punctuation, but Web filenames can contain dashes and underscores. So the filename can contain dashes, underscores, and periods (well, that's obvious, since a period precedes every filename extension), so you're probably best off just sticking with letters and periods for your filenames. For example, *resources.and.links.htm* is a valid filename for a Web page. Take a look at Table 3-1 for more filename examples.

Table 3-1	Kim Komando's Dot-Period Conversions			
Circumstance	*Dot or Period*	*Proper Usage*	*Improper Usage*	
www.dummies.com	Dot	www-dot-dummies-dot-com	www-period-dummies-period-com	
A time of mourning	Period	I'm in a period of mourning.	She mourned for her spouse for a long dot.	
Dorothy's nickname	Dot	Hello, Dot.	Hello, Period.	

on the test

One filename that you need to pay special attention to is the name for your primary Web page — the one people see when they first come to your Web site. Here's a simple rule that you should follow without question: Always name your main file either index.htm or index.html. Here's why.

When you enter a Web address without indicating a specific Web page, your Web browser automatically looks for a Web page with one of these two names. For example, if you go to your Web browser and enter www.komando.com, what you actually get is www.komando.com/index.html. By following this easy rule for naming your main Web page, typically called your *home page,* you simplify publicizing your Web address. Telling people that your Web address is *www.mycompany.com* is a lot easier than *www.mycompany.com/homepage.html*.

heads up

Something else to keep in mind about your index.htm or your index.html file: If you don't have one and someone types in your home page address, they get an actual index of all the different files on your site. So if my Web page (www.komando.com) or the Dummies Web page (www.dummies.com) didn't have index.html files, you'd just see a list of every text file, every picture, and every everything on the sites when you stopped by to visit. While that may be handy, keep in mind that there may be pieces of your Web page that you don't want visitors to know about. The bottom line? Protect yourself and have an index.html file.

heads up

The one last thing you need to think about when saving your documents is where you save them to. You guessed it — I've got another rule of thumb for this. (Right about now, you're probably wondering how many thumbs I have.) Simply stated, save all your Web files (and all the other supporting files — graphics, multimedia files, and so on) in the same folder on your hard drive. This makes linking from one file to another much easier, and also ensures that those links don't break when you upload your files to your ISP's Web server.

Notes:

☑ **Progress Check**

If you can do the following, you've mastered this lesson:

❑ Save your files in the proper format.

❑ Know the difference between a dot and a period.

like paying taxes on time, make sure you have an index.html file

Check, Please!

Lesson 3-3

heads up

When you finish creating your Web page or pages, you naturally want to make sure that you did a good job. My advice: Instead of waiting until you're all done, check your work as you go, after you finish each major task. Even if you end up using one of the Web page editors I describe in Unit 8, this is good practice. We all know that practice makes perfect, except in the case of Michael Jackson's plastic surgery. I just love seeing those before and after pictures. But I digress.

If you go too long without correcting an error in HTML coding, the error can snowball into a bigger and bigger problem. Suppose you create a link back to your home page at the bottom of one of your subsequent pages, and then decide to include that same link at the bottom of all your other pages (a good idea, indeed). The obvious shortcut here is to copy and paste that link from one document to the next.

However, if you make a coding error on that first link, then the link is wrong on every page you copy the link to. Instead of having to fix the problem just once, you may end up having to fix the problem ten different times on ten different Web pages. Ouch!

on the test

Doing a constant check is also a great excuse to stop working and see how cool your Mother-of-all-Sites is doing. The good news is that checking your work is easy, no matter what program you use to create your Web pages.

1 **Just launch your Web browser.**

2 **Choose File⇨Open.**

After you open one file, you can check all the other internal links for your Web site.

heads up

Unfortunately, every Web browser out there displays a Web page a little differently. Most of this has to do with the Web browser itself. However, your Web page visitors can have different settings on their browsers, which can affect the way your page looks. Take a look at Figure 3-3 for an example. The truth is, there's no way to guarantee *exactly* how your page will look on someone else's computer. The best way to avoid any problem in this area is to check your work with more than one Web browser. It's pretty easy to do, too. Just go to my Web site — www.komando.com — and download the browser(s) that you don't have. That way, you can get some idea of the different ways your Web page can appear.

heads up

I've got to say this one more time: *Don't forget to check your pages as you create them*. After you finish all your coding, give the whole project one more big check on your own system. Next, check it all again when you "go live" by putting your whole site on your ISP's Web server. You get to tackle that later.

Recess

heads up

We interrupt this lesson with a commercial break: Guests of Kim Komando's Web page stay at the Cyber Hotel, located in Cyberspace just seconds from the Info Superhighway.

☑ Progress Check

If you can do the following, you've mastered this lesson:

❑ Open your browser and test your HTML code.

❑ Understand why it's so important to save all the files for your Web page in the same folder.

❑ Know that there are certain things you should not do that include dressing as if you were 15 years younger, leaving price tags on presents, using the last square of toilet paper, cleaning your fingernails at the dinner table (gross), or taking the following quiz without getting up and dancing around the room.

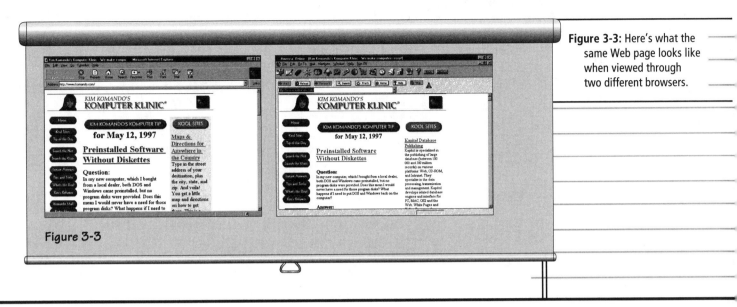

Figure 3-3

Figure 3-3: Here's what the same Web page looks like when viewed through two different browsers.

Unit 3 Quiz

Circle the letter of the best answer to each of the following questions. There may be more than one correct answer.

1. **Any HTML code that performs a function is called . . .**

   A. A tag   C. An anchor

   B. A marker   D. A miracle

2. **If a Web browser encounters HTML code that it doesn't understand, the browser . . .**

   A. Ignores the code

   B. Displays the code so you know where your mistake is located

   C. Crashes your system

   D. Displays an error message

3. **You can look at the HTML code on somebody else's Web page by . . .**

   A. Writing and asking the author for it

   B. Making an illegal copy of the Web page

   C. Putting on magic glasses

   D. Using your Web browser's <u>V</u>iew⇨Sour<u>c</u>e option

4. **In what format should you save HTML files?**

   A. Any word-processing format

   B. Text-only format

   C. Special Web format

   D. I didn't read the section

5. **What is the proper file extension for an HTML file?**

   A. .htm

   B. .html

   C. Both A and B

   D. Neither A nor B

6. **What is the correct name for your primary (home) page?**

   A. main.html

   B. home.html

   C. index.html

   D. start.html

7. **The easiest way to check your work is to . . .**

   A. Read through the HTML file line by line

   B. Ask someone else to read through the file for you

   C. Upload the files to your ISP

   D. Open the files with your own Web browser

Unit 3 Exercise

1. If you're using a word processor to create your Web pages, practice using the Save As command and saving your files as text only. Also, make sure you stick to the naming conventions discussed in this unit.

2. After you save some HTML files, open them in your Web browser and make sure they really look the way you want. If possible, try more than one Web browser.

Unit 4

. . . .

HTML To Go

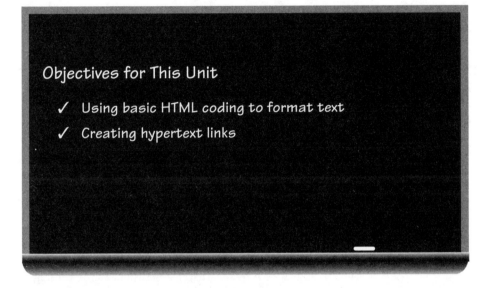

Objectives for This Unit

✓ Using basic HTML coding to format text

✓ Creating hypertext links

Prerequisites

▶ Knowing how HTML works (Lesson 3-1)

▶ Knowing how to save an HTML file (Lesson 3-2)

▶ Knowing how to test an HTML file (Lesson 3-3)

on the CD

▶ breaks.htm

▶ text.htm

▶ type.htm

▶ list.htm

▶ headings.htm

▶ horzrule.htm

▶ info.htm

▶ index.htm

▶ links.htm

▶ download.htm

*O*kay. The time has come to leave your old life behind and, perhaps for the first time in your life, learn how to do some real, live programming — HTML programming, that is. Speaking of living life to the fullest, my Uncle Norman lives every day as if it were his last. No such luck. He runs around all day, every day screaming, "I'm gonna die! I'm gonna die!" I wish he'd stop already.

Let's start at the very beginning and cover the essential HTML elements that you will use with almost every Web page you design. Remember, as you learned in Unit 1, any word processor will do, but save and test as you go along. You'd hate to have the best page you ever designed in your whole life not work or, worse, vanish into the intergalatic bit bucket because the power suddenly went out before you had a chance to save your work.

Figure 4-1: This is the top of my home page.

Title bar

Figure 4-1

Lesson 4-1

Getting a Better Title in Lieu of a Salary Increase

Two of the most important decisions you make when you create a Web page are the title and the colors you use for key elements. The hardest part is making up your mind about each category, because the coding for each is so simple.

Playing the title role with the <TITLE> tag

The <TITLE> tag tells your Web browser what text to display in the bar that runs across the top of every HTML page. The title should be the very first thing in your HTML document. For example, the title bar in Figure 4-1 (although you can't see the whole thing) reads: Kim Komando's Komputer Klinic – We make computers easy!

The HTML coding for that title looks like this:

```
<HEAD><TITLE>Kim Komando's Komputer Klinic - We make
            computers easy!</TITLE></HEAD>
```

Simple, eh? To create the title for your Web page, follow these instructions:

on the test

1 **Go to your word processor, or even Microsoft Notepad, and create a new document.**

2 **Type <HEAD><TITLE>.**

Type it exactly like this, all in caps and in those pointy angle brackets. You don't have to type HTML code in all caps, but doing so makes it easier to see in a document.

3 **Type the name of your title after the <HEAD><TITLE> HTML tags.**

You don't need to add any spaces before or after the angle brackets, just spaces in the text as you want it to appear.

4 **Type </TITLE></HEAD> at the end of the line.**

Remember, you don't need to add spaces in the HTML code.

Let me give you a little more detail about the second set of bracketed instructions with a slash in it. The slash tells your browser that the code ends. In other words, if the instructions start at the first bracket, or *open tag,* they end when the browser gets to the *close tag* with the slash.

Okay, save the page with an *.htm* extension the way I describe in Lesson 3-2. Now open your browser and choose File⇨Open. Find the page on your hard drive, and select it. Let me guess, you don't see a thing and you think you're doing something wrong. Check again. You see a blank document, but if you look up at the title bar, you see the title you just typed in.

heads up

Maybe you're wondering why you need two tags, *head* and *title,* just to create the title. Rather than bore you with a bunch of technical mumbo-jumbo about the *head* tag, I'll just tell you that you always need to format the title always this way. You're not likely to ever use the head tag for anything else. It's not that I don't believe you can understand this, but we have to move on.

Having trouble finding the document on your hard drive? If you saved it as a Text Only document and then changed the extension, your Web browser probably only reads it as a text document. When you go to the File/Open menu of your browser, click on the arrow next to the Files of Type line and select Text Files. After that, you should be able to find your document without a problem.

Coloring your text and life

When you want to change colors of your text, there's no need to call Ted Turner. All you need to do is include another line of HTML code right after your Title information. This tells the Web browser what color to use for various types of text. The four different types of text that you can adjust colors for are:

- ◆ **TEXT.** Aside from the three different kinds of links this list shows, all of the text on your page appears in whatever color you specify for *TEXT.* If you don't specify a color, the default is black.

- ◆ **LINK.** Except for the next two special kinds of links, any linked text on your page appears in the color you specify for *LINK.* If you don't specify a color, the default is normally blue.

- ◆ **ALINK.** This is short for *active link.* A link is active when you click and hold the mouse button on it. For whatever period of time you keep the mouse button depressed, the link appears in the color you specify for *ALINK.* If you don't specify a color, the default is normally red.

- ◆ **VLINK.** Most Web browsers have one handy feature: They keep track of where you've been. If a particular link leads to a page you've visited recently, that link is a *visited link* and is appears in a different color. If you don't specify a color, the default is normally purple.

You may have noticed that when I talk about default link colors in this list, I use the word "normally." That's because just about every Web browser gives you the ability to choose your own default colors for each kind of link. If you

Notes:

the title tag
requires two
different tags:
<HEAD> and
<TITLE>

Notes:

be careful picking colors — you want the combination to be attractive, not tacky

want to, you can tell your browser to display regular links in chartreuse, active links in magenta, and visited links in burgundy.

Here's my point. If you don't specify any colors for your links, there's no way to be absolutely sure what color those links appear on somebody else's Web browser. If you absolutely, positively want the visited links on your page to appear in purple no matter what, you have to specify purple as the color to use for visited links.

The tricky part is that on the Web, you specify a particular color by using a *hexadecimal code*. This is the pound sign (#) followed by six characters. For example, take a look at this line of code.

```
<BODY TEXT="#FF0000" LINK="#000000" ALINK="#ffffff"
          VLINK="#2b6718">
```

Careful, one digit off, and your browser will launch our intercontinental ballistic missiles. If you add the preceding line of code to your Web page, your regular text is a shade of red (#FF0000), your regular links are solid black (#000000), your active links are solid white (#ffffff), and your visited links are an ugly green (#2b6718). I hope you never use this color combination; I show it here just to demonstrate a point. Now that I think of it, it's kind of silly — I say don't do this by doing it.

on the CD

More color schemes (or *hex codes*) exist than Zsa Zsa and Liz Taylor have hex-husbands. So with millions of colors to choose from, how do you possibly figure out the right hex code? Well, you can use trial and error, but that may take you weeks to find the color you want. The easy way if you're a Windows user is to use a program called RGB Color Box, which comes with the CD-ROM at the back of this book. (If you're a Mac user, check out HTML ColourTool, available from MacUser Software Central, `http://www5.zdnet.com/mac/·download.html`.)

You can pick a color with this handy program, and RGB Color Box tells you the color's hex code equivalent. When you have the hex code for the color you want, just substitute your new hex code on the line of code I just gave you. If you're willing to live with the defaults for text or links or active links or visited links, just take that part out of the line of code. For example, if you want to use all those colors, except you're happy using the default for active links, type the following line of code:

```
<BODY TEXT="#FF0000" LINK="#000000" VLINK="#2b6718">
```

Adjusting text colors is fun, and it helps to give your page a more professional, color-coordinated look.

To test colors on your Web page, follow these steps:

1 **Go to the appropriate program and select the different colors you want.**

In RGB Color Box, click on the Generate Body Tag box to reveal the hex codes. Jot down the hex codes on a piece of paper, along with the names of the colors, so you won't forget them.

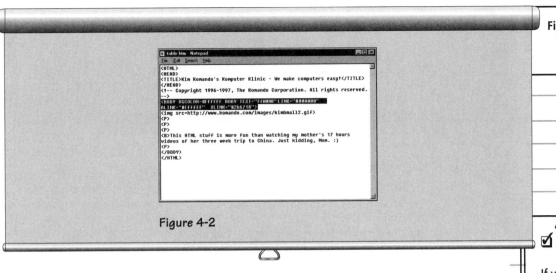

Figure 4-2

Figure 4-2: Check out where the color codes go inside your HTML code.

2 **Go back to the document that you already saved when you created your title.**

3 **Type in the lines of code that define your colors.**

My example was <BODY TEXT="#FF0000" LINK="#000000" ALINK="#ffffff" VLINK="#2b6718">. Yours won't be exactly the same as this because you probably picked sharper looking colors, but you get the idea. Remember, if you like the default colors for Body Text, for example, you don't have to add a hex code for it at all. See Figure 4-2.

4 **Save your document by choosing File⇨Save.**

You don't have to use the Save As function this time, because you already saved the file as an *.htm* document.

If you go back to your browser to check, you don't see anything different because you don't have any text in your document yet that these colors affect. Just hold your horses. You start seeing colors as we add more code.

☑ **Progress Check**

If you can do the following, you've mastered this lesson:

❑ Create an HTML document and put a title on your fledgling Web page.

❑ Use the RGB Color Box program to pick colors you'd like to use on your Web page.

❑ Give yourself a new title like webmaster or webmistress.

Giving Your Page Some Body (Text)

Lesson 4-2

on the CD

Body text sounds like it could be a new kind of tattoo. It's not. Body text in your HTML document is just like body text in your word-processing documents. Body text is basically the default format for text. Here's the format for what appears in Figure 4-3. You can find this among this book's CD files as text.htm.

```
<BODY>This is an example of body text.</BODY>
```

Any text that you place between these tags appears as plain old text. But before you try out this tag, you may want to check out the next tag, too.

Figure 4-3: This is what you see in your browser when you test some body text.

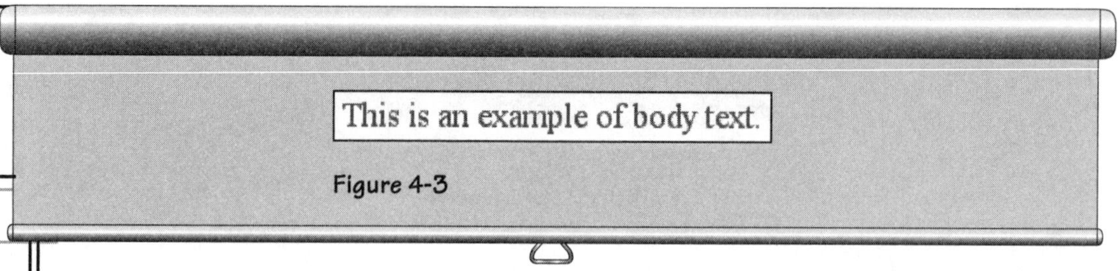

This is an example of body text.

Figure 4-3

Notes:

Line breaks

Your Web browser doesn't do anything unless you tell it to by using HTML code. With a word processor, you can type away all you want and use the return key to create paragraph breaks. However, in your Web browser, unless you include the HTML code for line breaks, that text shows up as one giant, run-together paragraph. Yucko. The solution to this mess is the following tag.

`<BR>`

heads up

Now that's what I call easy. When you get to the end of a paragraph, make sure you always type this code. Remember, this is one of the few lines of HTML code that doesn't require two tags. Just typing **
** at the end of the line does the trick.

1 **Go back to the word-processing document you're working in.**

2 **Type <BODY>.**

3 **Type in a bunch of text.**

It doesn't matter what it is — the text can be the lyrics to your favorite song or the Gettysburg Address. Just type a bunch.

4 **When you've rambled long enough to make a paragraph, type the <BR> tag.**

5 **Now go ahead and add another paragraph of text.**

6 **Type </BODY> when you're done.**

7 **Choose File⇨Save.**

8 **Go to your browser and open the document again.**

Each time you save new code in your word-processing document, you must reopen the document from your hard drive. In other words, the browser doesn't update and see all the changes you've made.

You should notice a few different things, as shown in Figure 4-4. First, two separate paragraphs of text appear; and if you selected a color for your text, you see it in that color.

9 **Call your mom again and tell her how impressive your programming is.**

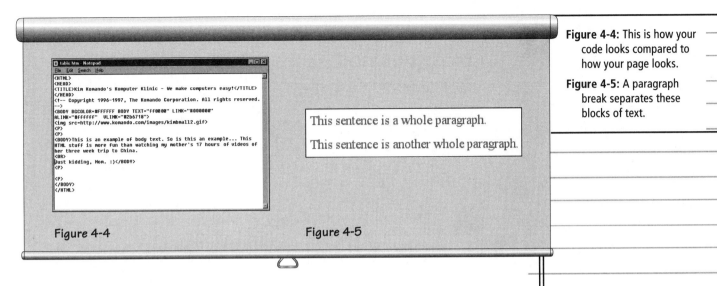

Figure 4-4: This is how your code looks compared to how your page looks.

Figure 4-5: A paragraph break separates these blocks of text.

Figure 4-4   Figure 4-5

Paragraph breaks

on the test

When you use the line break tag <BR>, your Web browser takes you down one line. However, just as in word processing, sometimes you want a little extra space between your paragraphs. If that's the case, use the following tag instead:

```
<P>This sentence is a whole paragraph.</P>
```

```
<P>This sentence is another whole paragraph.</P>
```

The big difference from a plain line break is that you need an opening and closing tag to specify a paragraph. Figure 4-5 shows what the preceding code looks like on a Web browser.

Notice the space between the two paragraphs. Your Web browser knows to add this space automatically. Give paragraph breaks another try:

1 **Go back to your word-processing document where you're creating your Web page.**

2 **Right after the first** <BODY> **tag, type** <P>**.**

3 **At the end of that paragraph where you originally typed the tag**
, delete the
 tag and type </P> **instead.**

4 **Type** <P> **where you want the next paragraph to start.**

5 **Type** </P> **where you want the paragraph to end.**

6 **Choose <u>F</u>ile⇨<u>S</u>ave to save the document and to check it out with your Web browser.**

You should see two paragraphs separated by spaces.

on the CD

If you need to see the final code, check out breaks.htm from the files that came with this book's CD.

Bold (but not necessarily courageous) type

Just because you make type bold in your word-processing document, don't be fooled into thinking this has anything to do with making type bold on your Web page. Just like everything else on your Web page, a Web browser will make type bold only if you tell it to do so using the right HTML tag. Bold type looks like this.

```
<B>This is bold type.</B>
```

on the test

As you're about to discover, some HTML tags duplicate the functions of other HTML tags. Exactly why this is so isn't really important. Call it poor planning on the part of the original developers of HTML, if you want. What is important is that you can use whichever one you want to produce the desired effect. For example, using the <STRONG> tag also produces bold type. It works like this.

```
<STRONG>This is another way to make your type bold.</
                    STRONG>
```

Before you boldly go to try out bold type, take a look at the next section.

Italic type

Italic type works pretty much like bold type. Here's the code.

```
<I>This is italic type.</I>
```

heads up

I just have one word of caution: Italics are great for added emphasis on a printed page, but if you've ever looked at italics on a computer screen, you know italic text is sometimes hard to read. For that reason, I suggest you don't go too crazy with italics. For the benefit of your cybervisitors, don't ever make an entire paragraph display in italics — that is, unless you're making a Web site to confound the devil.

on the test

One more point about italics: There are four — count 'em, four — other ways you can stress text as an alternative to italics. They are: *address, emphasis, citation,* and *variable.* The tags look like this.

```
<ADDRESS>This just makes text appear in italics.</AD-
                DRESS>
<EM>So does this</EM>
<CIT>And so does this.</CIT>
<VAR>And so does this</VAR>
```

The tags all do the same thing. Go figure.

Now, let's try them all out:

1 **Go to your word-processing document and pick out a line of text that you want to bold and a line that you want to put in *italics*.**

2 **Type <B> where you want the bold text to start, and then go to the end of the line and type </B> where you want the bold text to end.**

3 **Type <I> where you want the italics to start, and then go to the end of the line and type </I> where you want the italics to end.**

4 **Save your document.**

5 **Open the document in your browser and take a look at your bold and italic text.**

6 **Now, go back to your word-processing document and substitute the <STRONG> tag for the <B> tag and the <ADDRESS> tag (or any of the other italics tag options) for the <I> tag.**

7 **Choose File⇨Save to save your document and to check it out in your browser again.**

Your document should look exactly as it did before. (And don't accuse me of making you do useless work, either. Hey, you took algebra didn't you? Did you ever use that?)

> *here are a few different ways to do italic or bold type*

Blinking type

Of course, there are things you can do on a computer screen that you can't do on a printed page at all. I have yet to see a sheet of paper with blinking type on it. However, on your Web page — if you're using the Netscape Navigator browser — blinking type is easy to create. Keep in mind that if people visit your page and they're using Internet Explorer, they're not going to see this stuff blink (but I bet Microsoft fixes that someday with a new release). If you do want to give it a try, though, just use the following code:

```
<BLINK>This is blinking type.</BLINK>
```

heads up

I have to give you a big caution on this one, though. You may think it's cool that you can make words flash on your screen, but look at it from someone else's point of view. If you are reading a page of information and there's a little blob blinking in the corner of your eye the whole time, it can be like somebody continuously tapping a pencil on a desk. At first it may not seem like a big deal, but after a while, it's a real pain in the . . . well, you get the idea. But other folks may feel differently.

> *blinking type is visible only with the Netscape Navigator browser, not with Internet Explorer*

Monospaced type

Just about all of the text on your Web page appears in what's called a *proportional font*. A proportional font is one like Times or Helvetica where each letter takes up only as much horizontal space as it needs. If you want a different look, you can use a *monospaced font*. In a monospaced font, every character takes up as much horizontal space as every other letter. Courier, which creates a typewriter look, is an example of a monospaced font.

Notes:

Believe it or not, HTML offers five ways to create monospaced type: *teletype, preformatted, code, sample,* and *keyboard.* Here's what the tags look like.

```
<TT>This is the teletype tag.</TT>
<PRE>This is the preformatted tag.</PRE>
<CODE>This is the code tag.</CODE>
<SAMP>This is the sample tag.</SAMP>
<KBD>This is the keyboard tag.</KBD>
```

To check out what these different fonts look like, go back to your word-processing document:

1 Type in the preceding lines of code just as you see them.

2 Save the document and open it in your Web browser.

Now, you can decide if you like the look of any of these fonts and you can choose to use whichever you like best.

Indents

on the test

From time to time, you may want to indent a paragraph here and there to create a more visually interesting page. In HTMLspeak, an indented paragraph is a *block quote.* Therefore, it stands to reason that the tag for an indented paragraph looks like this:

```
<BLOCKQUOTE>This sentence will appear indented on a Web
            browser.</BLOCKQUOTE>
```

on the CD

Go ahead and try this out in your word-processing document. You know how to do it: Just add the <BLOCKQUOTE> tag to a section of your text. Save the document and check out the effect in your browser, or check out type.htm from this book's lesson files.

Lists

on the test

Oscar Schindler would be proud. If you have lists to include on your Web page, HTML gives you the option to format them as bulleted or numbered. As long as you get the code right, you don't have to worry about typing in the bullet characters or item numbers. Your Web browser takes care of that for you.

Here's a three-item list formatted with bullets.

```
<UL>
 <LI>This is the first item.
 <LI>This is the second item.
 <LI>This is the third item.
</UL>
```

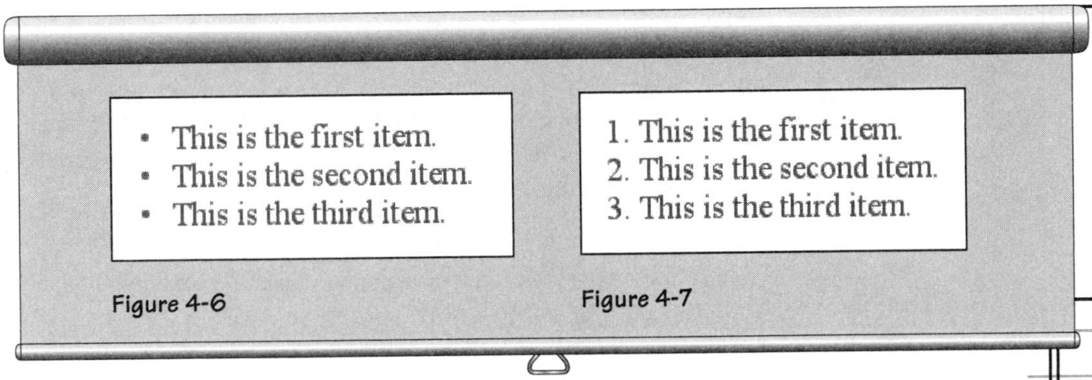

• This is the first item.
• This is the second item.
• This is the third item.

1. This is the first item.
2. This is the second item.
3. This is the third item.

Figure 4-6

Figure 4-7

Figure 4-6: The bullets appear automatically, which is very different from semiautomatic bullets.

Figure 4-7: Sequential numbers replace the bullet characters.

Notice that there is one set of tags to identify the whole list and another tag to mark each item in the list. Also, notice that you don't have to put a line break after each item. Figure 4-6 shows this code when viewed in a Web browser.

Here's the code for the same items displayed as a numbered list.

```
<OL>
 <LI>This is the first item.
 <LI>This is the second item.
 <LI>This is the third item.
</OL>
```

Again, there's a set of tags to mark the whole list, and a set to mark each item. Figure 4-7 shows what the preceding block of code looks like when you view it with a Web browser.

This will probably come as no surprise, but there are two other ways to create bulleted lists on your Web pages. The alternative tags for bulleted lists are: *directory* and *menu*. The *directory* tag looks like this.

```
<DIR>
 <LI>This is the first item.
 <LI>This is the second item.
 <LI>This is the third item.
</DIR>
```

The *menu* tag looks like this.

```
<MENU>
 <LI>This is the first item.
 <LI>This is the second item.
 <LI>This is the third item.
</MENU>
```

As with all the other "multiple choice" tags, you can use whichever one you want. Give it a try:

1 Decide if you want to test a bulleted list or a numbered list, and then go to your word-processing document.

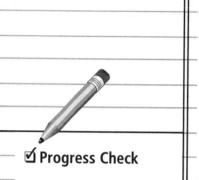

☑ **Progress Check**

If you can do the following, you've mastered this lesson:

❑ Enter body text into your fledgling Web page.

❑ Mix and match the code comfortably so you can create a basic page.

2 Think of an interesting list of items like names you would give your pet snake, if you had one, or list the three best haircuts that Hillary Clinton has had over the past few years.

3 Call your mom to consult about your list.

She probably won't answer the phone. Leave a message.

4 Go to the bottom of your word-processing document and type `<UL>`.

I give this example with the first bulleted list I talked about. You can test it out with this one or with any of the others.

5 Type `<LI>` and then the first item on your list.

Most programmers would type this on a separate line from the `<UL>` code, but you don't have to do that in order to get it to work. It just looks tidier that way.

6 Type `<LI>` again with the second item on your list.

7 Type `<LI>` again with the third item on your list.

8 When you finish your list, type `</UL>`.

9 Choose File⇨Save to save the document and view it in your browser.

10 If you want, go back to your word-processing document and try replacing the `<UL>` code to `<MENU>` or one of the other list codes.

11 Change tactics and call your dad.

If you need to check your finished product, compare it to lists.htm from this book's CD files.

Recess

Boy, you learned a lot in the last lesson. Now, take a break and explore your talents with these newfound skills. Make a page that contains the top 10 things that your in-laws, boss or parents do that you hate, or love, the most. Okay, maybe that's not a good idea, just in case they see your Web page. Instead, in a list, describe your last vacation and the top five things that you remember the most. Come on, don't get lazy on me now. Much like riding a bike and some other things in life, practice makes perfect.

Lesson 4-3

Getting Attention at the Head of the Class

Headings

Just like with your word-processing documents, you may want to start your Web page with a heading, and then break up the subsequent paragraphs with other headings. HTML has just what you need, offering six different levels of headings. This is what the heading tags look like.

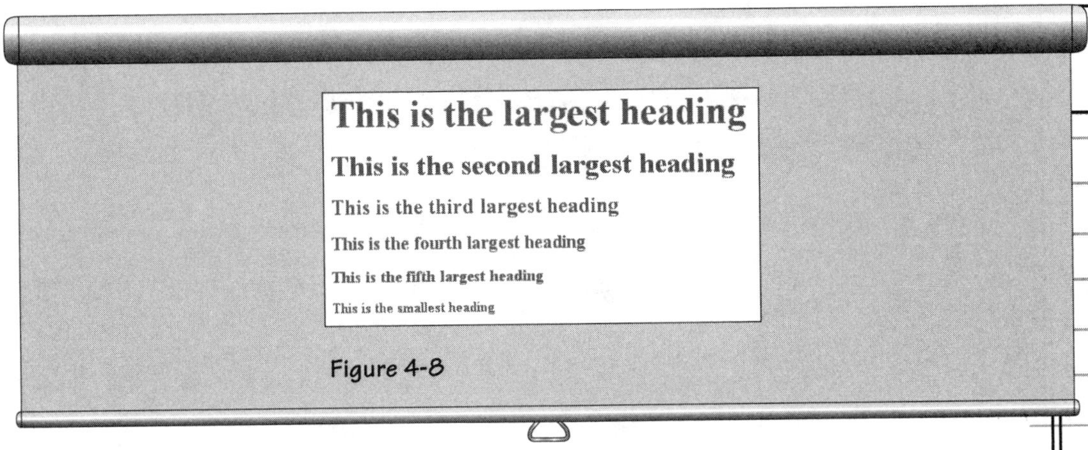

This is the largest heading

This is the second largest heading

This is the third largest heading

This is the fourth largest heading

This is the fifth largest heading

This is the smallest heading

Figure 4-8

Figure 4-8: Headings come in six sizes.

Notes:

```
<H1>This is the largest heading</H1>
<H2>This is the second-largest heading</H2>
<H3>This is the third-largest heading</H3>
<H4>This is the fourth-largest heading</H4>
<H5>This is the fifth-largest heading</H5>
<H6>This is the smallest heading</H6>
```

heads up

There's one other thing you need know about these heading tags: You don't have to use the line break tag <BR> to create a new paragraph after the heading. Your Web browser knows that a heading belongs on a separate line and therefore takes care of it for you without the extra line break tag. Figure 4-8 shows what the preceding codes for font sizes look like when you view it through a Web browser. Now that's one smart browser.

Play with different sizes of headings by following these steps:

1 **In your word-processing document, go to the beginning of the first paragraph.**

2 **Type <H1> (or whatever size heading that you want to test out).**

3 **Now type an incredibly funny and clever head.**

   Don't get stuck on this for too long. You have 15 seconds. I'm timing you.

4 **Type </H1> to finish the head.**

   If you used a different code at the beginning of the head, make sure the code you use here matches it.

heads up

5 **Go to the beginning of the second paragraph.**

6 **Repeat Steps 2 through 4.**

   This time, use a different heading size and yet another funny and clever title. (You have only 10 seconds to come up with this one.)

7 **Choose File⇨Save to save your document and to check it out in your browser.**

8 **Call your mother, collect, to brag.**

on the CD

The headings.htm file that came on this book's CD has all six heading sizes in one document, if you want to take a shortcut.

experimenting with different font sizes is a good way to add spark to your page

Notes:

Horizontal line (the shortest distance to my point)

on the test

In all of HTML coding, there is one and only one graphic element that you can create entirely from HTML code without having any external graphic file. That graphic element is the simple horizontal line, or *horizontal rule* in HTMLese. Here's an example of the code:

```
<HR>
```

Another example of horizontal rule is a king on his back. Never mind. On-ward! This code creates a horizontal rule that runs across the width of the window in your Web browser, regardless of how wide or narrow you happen to make that window. This is a handy bit of code for dividing up different sections on a page.

heads up

One thing you can't do is have a horizontal rule on the same line as anything else. If you're typing along and you put <HR> in the middle of a sentence, your Web browser displays the sentence on separate lines with the horizontal rule between them.

If you want to get really fancy with your horizontal rules, you can specify some other options in your HTML code. For example, you can determine the length of the rule as either a percentage of the horizontal space in the browser window, or as a fixed number of pixels, or dots, on the screen.

To specify the length of the line as 75 percent of the window width, for example, you would use this code:

```
<HR ALIGN=LEFT WIDTH="75%">
```

To specify the length of the line as 75 pixels (much shorter than the other one), you would use this code:

```
<HR ALIGN=LEFT WIDTH="75">
```

You may have noticed that both of these lines of HTML code include ALIGN=LEFT. That's because when the rule doesn't take up the whole width of the screen, you can also specify whether the rule aligns to the LEFT, the CENTER, or the RIGHT by adding the appropriate code.

You can also make your horizontal rules a specific number of pixels thick. For example, to make the first rule above 10 pixels thick, you use this code:

```
<HR ALIGN=LEFT WIDTH="75%" SIZE=10>
```

However, if you make a thicker than normal line, you may notice that it looks more like a box than a line. Why? Horizontal rules by default use what's called shading, as shown in Figure 4-9. With shading active, the line has no color and its edges are shaded to create a 3-D effect. To make the preceding rule solid black, you need to use this line of code:

```
<HR ALIGN=LEFT WIDTH="75%" SIZE=10 NOSHADE>
```

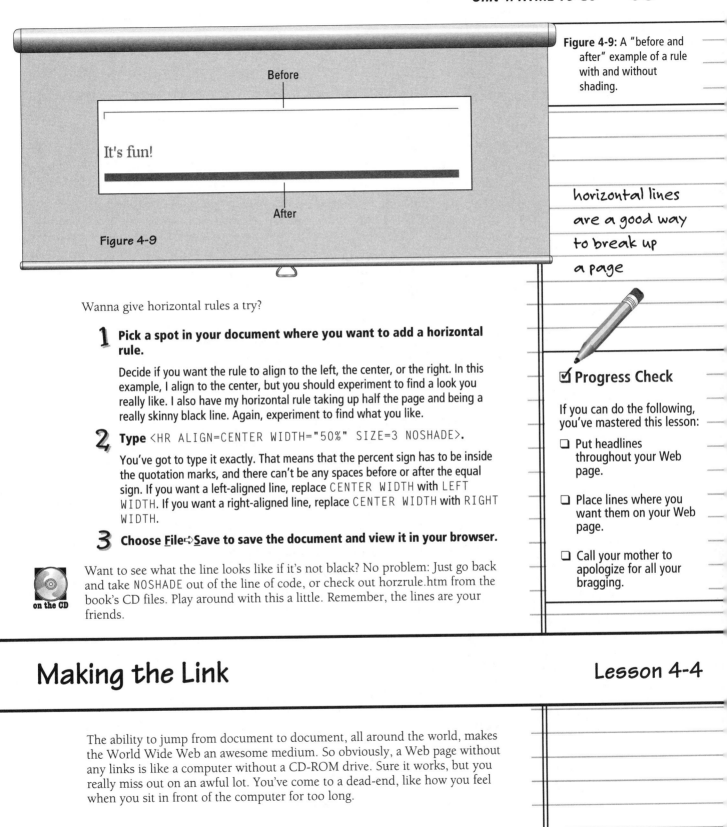

Before

It's fun!

After

Figure 4-9

Figure 4-9: A "before and after" example of a rule with and without shading.

horizontal lines are a good way to break up a page

Wanna give horizontal rules a try?

1 Pick a spot in your document where you want to add a horizontal rule.

Decide if you want the rule to align to the left, the center, or the right. In this example, I align to the center, but you should experiment to find a look you really like. I also have my horizontal rule taking up half the page and being a really skinny black line. Again, experiment to find what you like.

2 Type `<HR ALIGN=CENTER WIDTH="50%" SIZE=3 NOSHADE>`.

You've got to type it exactly. That means that the percent sign has to be inside the quotation marks, and there can't be any spaces before or after the equal sign. If you want a left-aligned line, replace `CENTER WIDTH` with `LEFT WIDTH`. If you want a right-aligned line, replace `CENTER WIDTH` with `RIGHT WIDTH`.

3 Choose File⇨Save to save the document and view it in your browser.

Want to see what the line looks like if it's not black? No problem: Just go back and take `NOSHADE` out of the line of code, or check out horzrule.htm from the book's CD files. Play around with this a little. Remember, the lines are your friends.

on the CD

☑ **Progress Check**

If you can do the following, you've mastered this lesson:

❑ Put headlines throughout your Web page.

❑ Place lines where you want them on your Web page.

❑ Call your mother to apologize for all your bragging.

Making the Link

Lesson 4-4

The ability to jump from document to document, all around the world, makes the World Wide Web an awesome medium. So obviously, a Web page without any links is like a computer without a CD-ROM drive. Sure it works, but you really miss out on an awful lot. You've come to a dead-end, like how you feel when you sit in front of the computer for too long.

on the test

There are basically four types of files you're likely to link to from your Web page:

- *Internal links,* which are links to other pages on your own site.
- *External links,* which are links to pages on another Web site.
- *Anchors,* which are links to other locations in the same document.
- *Links to downloadable files,* such as shareware programs that you want people to be able to download from your Web site. The links to the downloadable files have no specific name.

Your links aren't limited to other Web pages. You can also link directly to GIFs and JPEGs. That's material for Unit IV. *Don't look!* For now, let's discuss each one of these four types of links individually.

Internal links

When you create your Web site, keep all of the files for your Web site — HTML files, graphics, multimedia files, and so on — all in one folder, both on your own hard drive and on your ISP's computer after you upload the files. Using one folder makes it easy to deal with internal links, which are also known as *relative links.*

As you soon discover, when you create a link to an outside Web page, you must use the entire Web address, or URL (pronounced "you are el"), to create the link. But with an internal link, you use only the file name. Take a look at the following code to see what I mean:

```
<A HREF="info.htm">This text serves as a link to
            info.htm.</A>
```

If you type this code into your HTML document, clicking on the text between the tags tells your Web browser to look in the same folder that contains the current file for another file called *info.htm.* If the linked-to file isn't in the same folder as the current file, your Web browser can't find it. This type of link is often called a relative link — the location of the linked-to file is relative to the location of the current file.

on the CD

You use relative links to help people navigate your site. For example, at the bottom of all your subsequent pages, you may want to include code that looks something like this, which you can find as info.htm among this book's CD files.

```
<A HREF="index.html">Return to Home Page</A>
```

heads up

This code enables your Web site visitors to jump back to your first page. Notice that the filename must be in quotation marks — not your word processor's "curly quotes" either. Your Web browser won't understand them, in the way that you don't understand your own relatives. If you don't know how to change your "curly quote" function so you get quotation marks instead, you need to check the help files that come with your word processor.

Do a test run on a link by following these steps:

links are an important part of any Web page

1 **Nope. You're wrong. Don't go to that same old word-processing document you've been working in all along. Instead, I want you to create a totally new word-processing document.**

If you don't remember how, check out Lesson 3-1. (But tell me, how did you get this far in this unit?)

2 **To add a title to the new document, type** `<HEAD><TITLE>` **and then your title.**

You can use the same title you used for your other page, if you want, or you can create a totally new one.

3 **Now type** `</TITLE></HEAD>` **to finish it all off.**

4 **Add some text.**

Just use the old `<BODY>` code. Don't get too carried away. Type `<BODY>`, add a few lines, and then close the whole thing off by typing `</BODY>`.

5 **Choose <u>F</u>ile⇨<u>S</u>ave, but save this new document as an** *.htm* **file.**

heads up

Remember, you may have to save it as text, which is fine for now. If you do have to save it as a text file, *do not* change the extension to *.htm*. Just keep it as *.txt* for now) Call it *page2.htm* and save it in the same file where you saved the *index.htm* document you've been working on through this whole unit. This is very important: If you don't save it in the same file where the other document is, your link won't work.

6 **Go back to your first word-processing document (*index.htm*) and type this at the bottom of the page:** `<A HREF="page2.htm">This text serves as a link to my second page</A>`.

Let me break this down for you. The first part of the code, `<A HREF="page2.htm">`, tells the browser that you want to link to another page that you called *page2.htm.* (Make sure you give your page that name. If you can't save your file as an *.htm* document and save it as a *.txt* document instead, be sure that you use `"page2.txt"` instead of `"page2.htm"` in your code.) The second part of the code, `This text serves as a link to my second page`, is the actual link that you see on the page. The third part, `</A>`, is the final piece of the HTML code.

7 **Save your *index.htm* document and open it in your browser.**

You should see a line of underlined of text at the bottom of your page that reads, "This text serves as a link to my second page." If you changed the color of your links way at the beginning of this unit, the text will be in the color that you assigned. If you didn't give it a new color, the link will just be blue.

8 **Make a drum roll noise on your desk.**

9 **Click on the link.**

Your second page should appear in your browser screen. Congratulations! You have just created your first link!

on the CD

The finished product is among this book's CD file as index.htm.

If these steps didn't work, one of two things could be wrong. First, be sure that you saved the second document in the same file as the first document. If you didn't, your browser doesn't know where to look for it. Second, be sure you gave the file the right name in the link. If you haven't, go back and correct it.

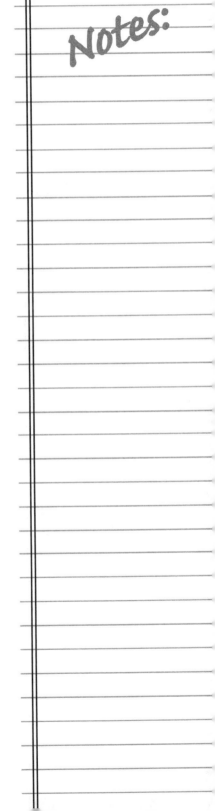
Notes:

Figure 4-10: This is a picture of what you get when you click a missing link.

HTTP/1.0 404 Object Not Found

Figure 4-10

External links

To modify a famous old saying, no Web page is an island. As a service to the people who come to visit your Web site, you owe it to them to provide some Web links to useful, related material. For example, if you want to guide your visitors to the absolutely most fantastic Web site in the history of the Internet, you can include this bit of HTML code in your document:

```
<A HREF="http://www.komando.com/">Kim Komando's Komputer
            Klinic</A >
```

Modest, aren't I? The only difference between this external link and an internal link is that this one specifies the entire Web address of the linked-to page. You can use this exact same code on any page, no matter where it is or what folder it's in, and it always leads to my home page. For this reason, this type of link is also referred to as an *absolute link*.

Ready to give it a try? It's really no different than creating an internal link.

1. **Go to the word-processing document you've been working in for most of this unit (index.htm).**

2. **At the bottom of the page, type this address:** <A HREF="http://www.komando.com/">Kim Komando's Komputer Klinic</A >.

   This links you to my page.

3. **Make sure you're connected to the Internet.**

   Before, you could check your code just by opening your browser, but not by having a live Internet connection. To check an external link, your Internet connection needs to be live.

4. **Choose File⇨Save to save your word-processing document and open it in your browser.**

   At the bottom of the page, you should see a link that says, "Kim Komando's Komputer Klinic."

5. **Click the link.**

   Hi! I should be smiling at you from your browser. It worked! Nice to see 'ya!

Missing links

Missing links. This is the unknown connection between man and ape. The answer to the mystery is quite simple: The link is not missing at all. It's the . . . wait. That's a different book. A missing link on a Web page is a clickable link that does not exist or for which you have an incorrect address. Take a look at Figure 4-10 to see what pops up on your screen when you click a missing link.

Anchors aweigh!

Overall, keeping individual Web pages as short as possible and splitting large amounts of information into several pages is a good idea. However, sometimes you just can't avoid large documents. Instead of forcing your visitors to scroll through page after page, you can help them jump right to a specific location in that document by using a special kind of link called an *anchor*.

An anchor actually requires you to type code in two places. First, identify the point in your document that will serve as the anchor itself. Next, create a link to that anchor from somewhere else — either in the same document, or even from another document.

Here is the code you need to create an anchor:

```
<A NAME="anchor1">anchor1</A>
```

Just position your cursor in your document wherever you want the anchor to be and then type in the preceding line of code. Note, however, that you can name the anchor whatever you want — you don't have to call it *anchor1*.

If the link you create is in the same document as the anchor, you must identify only the anchor name in the link. Here's an example:

```
<A HREF="#anchor1">This is a link to anchor1.</A>
```

If the anchor and link are in different Web pages on your site, the link looks something like the following code. As you can see, you create a relative link.

```
<A HREF="info.html#anchor1"> This is a link to anchor1 in
                a document called info.html.</A>
```

Technically speaking, you can use the same technique to link to anchors in Web pages on somebody else's Web site. Instead of creating a relative link, you just create an absolute link as I describe in the "External links" section. However, I can't think of too many instances where you'd be likely to link to anchors on somebody else's site. Sounds kind of codependent.

Next, you get to create an anchor on one page. Let me tell you when an anchor like this is really handy. Say your visitor was kind enough to read all the way to the bottom of a really long page and now she wants to see what's at the top again. If you have an anchor at the top of the page that she can just jump to, you save her a lot of scrolling time and she'll probably be pretty grateful.

1 **Go to the top of your word-processing document and type**
```
<A NAME="anchor1">welcome</A>.
```

Your anchor will be the word "welcome" at the top of your Web page. Well, aren't you friendly.

Notes:

anchors can make it easier for your visitors to navigate your page

2 **Go to the bottom of your word-processing document and type** `<A HREF="#anchor1">Go to the top of the page.</A>`.

3 **Choose File⇨Save to save your document and open it in your browser.**

You should see the word "welcome" at the top of your page. Now, chances are good that you see it right at the beginning of a paragraph of text. If you want to fix that, you know how. Just add the `<BR>` tag at the end of the anchor line. If you add the break, though, remember that you must save that document again and reopen it in your browser.

4 **Click on the line at the bottom of the page that reads, "Go to the top of the page." (The line looks like a link.)**

You jump to the top of the page.

You can now use that "welcome" anchor on subsequent pages as well. If you need to see my version, check out links.htm from this book's CD files.

Downloadable files

on the test

Say you find some hot, new program and you want to distribute it as shareware through your Web page. You can easily make programs and other such files available for download from your Web site.

Technically, you can put the program file in the same folder with your other Web files, create a clickable link to the program, and then upload the whole shebang to your ISP's Web server. When somebody clicks on the link, the Web browser downloads your file. The only problem is, depending on the type of file and the Web browser that's doing the downloading, the result may not always be one you want. For example, the Web browser may try to open your application program as a viewable file, and that's clearly not what you want.

I won't get into the details of how to create an FTP dropbox and how to put files into it. That's beyond the scope of this book and something your ISP should be able to help you with. However, once you have the file there, you can create a link from your Web page that automatically downloads the file using FTP (instead of HTTP). Here's what one such link looks like.

```
<A HREF="ftp://ftp.eudora.com/eudora/windows/3.0.1/light/
         eul301.exe">Eudora_Light for Windows </A>
```

on the CD

Adding this code (which you can find as download.htm from this book's lesson files) to your Web page creates a link to Eudora Light, a popular e-mail software from a company called Qualcomm.

As you can see, instead of *http*, this links starts with *ftp*. The FTP acronym tells the Web browser that it's about to receive an FTP file instead of a Web file. The next part of the link, *ftp.eudora.com*, tells the name of the FTP server. The rest of the information tells the exact location and name of the file (in this case, *eul301.exe*, located in */eudora/windows/3.0.1/light/*) to be downloaded.

This method may seem a little more complicated than you may have hoped for, but it's really the most reliable way to make downloadable files available from your Web site. Again, if you want to have downloadable files, your best bet is to contact your ISP directly.

if you really want to make download-able files available on your page, contact your ISP to find the easiest way to do it

☑ **Progress Check**

If you can do the following, you've mastered this lesson:

❏ Create an internal link on your own Web page.

❏ Make a link that jumps to another page.

❏ Set up an anchor.

❏ Differentiate between the different kinds of links.

Unit 4 Quiz

Circle the best answer to the following questions.

1. **The title on your Web page requires two sets of tags. They are:**

   A. ⟨HEAD⟩ and ⟨TITLE⟩   C. ⟨TITLE⟩ and ⟨BODY⟩

   B. ⟨HTML⟩ and ⟨TITLE⟩   D. ⟨TITLE⟩ and ⟨BR⟩

2. **Using paragraph breaks to separate paragraphs puts which of the following between each paragraph?**

   A. A horizontal rule   C. A slice of cheese

   B. Extra space   D. Nothing

3. **On Web pages, headings come in how many different sizes?**

   A. Two   C. Six

   B. Three   D. Ten

4. **The *address, emphasis, citation*, and *variable* tags can all be used to create what kind of type?**

   A. Bold   C. Blood

   B. Underlined   D. Italic

5. **The *strong* tag is another way to create which of the following type?**

   A. Bold   C. Blinking

   B. Underlined   D. Italic

6. **The term *block quote* means . . .**

   A. A paragraph that has a border around it

   B. An indented paragraph

   C. A paragraph that appears in reverse type

   D. A paragraph about Lego blocks

7. **On a Web page, a list of items can be . . .**

   A. Numbered   C. Numbered or bulleted

   B. Bulleted   D. None of the above

8. **The only graphic you can create with HTML code is . . .**

   A. The Komputer Klinic logo   C. A simple box

   B. A horizontal rule   D. A simple circle

Notes:

Notes:

9. **A link to another page on your site is called . . .**

   A. A relative link

   B. An internal link

   C. Either A or B

   D. Neither A nor B

10. **A link to another Web site is called . . .**

    A. An absolute link

    B. An external link

    C. Either A or B

    D. Neither A nor B

11. **An anchor . . .**

    A. Holds your place when you type HTML code

    B. Keeps your home page attached to any subsequent pages

    C. Lets you link to a specific location in a Web page

    D. Keeps your boat from floating away

12. **The best way to download a non-Web file is by . . .**

    A. HTTP

    B. FTP

    C. IBM

    D. Floppy disk

13. **Read my book . . .**

    A. When you're in the bathroom

    B. When you create a Web page

    C. When you're on a business trip with your laptop and modem, but you didn't install a WYSIWYG Web creation program on your laptop

    D. All of the above

Unit 4 Exercise

If you've followed my advice so far, you've tested and experimented with the different HTML tags as you have worked your way through this unit. Now, to close out this unit, you have one simple (yeah, right) assignment. Create your own Web page by using any or all of the HTML tags described in this unit. If something doesn't turn out just the way you want, just try it again.

As you create your page, try to get some idea of exactly where you may want to place some graphics later on. You won't actually be working with graphics until Unit 5, but it's probably a good idea to start thinking of graphics now.

Part II Review

Unit 3 Summary

▶ **HTML:** HTML (HyperText Markup Language) is the programming language that you need to know to create text, images and more in your Web page. Each individual piece of HTML code is called an HTML tag. You can see the HTML code of other people's Web pages by going to the View⇨Source menu of your browser.

▶ **Saving your Web page:** You need to save Web pages in a particular way. Save them as all-text documents, with either an .htm or an .html extension. If you don't save them in this way, your browser will not be able to read or identify the file.

▶ **Checking your work:** I can't emphasize how important it is to check and double-check and triple-check your work. The smartest thing to do is to check your work as you go. When you finish creating your page, check it in different browsers so you'll know that the page looks okay no matter who's viewing it.

Unit 4 Summary

▶ **HTML Essentials:** This unit covers all the basic HTML you should know. The unit starts with the title of your page and then goes on to talk about different ways to format text and how to create links. For a quick review of the different HTML tags, see the Cheat Sheet at the front of the book.

Part II Test

The questions on this test cover all the material presented in Part II (Units 3 and 4). Answers are in Appendix B.

True   False

T   F   1. HTML tags can have either one or two parts.

T   F   2. If your HTML tag is in angle brackets, your browser cannot understand it.

T   F   3. Checking the HTML code of someone else's Web page is unethical.

T   F   4. HTML consists of characters you create with the standard typewriter keys of your keyboard.

T   F   5. Every graphics and multimedia format has its own file extension.

T   F   6. If you check your HTML code as you go, you can catch errors earlier.

T   F   7. You can change the color of text and links.

T   F   8. Line breaks add extra space between paragraphs.

T   F   9. There are five different HTML tags to create italic text.

T   F   10. Internal links are thoughtful while external links are extroverted.

Multiple Choice

For each of the following questions, circle the correct answer or answers. Some questions may have more than one right answer, so read all the answers carefully.

11. **To check the HTML code of another Web page**

    A.   Write to the webmaster to ask for his or her secret recipe

    B.   De-engineer the entire page

    C.   Choose View⇨Source in your browser and have a look

    D.   Ask a psychic to tell you what the code is

12. **To save a Web page in the proper format**

    A.   Choose Save As and save the document as a Text file

    B.   Consult with your local environmental preservation group

    C.   Just choose Save in your word processor

    D.   Call technical support at your ISP to check the format they prefer

13. **The main file of your Web page should be called**

    A.   main.htm

    B.   index.txt

    C.   index.htm

    D.   index.html

14. **A Vlink is**

    A.   A veteran link

    B.   A visited link

    C.   A version link

    D.   A voluptuous link

15. **If you want to make text bold in your Web page, you would use this set of tags:**

    A.   `<B> </B>`

    B.   `<HEAVY> </HEAVY>`

    C.   `<STRONG> </STRONG>`

    D.   `<DARK> </DARK>`

Part II Test

16. **An internal link**

    A. Will allow visitors to jump from place to place in your Web site

    B. Will allow visitors to jump to other Web sites

    C. Is also called a relative link

    D. Is also called an interior link

Matching

17. **Match the tag with its function:**

    A. `<A HREF="info.html"> </A>`   1. Italics

    B. `<BLOCKQUOTE> </BLOCKQUOTE>`   2. Internal link

    C. `<ADDRESS> </ADDRESS>`   3. Anchor

    D. `<A NAME="anchor1"> </A>`   4. Indented paragraph

18. **Match the tag with its function:**

    A. `<B> </B>`   1. Bulleted list

    B. `<UL> </UL>`   2. Keyboard font

    C. `<OL> </OL>`   3. Numbered list

    D. `<KBD> </KBD>`   4. Bold font

19. **Match the file format with its correct extension:**

    A. GIF   1. .txt

    B. Wave sound files   2. .wav

    C. Window movies   3. .gif

    D. Text   4. .avi

Part II Lab Assignment

This exercise lets you see the code that went into creating a good Web page.

Step 1: Find a good Web page

Fire up your Web browser and call up the same Web page you used for the Part I Lab Assignment.

Step 2: Look for coded elements

Identify the elements on that Web page whose coding was discussed in Part II.

Step 3: Try to figure out the HTML code behind those elements

Write down the HTML you think that Web page designer used to create those elements.

Step 4: Look at the actual code used

Double-check your HTML estimates by using the View⇨Source function on your browser.

Getting Fancy

Part III

In this part . . .

Do any amount of cruising on the Internet and you're bound to stare closely at a particular Web page and say, "How'd they do that?" No, I'm not talking about sites that have pictures of typewriters dropped ten stories from the top of a building just to show the devastating results or about sites with pictures of, ahem, something that would make your mother blush. I'm talking about sites that are simply a work of art, complete with killer graphics, sounds, animations, tables, and more!

I still get chicken skin when I see sites such as these. (You know, chicken skin — that's when the hair sticks up on your arms. I got it now just writing about it.) In Part III, you'll read about what it takes to get attention on the Web and become a site worth remembering. You'll get into the artsy side of life and stretch that side of your brain. Then I'll exercise the other half of your brain and get you into using data and tables on a Web site. All of this exercising and stretching will make you one well-rounded person and Web page creator! Just remember, creating a Cézanne painting takes a lot of little brushstrokes. Accordingly, a lot of little things make for one heckuva Web site.

Your Picture-Perfect Web Page

✓ Learning which graphics formats work and which don't

✓ Finding pictures to use on your Web page

✓ Adding graphics to your page

✓ Using graphics as links

✓ Adding simple animation

✓ Deciding between a background color and a background image

Prerequisites

▶ A Web page design (Unit 2)

▶ The beginnings of a Web page (Unit 3)

▶ Text on your Web page (Unit 4)

on the CD

▶ image.htm

▶ image2.htm

▶ page2.htm

▶ backgrnd.htm

▶ GIFWeb

▶ GraphicConverter

▶ Paint Shop Pro

▶ Webimgs folder

*O*kay, so you know that the World Wide Web is a graphical medium. That obviously means that you need to add graphics to your Web pages — or risk the dreaded "boring page" syndrome, an ailment guaranteed to scare off potential visitors by the cybertruckload.

I don't deny that graphics are a little trickier than text, but graphics are not rocket science, either. Just read on to see just how easy it is to add graphics to your Web page.

Top 5% of the Most Boring Internet Sites

avoid this
dreaded
distinction

It's All in the Format   Lesson 5-1

If you've worked with a graphics, word processing or desktop publishing program — or any program that uses graphics — you realize that some programs accept graphics that are saved only in certain formats. For example,

☑ Progress Check

If you can do the following, you've mastered this lesson:

❑ Explain the difference between GIF and JPEG files.

❑ Identify which type of file you would use for which type of art on your Web page.

❑ Find the Paint Shop Pro program on your CD-ROM and start to get acquainted with it.

if you want to put high quality photos on your Web page, use the JPEG file format

it may be hard to find a Windows-based program that doesn't accept BMP (Windows *bitmap*) files, but not all of the lower end programs can use TIFF (*Tagged Image File Format*) files.

on the test

Well, the Web is no different. In fact, the Web offers built-in support for only two graphic file formats: GIF (*Graphic Interchange Format*) and JPEG (*Joint Photographic Experts Group*). So all of your images must be in one of these two formats. But which one? To answer that, you'll need to examine the different formats a little more closely.

on the test

GIF and JPEG image types fall under the category of *bitmapped images*, otherwise known as *raster images*. A bitmapped image is one composed of a bunch of dots. Each dot has a varying color and shade so that the dots collectively make up a picture. The opposite of a bitmapped image is a *vector-based image*, which is made up of separate graphic elements. Here's an example to demonstrate the difference.

If you have a vector-based image that includes a circle, you can remove the circle, using an image-editing program, by clicking your mouse on the circle and then pressing the Delete key. Nothing will look any different, except that the circle will be gone. However, if you have a circle in a bitmapped image, you must delete the circle using an eraser tool, and the result is a white space where you erased the circle. To finish the job, you have to add something else to where the circle used to be.

Anyhow, because both GIF and JPEG are bitmapped images, you're probably wondering what makes them different. The first area where they differ is in color capability. Perhaps you've already heard the terms *8-bit color* and *24-bit color*. Sometimes these terms are called *256 colors* and *millions of colors*, respectively. These terms refer to the amount of color information a graphic can contain. An 8-bit image can contain only 256 different colors, while a 24-bit image can contain millions of colors. GIF is an 8-bit color format, and JPEG is a 24-bit color format.

on the test

So what? Well, 24-bit color is considered *photorealistic color*. So if you present photographs on your Web site, you get a higher quality image if you use JPEG instead of GIF.

On the other hand, for simple non-photographic graphics, you're better off with GIF. Why? Because there's less color information in a GIF file, the files are normally smaller, too. And on the Web, unlike most everything in life, smaller is always better because the smaller the file, the quicker the download, and the faster your Web page appears on somebody's screen. Also, there are some nifty tricks (as you see in Lesson 5-5) you can do with GIFs that you can't do with JPEGs. Think of those tricks as your free GIFt just for buying this book.

The one thing that both of these formats have going for them is that they're both highly compressed. Saving a graphic in one of these formats generally results in a much smaller file compared with the same graphic saved in just about any other format. ***Remember:*** Smaller files mean faster downloads.

All of your graphics must be in either GIF or JPEG format. If you have existing graphics in other formats, you need to convert them. If you use a program like Adobe Photoshop, conversion is easy. Just open the graphics file and save it as GIF or JPEG. That's a must. Remember, though, with graphics files, you can't just change the extensions the way you would if you wanted to change a *.txt* file to an *.htm* file. You have to use some kind of program to convert them.

on the CD

If a $700 program isn't in your budget, though, give Paint Shop Pro for Windows or GraphicConverter for the Macintosh a try. There are shareware programs that can handle conversions from most popular file formats. To make life easier for you, I include them on the CD-ROM at the back of this book. Isn't that nice of me?

The Hunt for Good Art   Lesson 5-2

So where do you find all the wonderful graphics to put on your Web page? All sorts of places. For starters, you can get them from yourself.

The do-it-yourself approach

If you want to remain analog, that is if you want to use your own photographs, you have plenty of options. If you don't own any camera at all (or you're in the market for a new one), you may want to consider a digital camera. Instead of capturing the moments of your life on film, these spiffy little cameras capture images in digital format that you can download right onto your computer. Digital cameras are a bit costlier than an Instamatic, but prices are dropping.

If you're committed to good, old-fashioned film, you can always have your prints developed onto Photo CD instead of paper. Photo CD is a CD-ROM-based format that Kodak created specifically as a digital alternative to paper-based photographic development. Any current model multimedia PC can read these CDs. After you have the photos put onto a Photo CD, however, you'll still need to convert them to JPEG.

Don't worry. I take you through the steps of converting an image file to GIF format. This isn't like a ritual conversion or anything, so don't get too nervous about that. Just follow the bouncing ball and you'll do just fine.

on the CD

1 **Install the Paint Shop Pro (if you use Windows) or GraphicConverter (for Mac) program from the CD-ROM that comes with this book.**

See Appendix C, "About the CD," if you have not already installed the programs on the CD.

2 **Run the graphic program.**

3 **In the graphic program, choose File⇨Open.**

Notes:

When you do this, you'll see a dialog box that's a lot like the dialog box you'd use to open a file in your word processing program. (If you haven't installed the exercise files as described in the About the CD appendix, please do so now to get them copied to your hard drive.) In the Webimgs folder, inside the 101CWP folder on your hard drive, are a whole bunch of different file format images.

4 Pick any one of the images and open the image.

After you find a file you like the name of, just double click on it. The file will open right up in your graphics program.

5 Choose File⇨Save As.

I want you to call your image *image.gif*. I know that's boring, but it helps later when you're trying to add this image to your Web page.

6 Select the file type in the Save As box.

If you're using Paint Shop Pro, click on the item in the Save As box next to the line that reads "Save as type." If you are using GraphicConverter, click on the Format pop-up list box. Scroll around until you find the GIF option, and then select the GIF option by clicking on it.

7 Use the Save As box to open up the folder where you want to store your image.

Put your image in the same folder where you're keeping the HTML word-processing documents that you were working on in Unit 4. If you don't save it there, then nothing you do in the rest of this unit works.

8 Click on Save.

That's it! You just saved your image.

9 Choose File⇨Exit (in Windows) or File⇨Quit (on a Mac) to quit the graphics program you're using.

heads up

You can save your image in JPEG format just as easily. In Step 6, you just choose the *.jpg* extension (Mac users: JPEG/JFIF Format) format instead of GIF.

Now what about those precious photographs from years gone by, the ones pasted in the photo albums that haven't seen the light of day for 10 years? (You know, those "I-was-so-much-thinner" photos.) The answer to this problem is a scanner — that wonderful device that can take a picture of any paper-based image and pop it onto your computer screen. If you don't own a scanner, you may want to consider buying one. Prices have dropped considerably in the past year or two. If buying a scanner is not an option, make friends with somebody who owns a scanner and ask your new pal to scan your photos for you. If you're just not the friendly type (it's okay, a lot of us have lost our friends by spending too much time on the PC), you may have to spend a few bucks at a local service bureau that specializes in computerized output. The service bureau can do the scanning for you, too. And you don't have to be friendly — but you really should be.

If you're the artistic type, you can create images in your favorite graphics program and use them to your heart's content. Unfortunately, my many talents just don't extend to art. If you're like me, you may have to look elsewhere for your graphics. Just read on.

In search of graphics

All kinds of graphics are available from all kinds of places. The problem is that quality varies widely. The trick is to find good graphics that you can legally use on your Web page.

on the CD

Just to get you going, I include some sample images on the CD-ROM included with this book. They're the same ones that you chose from in the last lesson when you converted a file. Feel free to use the images at will on your Web page. But where do you go from there?

I suggest you start by looking at what you already have. Do you own a graphics or desktop publishing program? Many of these types of programs come with free collections of *clip art*, a term that stems from the fact that such artwork used to come in book format from which you could clip the image and paste it onto your paper document for reproduction. Take the time to go through the clip art you already have, and you may discover that your search ends right there.

Or maybe not. If you feel the need to look outside your own software collection, you should know that many companies now offer huge collections of *royalty-free* clip art on CD-ROM. By royalty-free, I mean that after you purchase the CD-ROM, you have the legal right to use the images on your own Web pages just about any way you want. However, before you use any image from such a collection, read all the fine print regarding what you can and can't do, because the exact rules are likely to vary from one company to the next.

on the test

You can also find plenty of royalty-free artwork on the Web, but you have to be very careful. Remember when you read about copying somebody else's HTML code in Lesson 3-1? Don't think for a minute that you can do the same with any graphic you happen to find on the Web. Unlike HTML code, the artist who created any given graphic owns an exclusive copyright to that graphic. Unless it specifically states somewhere on the Web page that you have the right to use a particular graphic, you have to assume that you have no right to the graphic and, therefore, can't use it on your Web page. Plenty of lawsuits have been brought against well-meaning people who wrongly assumed that the Web was a free-for-all and anything on it was automatically in the public domain. Don't let yourself get tangled in a web of lawsuits.

heads up

Here's a tip that may be helpful: You can tap into Web-based search engines specifically designed to help you locate the graphics you need. You can find one such search engine, shown in Figure 5-1, called Clip Art Searcher, at `http://www.webplaces.com/search/`.

No matter how good the artwork is, there's always one drawback to using mass-marketed clip art. You never know how many other people are going to use the same art on their Web pages, meaning that your Web page may suffer from an apparent lack of originality.

The answer to this problem, albeit a sometimes expensive answer, is a freelance graphic artist. In other words, hire someone who can create custom artwork for you to use exclusively on your Web site. This option is strictly budgetary; if it makes economic sense, a freelance artist really is the way to go.

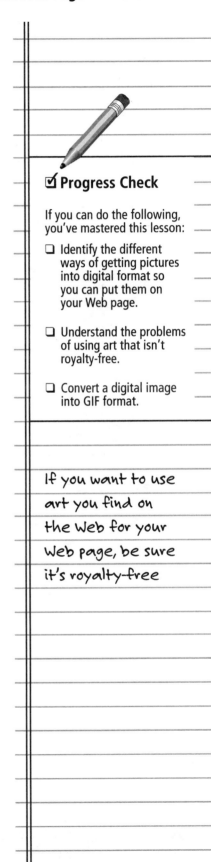

☑ Progress Check

If you can do the following, you've mastered this lesson:

❑ Identify the different ways of getting pictures into digital format so you can put them on your Web page.

❑ Understand the problems of using art that isn't royalty-free.

❑ Convert a digital image into GIF format.

If you want to use art you find on the Web for your Web page, be sure it's royalty-free

Figure 5-1: The Clip Art Searcher Web page helps you locate royalty-free art on the Web.

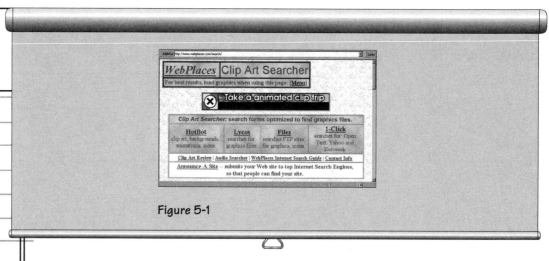

Figure 5-1

Best of all, if you use your favorite Web search engine, you have a wide selection of graphic artists who are looking for work. You aren't just limited to the ones you happen to know in your own geographic area. If you want to search for a firm or an artist looking for work, it's easy. Just use your favorite search engine such as Yahoo! and use the search phrase `web designer`. Guaranteed, you'll find lots of people willing to help you create art for your Web page, for a price. To save some bucks, try contacting the art department at a local college or university. There, you can usually post a job opening or speak with an instructor who may have the perfect student willing to help you, for peanuts.

Lesson 5-3   Putting an Image on the Page

Let's assume that you've found the images you want to include on your page and you've converted them to either GIF or JPEG. What's next?

heads up

First, you have to make sure you've put your images in the right place and have given them appropriate names. Remember when I told you to put all the files for your Web site in the same folder on your hard drive? That goes for graphics, too. And like your HTML files, your graphic files have to have the right file extensions. All of your GIF files must end with *.gif* and all of your JPEG files must end with *.jpg*.

Now I'm going to walk you through the steps of putting an image into your Web page. Here we go. Take a deep breath. This is going to be easy.

1 **Open the word-processing document you've been using as you went through all the steps of learning HTML code.**

   You should have called the document *index.htm.*

2 After you open index.htm, position your cursor wherever you want your image to be.

Think about where you want to put the image that you converted into GIF format in the last lesson. Do you want it at the top of the page or at the bottom or in the middle? Doesn't matter to me, as long as it's after the first HTML tag. Just figure it out and position your cursor. Where you put the coding is where the picture will end up — relative to the other elements — in the final Web page. Just keep that in mind when you choose your spot.

3 Now type this line of HTML code: `<IMG SRC="image.gif">`.

Remember that you should have called your GIF image *image.gif.* If you didn't, that's okay, but you need to change this line of code so the name of the file (that's the stuff in quotation marks) has the same name as your GIF image. And don't forget the quotation marks: Without them, this won't work.

4 Save your file and open it in your Web browser.

Voilà! A picture. Smile for the camera.

on the CD

If you need to see how I did it, check out image.htm from the book's CD files. Pretty nifty, huh? But I know you, that's not enough for you. Now you want to do all kinds of tricks with your picture. Start with a simple one.

1 Go back to your HTML word-processing documents.

2 Find the code where you added your picture, and type `<BR>` **before and after the code.**

If you remember from Lesson 4-2 on HTML, this tag creates a line break so your picture is on a line by itself. (Greedy picture, doesn't want to share!)

3 Save the file and re-open it in your browser to check it out.

on the test

You can also include your image *inline* with other text, meaning that your image and your text appear on the same line. If you do that, you have several alignment options to choose from.

- **TOP.** This option aligns the top edge of the graphic with the line of text in which it appears. Figure 5-2 shows a top-aligned graphic. The code for this is `<IMG SRC="image.gif" ALIGN=TOP>`.

- **MIDDLE.** This option aligns the vertical center of the graphic with the line of text in which it appears. Figure 5-3 shows a middle-aligned graphic. The code for this is `<IMG SRC="image.gif" ALIGN=MIDDLE>`.

- **BOTTOM.** This option aligns the bottom edge of the graphic with the line of text in which it appears. Figure 5-4 shows a bottom-aligned graphic. The code for this is `<IMG SRC="image.gif" ALIGN=BOTTOM>`.

- **LEFT.** This option aligns the graphic on the left and wraps multiple lines of text around the right side of it. Figure 5-5 shows a left-aligned image. The code for this is `<IMG SRC="image.gif" ALIGN=LEFT>`.

- **RIGHT.** This option aligns the graphic on the right and wraps multiple lines of text around the left side of it. Figure 5-6 shows a right-aligned graphic. The code for this is `<IMG SRC="image.gif" ALIGN=RIGHT>`.

You can align an image with text on a Web page lots of different ways

Figure 5-2: This is a top-aligned graphic.

Figure 5-3: This is a middle-aligned graphic.

Figure 5-4: This is a bottom-aligned graphic.

Figure 5-5: This is a left-aligned graphic.

Figure 5-6: This is a right-aligned graphic.

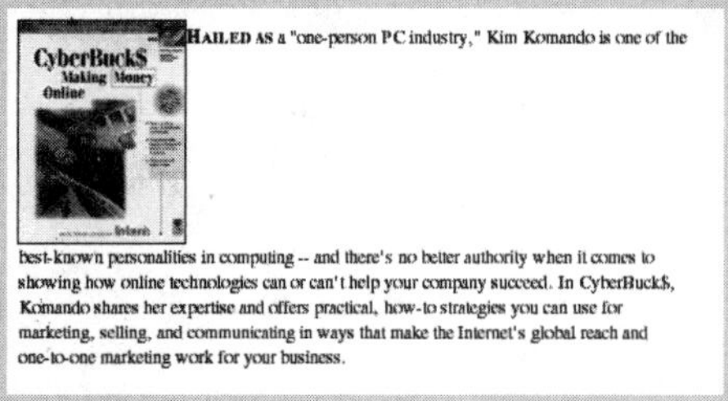

☑ Progress Check

If you can do the following, you've mastered this lesson:

❑ Add an image to your practice Web page.

❑ Align your image any way you want.

Figure 5-2

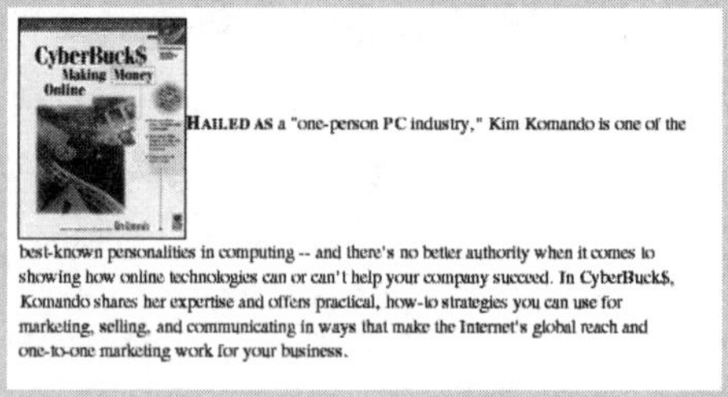

Figure 5-3

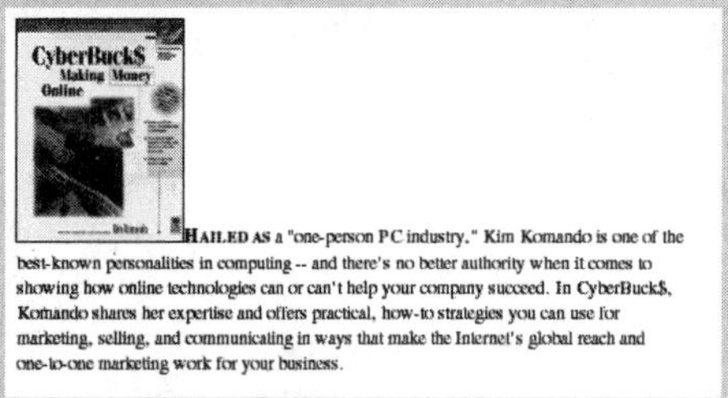

Figure 5-4

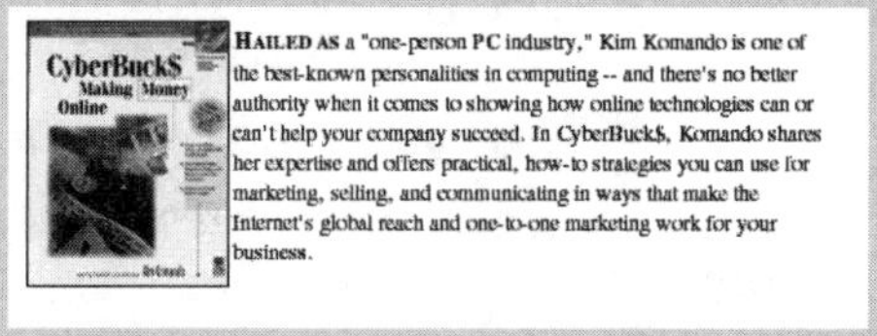

Figure 5-5

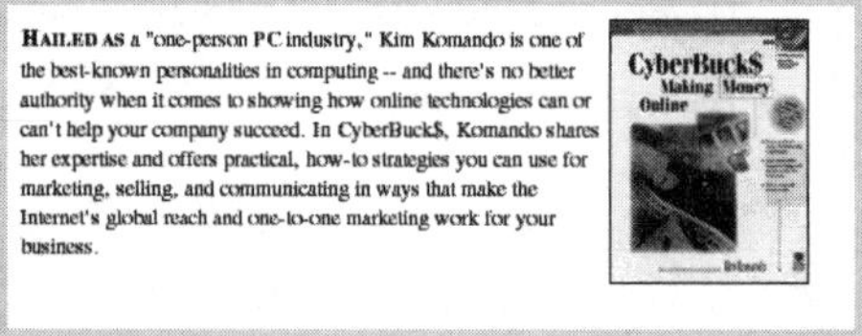

Figure 5-6

Are you revved up to give alignment a try?

1 Go back to your word-processing document.

Using the previous example, the correct code for a left-aligned graphic would be `<IMG SRC="image.gif" ALIGN=LEFT>`.

2 You can just add `ALIGN=LEFT` to the line of code you already have.

Remember that there has to be some body text near the image or else it won't have anything to align with.

For any other alignments shown above, substitute the appropriate term for `LEFT`.

Recess

Take a break and muse upon this: *Virtual reality. . . .What a concept.*

The Graphical Link

on the test

In addition to using graphics to decorate your page, you can also use them as buttons to activate hypertext links. To do that, you simply treat the code you used to get the graphic onto your page as if it were text that you wanted to use as a link. Using that same `image.gif` file I refer to in Lesson 5-3, the code to make that graphic into a clickable link to a file called *page2.htm* would be:

```
<A HREF="page2.htm"><IMG SRC="image.gif"></A>
```

Stretch your memory back to Units 3 and 4 for a minute and it will be easier to figure out what this code really means. The first and last set of bracketed instructions tell your browser that it's looking at a link. The difference here is that this time, the link itself is a bracketed code that tells the browser to go get the image you want to use as the link. Does this seem confusing? You may want to take a look back at Part II to do a refresher on links. I'll wait.

Are you back? Okay, let's give it a try:

1 **Go to that ol' word-processing document.**

Find the place where you put your image on that page.

2 **Type** `<A HREF="page2.htm">` **before the line of code that adds your image.**

Remember that *page2.htm* is that second page you created for your Web page back in Unit 4. Remember also that you may not have been able to save it as an *.htm* file. That's fine. If you saved it as a *.txt* file, just make sure that the HTML code you add here has the proper name for the file. But as you learned in Lesson 3-2, you should get in the habit of naming your HTML files with the right file extension, .htm or .html.

3 **Type** `</A>` **after the line of code that adds the image.**

4 **Save your document and open it in your Web browser.**

5 **Click on the image, and you should jump to that second page of your Web site.**

on the CD

My version of this link document is page2.htm, from the CD lesson files. I should point out one thing about linked graphics. When you view a linked graphic in your Web browser, a colored border appears around the graphic. The color of the border is whatever color you specify for that type of link: *LINK, ALINK,* or *VLINK.* (See Lesson 4-1.). You probably already noticed that color similarity when you just made your picture into a link. However, depending on the design of your page, you may not want a colored border around the graphic.

Personally, I think a border around an image isn't really very flattering. If you're like me and you'd rather do without all the bells and whistles, just follow along to add this code to remove a border:

Notes:

Notes:

on the test

1 **Go to your HTML word-processing document.**

2 **Go back to the line where you turned your picture into a link, and after** `image.gif`**, type** `BORDER=0`.

The whole line of code now looks like this:

```
<A HREF="page2.htm"><IMG SRC="image.gif" BORDER=0></
    A>.
```

Make sure everything is perfect. Remember, any kind of programming code is pretty unforgiving. If you so much as leave out a quotation mark, your browser won't know what you want to do.

3 **Save the document and go back to view it in your browser.**

on the CD

Your picture won't have a border any more. If you want to check out my version, check out image2.htm on the CD lesson files.

No discussion of linked graphics is without the mention of *image maps*. An image map is one of two things: A "Map to the Stars' Homes" in Hollywood, or a single graphic that can activate multiple hypertext links. Let's deal with the latter. Exactly which link gets activated depends on exactly where you click on the graphic.

Image maps are pretty complicated beasts — so much so that I'm going to save a longer discussion of them for Unit 6. But because image maps have to do with images, I give you a little flavor of what they are here in this unit.

The deal with image maps is that you need a separate program to help you create them; creating image maps on your own is virtually impossible. When I explain how image maps work, you'll understand why.

Each clickable area on an image map is a *hot spot*. Get your mind out of the gutter now. These hot spots are defined using a series of coordinates – that's like a location on your Web page, kinda like the coordinates you'd use when you were reading a map, except these seem a little more cryptic. For example, one hot spot on an image map may be defined as follows:

```
<AREA SHAPE="rect" COORDS="68,70,140,115">
```

This line of code indicates that the hot spot is rectangular in shape and uses the four points specified here as its corner points. The hardest part of all this — one that especially requires the aid of a separate program — is figuring out the coordinates.

To make matters more complicated, there are two kinds of image maps: server side and client side. Server-side image maps reside on your ISP's Web server to figure out which Web page to display based on where somebody clicked on the image map. The server-side method is older and more common, but it's also less efficient (as older common things usually are — like the 286 in my garage).

When you use a client-side image map, the viewer's Web browser can figure out for itself which page to request based on the spot where the viewer clicked. This is a newer, more efficient way to do image maps.

☑ Progress Check

If you can do the following, you've mastered this lesson:

❑ Turn an image into a link on your Web page.

❑ Explain what an image map is to your grandmother. (Okay, that's too tough. Try your sister instead.)

If you decide to explore the wonderful world of image maps, I urge you to find a program that helps you create client-side image maps. Client-side image maps are much easier for both you and your cybervisitors to deal with, and virtually all major Web browsers support them. I talk more about all of this in Unit 6.

Cool GIF Tricks: Animations and Transparencies

Lesson 5-5

on the CD

You can do some cool stuff with GIFs that you can't do with JPEGs. One of them is color transparency. If you have the right software to help you out, such as GifWeb (for Windows) or GraphicConverter (for Macs), which are both on the CD-ROM, (again, you're welcome) you can make any one color in any GIF image transparent when you view that image through a Web browser.

Why is this important? Let's say you want to include your company logo on your Web page. If you bring your logo directly in from the graphics program, it's probably going to have a white square around it, like the one shown in Figure 5-7.

However, using GifWeb or GraphicConverter, you can modify the GIF image so that all white comes through on your Web browser as transparent. The result is something like Figure 5-8.

You have to be careful, though. Transparency works according to color, not area. In other words, if you make white transparent, all the white in your image becomes transparent, including any white portions of the image itself. One way around this is to use your graphics program to make the area you want to be transparent some odd color. Then use your program of choice to make that off-color transparent.

Wanna give transparencies a try? Easy enough.

on the CD

1 **If you haven't already installed GifWeb (for Windows) or GraphicConverter (for Macs), follow the instructions in the About the CD appendix in the back of the book.**

2 **Start GifWeb or GraphicConventer up.**

3 **Under the File menu, click on Open Image (GifWeb) or Open (GraphicConverter), and then go to the folder on your hard drive where you're storing all your goodies for your Web page and open the screen shot that you converted into a *.gif* file earlier.**

In you are using GifWeb, skip to Step 5. GraphicConverter users have a preliminary step.

4 **If you're using GraphicConverter, click the transparency tool button on the floating toolbar to the right of the image. The tool looks like a wand with a diamond.**

Figure 5-7: You probably don't want this black box.

Figure 5-8: That nasty black square is gone for good.

Figure 5-7   Figure 5-8

5 **Click on the background that you want to render transparent.**

When you click on the color in GifWeb, a Background box appears on the left side of the screen, displaying the color that you have selected. (**Note:** If a second "Change to" colored button is displayed, the background consists of more than one color. You have to change the background to one color. Go to the Help menu and click on Online Help for more information.) When you click on the color in GraphicConverter, the color disappears from the area surrounding the image.

6 **In GifWeb, a dialog box appears telling you the operation is complete; click on OK. If you're using GraphicConverter, choose File⇨Save As.**

Both programs bring up a Save As dialog box.

7 **In the Save As dialog box, specify the name and location for the file, and click on OK.**

GifWeb brings up another dialog box telling you the file has been saved. Just click OK to dismiss the message. Once you click OK in the Save As box in GraphicConverter, you'll be returned to the program.

8 **To quit the program, choose File⇨Exit (in Windows) or File⇨Quit (on a Mac).**

But you're in luck. The Gif Construction Set program that you were just working with does animated GIFs as well as transparencies. If you want to create animated GIFs, open the Quick Start file in the Gif Construction Set folder. The file gives you step by step instructions on creating an animated GIF (as well as transparencies, if you want more information).

☑ Progress Check

If you can do the following, you've mastered this lesson:

❏ "Erase" a color from your GIF file so you can create a transparency.

❏ Think about other things in your life that you want to erase.

Lesson 5-6   The Lowdown on Backgrounds

As you may have already realized from your own Web surfing, it's possible (and common) to include a background on your Web page. You can do this two ways. You can specify a solid color using hex codes, as you learned to do with text colors in Lesson 4-1. Or you can specify a repeating graphic or logo to use as a background. Exactly how many times it repeats depends on the size of the graphic and the size of the browser image. The graphic repeats as many times as it needs to fill the window. Here's how to do either one.

Back in Lesson 4-1, you learned how to specify link colors. To refresh your memory, this is the coding example I used.

```
<BODY TEXT="#FF0000" LINK="#000000" ALINK="#ffffff" _
        VLINK="#2b6718">
```

To translate: The Body Text is red, the Link is black, the Active Links are white, and the Visited Links is an awful shade of green. If you want to specify a background color, you just have to add a little code to this line of codes. For example, to make the background color a light pink, type this code:

```
<BODY BGCOLOR="#e19eb8" TEXT="#ee0202" LINK="#000000" _
        ALINK="#ffffff" VLINK="#2b6718">
```

This would be a site to test for color blindness. If you don't get ill from this test, then you are color-blind. Want to take the test?

1 **Check out the hex codes for a color you like using the handy-dandy program RGB or some other method. Jot down the hex code on a piece of paper.**

If you don't want to bother with this step, you can just use that lovely light pink color that I'm using.

2 **Go back to your *index.htm* file and find the line of code that you added in Unit 4 to specify colors for text and links, and then, if you're using the same color as I, type in this line of code inside the bracket where you specified other colors.**

```
Add BODY BGCOLOR="#e19eb8"
```

Remember, you may not be using the same hex code that I'm using, so your code may be slightly different than mine.

3 **If you didn't add a whole line to experiment with color back in Unit 4, just add the line of code for background color inside of pointy brackets.**

4 **Save your document and go view it in your browser.**

Suppose that instead of a solid color, you want to use a graphic named *image.jpg* (or *image.gif*, for that matter) as a repeating image for your background. I did this with backgrnd.htm, one of the files on your CD. Now your line of code would look like this:

```
< BACKGROUND="image.jpg" BODY TEXT="#ee0202" _
        LINK="#000000" ALINK="#ffffff" VLINK="#2b6718"
        >
```

☑ Progress Check

If you can do the following, you've mastered this lesson:

❏ Change the color background of your Web page.

❏ Add a background image to your Web page.

Notes:

on the CD

You can give that a try if you want, but the image you chose is probably pretty busy, and it may not look too good. Still, go ahead and add BACKGROUND= "image.jpeg" to your HTML document, save it, and have a look. You can take it right out again if you don't like it. And I included nearly 200 background images for you to try out in the Webimgs folder that came with the CD!

on the test

Technically, nothing prevents you from specifying both a background color and a background image. However, if you do, the image takes priority over the color; the color displays only until the image has been downloaded. Color preferences are a personal thing. Just use colors that blend together nicely and don't clash.

be careful that your background images aren't too visually busy

extra credit

Other graphic considerations

I remember when desktop publishing first became the rage. Suddenly, people had dozens of fonts to choose from. But instead of choosing, some people decided to use them all — in the same document! The result: ugly documents that may as well have been rubber-stamped with the word *amateur*. (Or should I say AMATEUR?)

I've noticed this same disturbing trend with graphics on the World Wide Web. Some starting Web designers are so thrilled to be able offer stunning photos and gigantic image maps and catchy GIF animations that they go overboard.

Not only does this make a page look ugly and amateurish, it's also very rude to would-be visitors. The more graphics you put on a page, the longer it takes to download and the more of your visitor's time you waste.

As far as the looks of your graphics go, only you can be the judge of how much is too much. However, when it comes to download times, I do have another of my many rules of thumb: Keep your main graphic to under 60K in size, and make any other supplemental graphics (buttons, icons, and so on) as small as is reasonably possible. Now if you can keep your entire Web page to 60K or less, you get a gold star.

Unit 5 Quiz

Here's another quiz to keep you sharp. Choose the best answer.

1. **What are the two common graphic formats on the Web?**

    A. TIFF and JPEG   C. TIFF and GIF

    B. GIF and BMP   D. GIF and JPEG

2. **GIF stands for . . .**

   A. Graphic Industry 　C. Graphic Input File
   Foundation

   B. Graphic Interchange 　D. Get It Free
   Format

3. **A bitmapped image is a collection of . . .**

   A. Dots 　　　　　　　C. Points on a map

   B. Individual graphic 　D. GIF images
   elements

4. **24-bit color . . .**

   A. Is photorealistic color 　C Is used in JPEG images

   B. Consists of millions 　　D. Is all of the above
   of colors

5. **If you find a graphic you like on some other Web page, you can . . .**

   A. Always use it 　　C. Use it if you give credit to the creator

   B. Never use it 　　D. Use it if you have permission

6. **How many ways are there to align a graphic with text?**

   A. Two 　　　　C. Eight

   B. Five 　　　　D. Nine

7. **A graphic can serve as a hypertext link . . .**

   A. Whenever you want it to

   B. Only when it looks like a button

   C. Only if it has a colored border around it

   D. On alternate Tuesdays

8. **The bit of code to turn the border off on a linked graphic is . . .**

   A. BORDER=NONE 　　　C. BORDER =ZERO

   B. BORDER=TRANSPARENT 　D. BORDER=0

9. **In a transparent GIF, what is always transparent?**

   A. The area around the graphic 　C. Any white area

   B. The color you specify 　　　　D. All text

10. **An animated GIF uses how many GIF images to create the illusion of animation?**

    A. Two or more 　　C. As many as you want

    B. At least five 　　D. None

Notes:

Notes:

11. **If you specify both a background color and a background image, after your page loads, you . . .**

    A. See only the background color

    B. See only the background image

    C. See both the background color and background image

    D. See neither the background color nor the background image

12. **Generally, your main image should never be larger than . . .**

    A. 60K   C. 25K

    B. 100K   D. A bread basket

Unit 5 Exercises

1. Accumulate graphics from various sources and convert them all to GIF or JPEG as appropriate. Experiment with putting them in sample Web pages and see how they look. Try different alignment options.

2. Come up with some small graphics to use as buttons, and then use them as links to other pages on your site. Test them out in your Web browser. See if you like them better with or without the colored border.

3. Experiment with both background colors and background images. Remember that this will appear in the background *behind other text and graphics*. Once you find a background you like, fill up the page with text to make sure your visitors will still be able to read the text when it's set against the background you chose.

4. Fiddle around with the programs I've supplied for the cool GIF tricks. See if they strike your fancy.

Advanced HTML

Objectives for This Unit

✓ Generating links to Internet services outside of the Web

✓ Creating fill-in-the-blank forms on your Web page

✓ Setting up an HTML table

✓ Splitting a single Web page into frames

✓ Using image maps

Prerequisites

▶ Know the basics of HTML code that allow you to create a run-of-the-mill Web page (Units 3-5)

▶ A need to move beyond the basics and get into some advanced uses of HTML

Don't be frightened by the title of this unit. Virtually all HTML is pretty easy after you get the hang of it (then again, so is brain surgery). Let me try again. If you've made it this far without any major difficulty, you won't have any problem at all working your way through this unit. The only difference is that instead of relying on one HTML tag to do one separate thing, most of the techniques in this unit use a combination of tags to produce a result. Keep in mind, too, that if you choose to use one of the programs that I cover in Unit 8, that program may do all of this for you. With one of those programs, you may never need to know this much HTML. But creating Web pages is like driving a car. You don't really need to know how to check the oil in your car in order to drive a car. If you do, though, you're better able to take care of your car and know when the car is about ready to blow up because the oil is low.

I assure you that this is all simple stuff — no harder than anything else in this book. Just follow along to see what I mean.

on the CD

▶ email.htm
▶ ftp.htm
▶ gopher.htm
▶ newsgrp.htm
▶ form.htm
▶ tables.htm
▶ index.htm
▶ test1.htm
▶ test2.htm
▶ LiveImage
▶ ImageMapper

Lesson 6-1   # A World Outside the Web

Notes:

There's a lot more to the Internet than just the World Wide Web. You've already covered some of the services a little bit, but not all of them. To make sure you're all on the same page (such a pun, eh?), the Internet includes, but is not limited to:

- **E-mail:** Sends electronic messages between individuals and/or groups
- **File Transfer Protocol (FTP):** Transfers files between computers on the Internet. (You learn more about this in Unit 11 when I show you how to actually post your work to the Web.)
- **Gopher:** Retrieves text-based information on the Internet
- **Usenet Newsgroup protocols:** Posts messages to a newsgroup, which is like a giant e-mail center where people can read and respond to messages
- **Telnet:** Connects to and operates a remote computer on the Internet using a character-based interface

What you may not realize is that you can create links to any of these services from within your Web page. Sometimes the Web browser can handle these links itself, and other times the link is a little too tough for the browser to handle on its own. In these cases, the Web browser launches some external program to negotiate the link. If this sounds a little confusing, just keep reading and you see just how confusing it isn't. (Wait, was that confusing?)

Automatic e-mail

All of the major Web browsers come with some sort of e-mail program. Although many people find that these add-ons aren't as fully featured as stand-alone e-mail programs, the add-ons still come in handy for sending e-mail on the fly as you browse the World Wide Web.

There's a special kind of e-mail link you can put on your Web page that's called a *mailto* link. A mailto link lets your visitors automatically set up a new e-mail message to you right from your Web site. That way, if someone wants to send you an e-mail message as they visit your page, he or she doesn't have to fiddle around copying and pasting your e-mail address into a new message. By doing this, you get more mail telling you how great your site is and how great its creator is. Your self-esteem soars. You approach problems with a new verve. You are invincible. Do you see how much you need this *mailto* link?

I think every Web site in the world should have a mailto link that goes directly to the site's owner. It's a good way to get feedback from your visitors, and I just think it's polite. Follow these simple steps and you see just how easy it is to create one of these links.

a mailto link allows people to send you email messages automatically

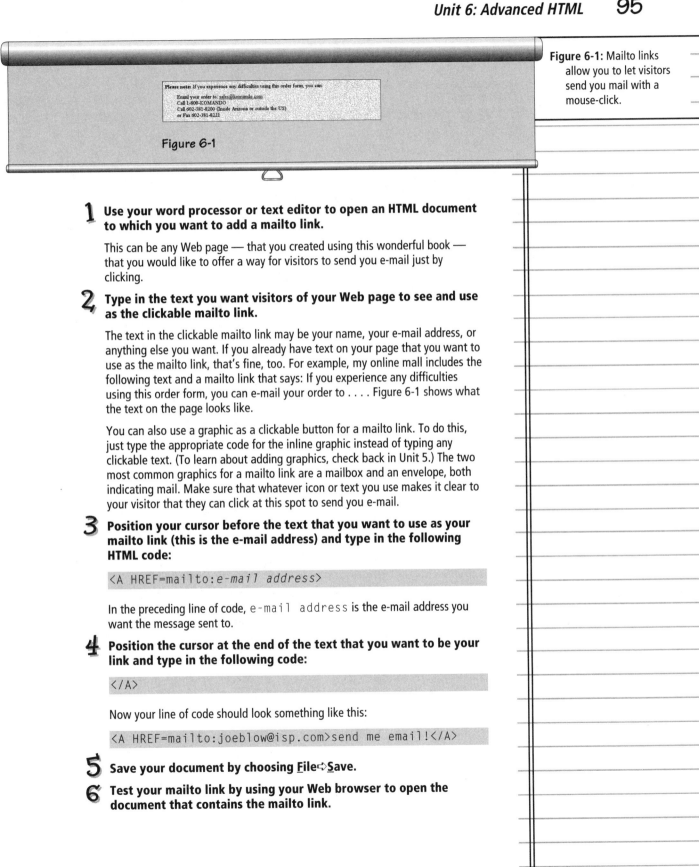

Figure 6-1

1 **Use your word processor or text editor to open an HTML document to which you want to add a mailto link.**

This can be any Web page — that you created using this wonderful book — that you would like to offer a way for visitors to send you e-mail just by clicking.

2 **Type in the text you want visitors of your Web page to see and use as the clickable mailto link.**

The text in the clickable mailto link may be your name, your e-mail address, or anything else you want. If you already have text on your page that you want to use as the mailto link, that's fine, too. For example, my online mall includes the following text and a mailto link that says: If you experience any difficulties using this order form, you can e-mail your order to . . . . Figure 6-1 shows what the text on the page looks like.

You can also use a graphic as a clickable button for a mailto link. To do this, just type the appropriate code for the inline graphic instead of typing any clickable text. (To learn about adding graphics, check back in Unit 5.) The two most common graphics for a mailto link are a mailbox and an envelope, both indicating mail. Make sure that whatever icon or text you use makes it clear to your visitor that they can click at this spot to send you e-mail.

3 **Position your cursor before the text that you want to use as your mailto link (this is the e-mail address) and type in the following HTML code:**

```
<A HREF=mailto:e-mail address>
```

In the preceding line of code, `e-mail address` is the e-mail address you want the message sent to.

4 **Position the cursor at the end of the text that you want to be your link and type in the following code:**

```
</A>
```

Now your line of code should look something like this:

```
<A HREF=mailto:joeblow@isp.com>send me email!</A>
```

5 **Save your document by choosing File⇨Save.**

6 **Test your mailto link by using your Web browser to open the document that contains the mailto link.**

Figure 6-2: The mailto link created this message window automatically.

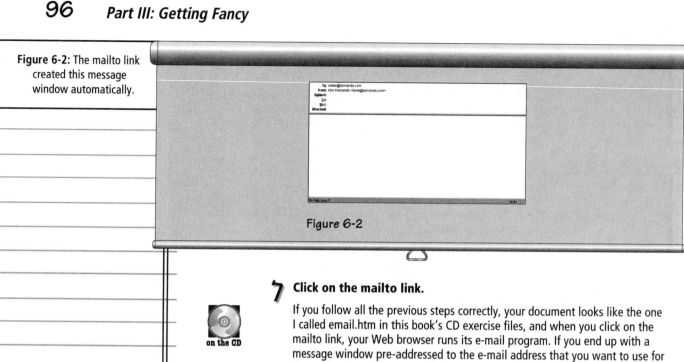

Figure 6-2

7 Click on the mailto link.

If you follow all the previous steps correctly, your document looks like the one I called email.htm in this book's CD exercise files, and when you click on the mailto link, your Web browser runs its e-mail program. If you end up with a message window pre-addressed to the e-mail address that you want to use for the mailto link, you know that you succeeded in creating the link. Figure 6-2 shows what the message window looks like.

Files galore (or a James Bond girl who never was)

Your Web browser can handle some non-Web services. A mailto link is an example of one type that the Web browser can't handle directly; the browser must run a separate e-mail program to get the job done.

On the other hand, all major Web browsers can handle FTP downloads on their own. That means you can create a link that automatically causes your Web browser to download a particular file. I briefly talk about this in Lesson 4-4. I tell you there that you need to contact your ISP if you want to find out where you should post an FTP, or downloadable, file. I'm not going to go into FTPs in any more detail now, but I do tell you how you can create a link that gets your visitors to any FTP file, whether you've posted the file yourself or you are downloading a file from someone else's FTP site.

Before you get started with these steps, you need to know the following information:

♦ **The name of the FTP server where the file resides.** This may be something like *ftp.company.com*. If you posted your own file to an FTP server, you know this address already. Otherwise, use your Web browser to locate the file you want to download and then begin to download the file. When you do, the address of the file appears in the address line of your browser.

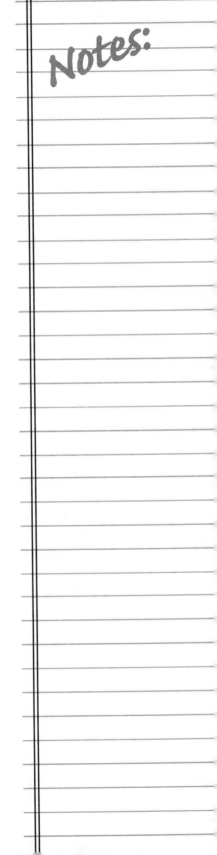

▸ **The complete path name that leads to the file.** By path name, I mean the exact folder or directory where you can find the file. The path name may look something like */pub/files/misc*. The path name is also in the address line of your browser.

▸ **The exact name of the file.**

heads up

Here's a shortcut to get all the FTP address information you need: When you download an FTP file, just copy the whole address from the address line in your browser and paste it into your HTML document. That way, you don't have to worry about the path name or specific name of the file — it's all right there for you.

After you have all that information together, you are ready for these simple steps:

1 **Use your word processor or text editor to open the HTML document you've been practicing in.**

2 **Type in the text you want to use as the clickable FTP link.**

Often, this text is a name or other description of the file.

heads up

You can also use a graphic as a clickable button for an FTP link. To do this, just type in the appropriate code for the inline graphic instead of any clickable text.

3 **Position the cursor at the beginning of the text (or before the code for the inline graphic) and type in the following HTML code:**

```
<A HREF=ftp://FTP address>
```

In this code, `FTP address` is the server name, location and name of the file. The FTP address looks something like this:

```
ftp.company.com/pub/files/misc/program.exe
```

where `program.exe` is the name of the file to download.

4 **Position the cursor at the end of the linked text (or at the end of the code for the inline graphic) and type in the following code:**

```
</A>
```

Now your line of code should look something like this:

```
<A HREF=ftp:// ftp.company.com/pub/files/misc/
          program.exe > Click here to download
          Program.Exe.</A>
```

5 **Save your document in the normal manner, open your Web browser, and then open your practice HTML document.**

My version can be found under ftp.htm with the files that came with this book's CD.

on the CD

6 **Establish your connection to the Internet.**

7 **Click on the FTP link.**

After a few seconds, your Web browser lets you know one way or another that the file is downloading. Take a look at Figure 6-3 for an example of a download. As long as the download starts up correctly, you don't need to wait for it

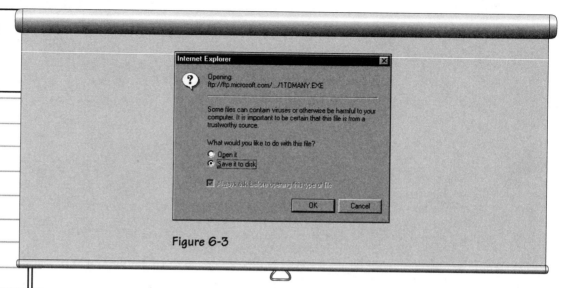

Figure 6-3

to finish. After you're satisfied that it's working, you can cancel the download by clicking on Cancel in the download dialog box.

All of these steps are based on the assumption that the file you're linking to is on an *anonymous FTP site*. An anonymous FTP site is one that anyone can access without entering a unique password and user ID. However, you can create a link to a file on a *non-anonymous FTP site*, as long as you include an appropriate user ID and password in the link. Here's what one of these links may look like.

```
<A HREF=ftp://joeblow:kokomo@ftp.company.com/pub/files/
                     misc/program.exe>
```

where *joeblow* is the user ID and *kokomo* is the password. Of course, the whole idea of using a password is to keep the general public out, so you're not too likely to use this sort of link on a public Web page.

Looking for Gopher holes

Before the World Wide Web came along, many people expected Gopher to become the next big thing on the Internet. In fact, some people had already figured out how to operate "Gopher malls," which allowed people to do their shopping via Gopher much like people shop on the Web today. Well, the World Wide Web came along and ruined any chances that Gopher had of becoming the hot technology.

Nevertheless, Gopher is still a good way to archive and retrieve text-based information, and there is no shortage of Gopher sites (called Gopher holes — really) on the Internet. Creating a link to a Gopher document is much like creating an FTP link. The main difference is that instead of downloading the file onto your hard disk as FTP does, a Gopher document is simply displayed in your Web browser's window. If you want to save it after looking at it, you can.

chances are good that you won't have your visitors download files from anonymous FTP sites

Gopher is a text-based format on the Internet

Just like with an FTP link, you need the following information before you start:

> **The name of the Gopher server where the file resides.** This may be something like gopher.company.com.

> **The complete path name that leads to the file.** By path name, I mean the exact folder or directory where the file is located. That may look something like */pub/files/misc.*

> **The exact name of the file.**

After you have all that information together, you're ready for these simple steps:

heads up

1 Open the practice HTML document that you've been working in and type in the text you want to use as the clickable Gopher link.

Often, this text is a name or other description of the file.

As with FTP, you can also use a graphic as a clickable button for a Gopher link. To do this, just type in the appropriate code for the inline graphic instead of any clickable text.

2 Position the cursor at the beginning of the text (or before the code for the inline graphic) and type in the following HTML code:

```
<A HREF=gopher://Gopher address>
```

In this code, *Gopher address* is the server name, location, and name of the file. The address looks something like this:

```
gopher.company.com/pub/files/misc/sample.txt
```

where *sample.txt* is the name of the file to view.

3 Position the cursor at the end of the linked text and type in the following code:

```
</A>
```

Now your line of code should look something like this.

```
<A HREF=gopher:// gopher.company.com/pub/files/misc/
        sample.txt > Click here to view
        SAMPLE.TXT.</A>
```

4 Save your document in the normal manner and get ready to test your link. Start by using your Web browser to open your practice HTML document.

My version of the document is gopher.htm, and came with this book's CD.

on the CD

5 Establish your connection to the Internet and click on the Gopher link.

After a few seconds, your Web browser loads the Gopher document in much the same way that it loads a regular Web document. Figure 6-4 shows what a Gopher document looks like.

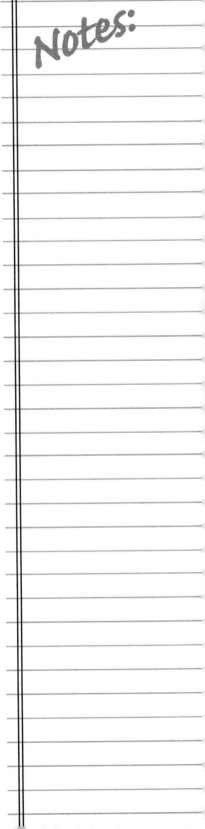
Notes:

Figure 6-4: A Gopher document looks much like any other Web document, less the graphics.

Figure 6-4

linking to a newsgroup is a good way to lead your cybervisitors to more information about topics that interest them

☑ Progress Check

If you can do the following, you've mastered this lesson:

❑ You know how to create a link to a Gopher or newsgroup site.

❑ You know how to link to an FTP site for file downloads.

❑ You understand the importance of soliciting feedback about your site, and you know how to create a mailto link.

❑ You realize that I will never run out of terrible puns.

All the news that's fit to report and lots of stuff you wouldn't care to read

At this writing, there are more than 25,000 Usenet newsgroups, and by the time you read this, there are likely to be thousands more, each one covering a different topic than any other newsgroup.

While your Web browser doesn't offer direct support for Usenet newsgroups, all of the major browsers come with some sort of add-on newsreader, much like they all come with e-mail programs. This all means that you can create a link to a specific newsgroup. When visitors click on that link, their Web browsers automatically start their add-on newsreader and then load the newsgroup you specify.

Newsgroup links can be a nice little addition to your Web site. With so many newsgroups out there, chances are you can find at least one that relates to the topic of your Web site. By creating a direct link to relevant newsgroups, you help to keep your visitors informed about the topics that are important to you. (And assumely your visitors, too.)

The only thing you need before you get started is the exact name of the newsgroup you want to link to. After you have that, just follow these steps.

1 **Open your practice HTML document and type in the text that you want to use as the clickable newsgroup line.**

If you're smart, you'll use the name of the newsgroup itself. (Hey, it's just a suggestion . . . .)

2 **Position the cursor at the beginning of the text that you're using as your link and type in the following HTML code:**

```
<A HREF=news:newsgroup>
```

In this code, newsgroup is the exact name of the newsgroup. The name looks something like this:

```
alt.computers.windows95
```

3 **Position the cursor at the end of the linked text and type in the following code:**

```
</A>
```

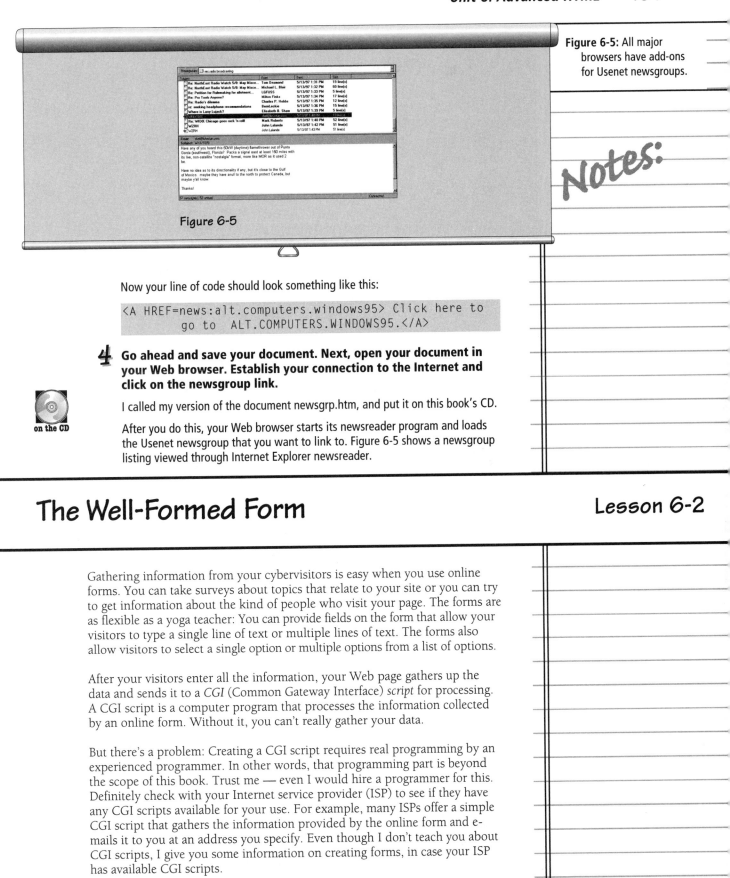

Figure 6-5: All major browsers have add-ons for Usenet newsgroups.

Figure 6-5

Notes:

Now your line of code should look something like this:

```
<A HREF=news:alt.computers.windows95> Click here to
          go to  ALT.COMPUTERS.WINDOWS95.</A>
```

4 **Go ahead and save your document. Next, open your document in your Web browser. Establish your connection to the Internet and click on the newsgroup link.**

on the CD

I called my version of the document newsgrp.htm, and put it on this book's CD.

After you do this, your Web browser starts its newsreader program and loads the Usenet newsgroup that you want to link to. Figure 6-5 shows a newsgroup listing viewed through Internet Explorer newsreader.

The Well-Formed Form

Lesson 6-2

Gathering information from your cybervisitors is easy when you use online forms. You can take surveys about topics that relate to your site or you can try to get information about the kind of people who visit your page. The forms are as flexible as a yoga teacher: You can provide fields on the form that allow your visitors to type a single line of text or multiple lines of text. The forms also allow visitors to select a single option or multiple options from a list of options.

After your visitors enter all the information, your Web page gathers up the data and sends it to a *CGI* (Common Gateway Interface) *script* for processing. A CGI script is a computer program that processes the information collected by an online form. Without it, you can't really gather your data.

But there's a problem: Creating a CGI script requires real programming by an experienced programmer. In other words, that programming part is beyond the scope of this book. Trust me — even I would hire a programmer for this. Definitely check with your Internet service provider (ISP) to see if they have any CGI scripts available for your use. For example, many ISPs offer a simple CGI script that gathers the information provided by the online form and e-mails it to you at an address you specify. Even though I don't teach you about CGI scripts, I give you some information on creating forms, in case your ISP has available CGI scripts.

forms are helpful
tools to get
feedback from
your cybervisitors

The FORM tag

The opening and closing FORM tags surround all of the HTML code that makes up an online form. But before I tell you about all that HTML code, let me give you a little more information about the FORM tags themselves. The opening FORM tag has to have some information that tells the form which CGI script to send the results to. Therefore, the opening FORM tag may look something like this:

```
<FORM METHOD="POST" ACTION="/cgi-bin/mailto?you@your-
                isp.com:/Form_Input">
```

The two important *attributes* in this tag are METHOD and ACTION. An attribute is basically just a way for the Web browser to get additional information about a tag. The METHOD attribute tells the Web browser how to send information to a CGI script — via POST or GET. There's no point in going into the technical differences between the two here. The important thing is that you need to find out from the person who wrote the CGI script which one to use. POST is more common than GET.

The other attribute is ACTION. This simply tells the online form the exact location of the CGI script where it should send the data. In the example above, the name of the CGI script is mailto (a common name for the type of script that e-mails form results to you). The location for the CGI script is in a folder called /cgi-bin (a common folder name for those that house CGI scripts).

heads up

Now, you may notice that I don't explain all the code in my example. In the example, a question mark and some other information follows mailto. For this particular CGI script, *you@your-isp.com* tells the CGI script the e-mail address to send the results to. *Form_Input* tells the CGI script what text to use for the subject line of the e-mail message. Basically, anything beyond the CGI script name is information that's used by that particular CGI script. You must get all that information from the person whose CGI script you're using.

Keep in mind that the items I discuss in the preceding paragraph are unique to this particular CGI script. Other CGI scripts may use other, extra criteria, or none at all. Again, check with the author of the script.

Now remember, that's only the opening <FORM> tag. When you're all done with your form, you need to conclude with </FORM>.

Don't worry about that now. I'll tell you when it's time to add that tag.

Creating a form

I suppose the best way to figure out how to create a form is to actually create one. So that's what you're about to do. You're going to create a form that:

- Asks for your visitor's name and e-mail address
- Lets the visitor specify one or more areas of interest
- Lets the visitor specify if they'd like to receive more e-mail on the topic

- Lets the visitor indicate what part of the country (or world) they're from

- Leaves some room for your visitor to type some additional comments

- Allows the visitor to reset the form to blank so they can start over

- Allows the visitor to submit the form

You may think it's overkill for me to show you all these different options. Well, maybe it is. Can I help it? They don't call me Komando for nothing. But I also want to be sure that you have lots of options — that you can create a form with single-line fields or checkboxes, if you want. With so many things to get through, you don't have any time to dawdle, so jump right in!

1 Open a fresh document by choosing File⇨New in your word processor or text editor.

Most times, a form is on it's own HTML document, so you need to create a new one to go through these steps. If you want, you can add a title and the `<BODY>` tag. (Check back with the HTML chapter if you forget how to add a title.) But you don't need to add anything if you're just doing this for practice.

2 Type in the `<FORM>`tag in accordance with whatever CGI script you're using.

Remember, the `<FORM>` tag looks something like this:

```
<FORM METHOD="POST" ACTION="/cgi-bin/mailto?you@your-
          isp.com:/Form_Input">
```

This, of course, assumes that you already have a CGI script lined up and ready to use. If you don't, and you just want to practice creating forms, that's easy enough. Just type in the FORM tag with no attributes so it looks like this:

```
<FORM>
```

3 Press Enter a couple of times to give yourself some space.

Remember that these extra returns don't affect the appearance of your Web page.

4 Type the following code:

```
<P>Name:<BR>
<INPUT TYPE=text NAME="visitorname" SIZE=25>
```

This code creates a field where a person visiting your Web page can type his or her name, and for teenagers to type dirty words. Visitors see a line with the word "Name" and then under it a blank white bar where they can type their name.

Some of this code probably looks familiar to you already. You learned about the `<P>` (paragraph) and `<BR>` (line break) tags back in Lesson 4-2. So now, I tell you about the rest of it. The name *visitorname* is the field name that the CGI script uses to identify the information entered in that field. (Depending on the CGI script that you use, you may have to use a particular field name so the script can understand what fields you're putting in your form. Again, check with the CGI programmer). The size (25) tells the form how many characters wide to make the field. If you don't think that 25 characters is long enough, go ahead and make it longer. Keep in mind that you can always change it after you take a look at it in your Web browser.

Notes:

5 **Now it's time to add the next field. Press Enter to type on a new line and then type in the following lines of code:**

Remember that pressing Enter just keeps things tidy — it's the <P> and <BR> tags that actually make the line breaks for you. (What can I say? I like things tidy.)

```
<P>E-Mail Address:<BR>
<INPUT TYPE=text NAME="email" SIZE=15>
```

This code creates another field for your visitor to add an e-mail address.

6 **On to the next field. Type in the following block of code:**

```
<P>What types of music do you like?<BR>
<INPUT TYPE=checkbox NAME="classics">Classical<BR>
<INPUT TYPE=checkbox NAME="blues">Blues<BR>
<INPUT TYPE=checkbox NAME="rock">Rock and Roll<BR>
<INPUT TYPE=checkbox NAME="country">Country and
          Western<BR>
<INPUT TYPE=checkbox NAME="soul">R&B/Soul<BR>
<INPUT TYPE=checkbox NAME="jazz">Jazz<BR>
```

Note: If you want, you can also add:

```
<INPUT TYPE=checkbox NAME="dull">Muzak<BR>
```

All right. Now this is another kind of option altogether. The last two fields you created let visitors write in whatever they want. This option creates a column of checkboxes instead. Visitors can check as few or as many of these options as they want.

Another way to list options

As an alternative to checkboxes, you can also present options as a scrolling list. A scrolling list appears as a separate little window with a scroll bar. To choose an option, your visitor just highlights it on the list. If you want to make a scrolling list out of the favorite music list that I just showed you, change the code to:

```
<SELECT NAME="music">
<OPTION>Classical
```

```
<OPTION>Blues
<OPTION>Rock and Roll
<OPTION>Country and
 Western
<OPTION>R&B/Soul
<OPTION>Jazz
```

That's all there is to it.

Next, you're going to figure out how to create a field with *radio buttons.* Unlike a checklist, radio buttons let a person choose only one option in a list.

7 **Type the following code to give visitors a yes or no option:**

```
<P>Would you like to receive additional information
             by e-mail?<BR>
<INPUT TYPE=radio NAME="info">Yes<BR>
<INPUT TYPE=radio NAME="info">No<BR>
```

Notice that both of the field names have the same name. This is how the online form knows which radio buttons are grouped together, and therefore makes sure that the person visiting your Web page selects only one option from that group. Pretty smart form, huh?

By now, you want some real feedback from your visitor. You want to give them a chance to really write some stuff. So, it's time to create a free-form text area.

8 **Type in the following code to create a free-form area:**

```
<P>Additional Comments:<BR>
<TEXTAREA NAME="comments" ROWS=4 COLS=40> </TEXTAREA>
```

This code creates a free-form text area that has four lines and is 40 characters wide. If you type any text between the opening and closing tags, the text appears as pre-entered text in the text area. (This area is where visitors tell you that they don't like questionnaires, focus groups, or surveys.)

Now you are going to write the code that lets your visitor either send you the form or clear it all out and start over again. This option is a must for those indecisive types.

9 **To create sending options, type this code into your HTML document:**

```
<P><INPUT TYPE="submit" VALUE="Send It Now! "> <INPUT
        TYPE="reset" VALUE="Oops! I Goofed">
```

This code creates two buttons. Clicking on the "Send It Now!" button allows your visitor to send the entered information to the CGI script that you entered in the opening FORM tag. The "Oops! I Goofed" button clears all entries on the form and lets the person start over again. Of course, you don't have to call your buttons "Send It Now!" and "Oops! I Goofed." You can call them whatever you want.

You're almost to the end of your form. Remember how way back in Step 1 you typed a beginning code for your form? Well, as with any HTML code, you need a closing tag.

10 **Type in the following code to create the closing tag:**

```
</FORM>
```

That's about all there is to it!

Now, to be sure you got all the steps right, I put all the pieces together for you. After you're done with the preceding steps, the form part of your HTML document should look like this:

it's smart to give your visitors the option of clearing their form so they can start over

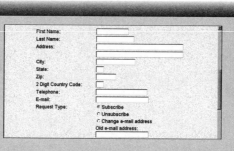

Figure 6-6: This is how a finished form looks in Internet Explorer.

Figure 6-6

```
<FORM METHOD="POST" ACTION="/cgi-bin/mailto?you@your-
          isp.com:/Form_Input">
<P>Name:<BR>
<INPUT TYPE=text NAME="visitorname" SIZE=25>
<P>E-Mail Address:<BR>
<INPUT TYPE=text NAME="email" SIZE=15>
<P>What types of music do you like?<BR>
<INPUT TYPE=checkbox NAME="classics">Classical<BR>
<INPUT TYPE=checkbox NAME="blues">Blues<BR>
<INPUT TYPE=checkbox NAME="rock">Rock and Roll<BR>
<INPUT TYPE=checkbox NAME="country">Country and
          Western<BR>
<INPUT TYPE=checkbox NAME="soul">R&B/Soul<BR>
<INPUT TYPE=checkbox NAME="jazz">Jazz<BR>
<P>Would you like to receive additional information by e-
          mail?<BR>
<INPUT TYPE=radio NAME="info">Yes<BR>
<INPUT TYPE=radio NAME="info">No<BR>
<P>Additional Comments:<BR>
<TEXTAREA NAME="comments" ROWS=4 COLS=40> </TEXTAREA>
<P><INPUT TYPE="submit" VALUE="Send It Now!"> <INPUT
          TYPE="reset" VALUE="Oops! I Goofed.">
</FORM>
```

Go ahead and save your HTML document and open it in your browser. My version of the document, called form.htm, is included on this book's CD. Once you get fancy, you can make forms for people to subscribe to your mailing list with something that looks like the screen in Figure 6-6. Congratulations! Now that you've created a simple form, you can use the same techniques to create any online form you may happen to need.

☑ Progress Check

If you can do the following, you've mastered this lesson:

❑ Explain how forms work.

❑ Understand that you're probably not going to be able to do your own CGI programming.

Recess

It's time for the HTML-Pokey! All together now . . .

Put your form tag in, take your form tag out
Put your mailto link in, and shake the HTML all about
You do the HTML-Pokey, and you turn your Web page around
That's what it's all about!

Laying the Data on the Table

Lesson 6-3

If you've used almost any word processor, you may know that the ability to create nicely formatted tables is a useful feature. Unfortunately, in the early days of the World Wide Web, the closest that HTML came to tables was what the computer sat on. Sure, you could format tabular data a little bit using monospaced type, but that was pretty ugly. Your other option was to create the table as a graphic, but that could waste lots of download time.

Thankfully, those table-less days are gone forever. Now, creating tables is as easy as can be. The first thing you do in this lesson is create a basic table. Then later on, you get to fine-tune your tables for a custom look.

Creating a basic table

Let's suppose for a moment that a law firm that has five partners wants you to publish a company phone directory on your Web site. For the sake of illustration, name these lawyers Joe Blow, Jane Doe, Fluffy Snow, Edgar Poe, and To and Fro. It would be the law offices of Blow Doe Snow Poe and Fro. Follow these steps to make a table out of the lawyers' phone numbers.

1 First, open your practice HTML document and figure out where you want your table located. Then type the following:

```
<TABLE>
```

This code tells your Web browser that what follows is going to be a table. I bet you guessed that already. It also tells your Web browser to put a thin border around the table contents.

2 Now add a title, or caption, for your table. To keep things tidy looking, hit the enter key so you're on the next line, and type:

```
<CAPTION>Employee Phone Directory</CAPTION>
```

Obviously, you don't have to call your table the Employee Phone Directory. That's just what I use as an example.

Notes:

3 **To indicate the start of the first row of the table, hit your Enter key and then type:**

```
<TR>
```

Because HTML defines tables as a series of rows, you need to use this tag at the beginning of each new row.

Now you need to create the fields for your table. Since this is a phone listing, you need a column for the name of the person and another column for their phone number.

4 **Go ahead and type the following to create the columns:**

```
<TH>Employee Name</TH><TH>Telephone Number</TH></TR>
```

The `<TH>` tag is used for column and row headers. Text that uses this tag usually appears as bold and centered. Just a friendly reminder: always remember to use close tags in your HTML..

5 **Now it's time to add all the information for your table. First, hit Enter so all your HTML coding is tidy and legible. Now go ahead and type in this code:**

```
<TR><TD>Joe Blow</TD><TD>555-1201</TD></TR>
<TR><TD>Jane Doe</TD><TD>555-1202</TD></TR>
<TR><TD>Fluffy Snow</TD><TD>555-1203</TD></TR>
<TR><TD>Edgar Poe</TD><TD>555-1204</TD></TR>
<TR><TD>To and Fro</TD><TD>555-1205</TD></TR>
```

The `<TD>` tag identifies the contents of regular table cells. And remember, you don't have to use this silly list of names. If you want to add your own data, that's fine, too.

You're such an HTML pro by now, you can guess what the next tag is. Remember how you started by typing in a tag that let your browser know that a table was coming up? Well, now you've got to tell it that the table ends.

6 **Type this final tag to end the table:**

```
</TABLE>
```

You're done! Not too painful, eh?

Now your HTML document should look something like this:

```
<TABLE>
<CAPTION>Employee Phone Directory</CAPTION>
<TR>
<TH>Employee Name</TH><TH>Telephone Number</TH></TR>
<TR><TD>Joe Blow</TD><TD>555-1201</TD></TR>
<TR><TD>Jane Doe</TD><TD>555-1202</TD></TR>
<TR><TD>Fluffy Snow</TD><TD>555-1203</TD></TR>
<TR><TD>Edgar Poe</TD><TD>555-1204</TD></TR>
<TR><TD>To and Fro</TD><TD>555-1205</TD></TR>
</TABLE>
```

Figure 6-7

Employee Phone Directory	
Employee Name	**Telephone Number**
Joe Blow	555-1201
Jane Doe	555-1202
Fluffy Snow	555-1203
Edgar Poe	555-1204
To and Fro	555-1205

Figure 6-8

Employee Name	**Telephone Number**
Joe Blow	555-1201
Jane Doe	555-1202
Fluffy Snow	555-1203
Edgar Poe	555-1204
To and Fro	555-1205

Figure 6-7: This is how your table looks in Internet Explorer.

Figure 6-8: This border is a little fatter than the default.

heads up

As you may have noticed, in Step 3, you put the <TR> tag on a separate line, while in Step 6, you put the <TR> tag on the same line as the cell contents. The truth is that your Web browser doesn't really care which way you do it. It's all a matter of whatever looks the best to you and seems the easiest to work with. You should try to make your HTML code as tidy as possible, though. That way, if there's some sort of mistake, you can go back and read through it to figure out where you made the error. You want to avoid any mistakes or Blow Doe Snow Poe and Fro can sue your butt.

Go ahead and save your HTML document and then view it in your Web browser. What you'll see should look like the table in Figure 6-7.

catching mistakes is easier if you keep your HTML code tidy

Simple table formatting

There are a few different attributes that you can add to the <TABLE> tag that affect the appearance of your table. They are:

▶ **<BORDER>.** Most Web browsers add a 2-pixel-wide border around HTML tables by default. However, you can control the thickness of the border by using a number value with this attribute. For example, if you want the border to be 8 pixels wide, you add this attribute into your table tag:

```
<TABLE BORDER=8>
```

If you want no border at all, you need to use a zero for the border width. Figure 6-8 shows the previous table with an 8-pixel border.

▶ **<WIDTH>.** If you don't specify a particular width for your table, your Web browser adjusts the width according to the contents of the table. However, you can specify the width of the table as either a percentage of the screen or as a set number of pixels. If you can, make sure a table isn't any wider than the screen. That way, your visitors don't have to scroll over to see the whole table. Because different visitors use different screen settings, it's not always possible to know how they will see anything. Of course, you can use this to your advantage. How? By making a really wide table and putting all the horrible facts at the end. Here's what I mean:

Notes:

Date	Action	Money-Saving Technique	Saved	Results
6/12/97	Installed hard disk	Did self	$300.00	Computer doesn't work
11/23/97	Bought car	Paid cash	Interest payment	Car is lemon
12/28/97	Bought stock	Avoided broker	Saved commission	Owe loan shark

At any rate, for a set number of pixels, you just add the number to the `<TABLE>` tag; for a percentage, you add the number and the percent sign. That means this attribute could look like:

```
<TABLE WIDTH=250>
```

or

```
<TABLE WIDTH=50%>
```

- ◆ **`<CELLSPACING>`.** This attribute controls the amount of space between each cell in the table. This space is expressed as a certain number of pixels. Using 5 pixels as an example, the format is:

```
<TABLE CELLSPACING=5>
```

I wish I could tell you how much space 5 pixels makes on the screen, but again, it really depends on the resolution of your monitor. And that means that every person coming to your site may see everything a little differently. Experiment with pixel numbers, though, so you get a feel for what it means. Figure 6-9 shows the previous table with 5-pixel cell spacing, the table width set to 50 percent.

- ◆ **`<CELLPADDING>`.** This attribute controls the amount of space between the contents of the cell and the edge of the cell. If you don't use any cell padding, you may find that the text you enter in a cell appears too close to the edge. Using 3 pixels as an example, your new `<TABLE>` tag looks like:

```
<TABLE CELLPADDING=3>
```

Figure 6-10 shows the previous table with 3-pixel cell padding.

And what if you want to throw all those attributes into your table? Not a problem. Just add all the attributes into your tag, and it looks something like this:

```
<TABLE BORDER=8 WIDTH=50% CELLSPACING=5 CELLPADDING=3>
```

See. It's not as hard as it may have sounded at first.

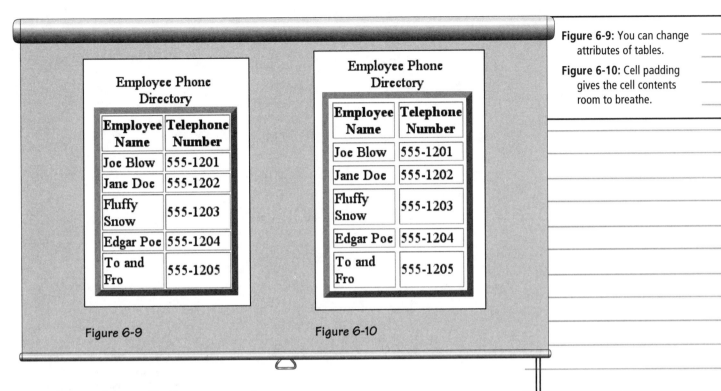

Figure 6-9

Figure 6-10

Figure 6-9: You can change attributes of tables.

Figure 6-10: Cell padding gives the cell contents room to breathe.

Simple cell formatting

heads up

Just as there are attributes that you can use in the `<TABLE>` tag that affect the entire table, you can add other attributes to the `<TD>` and `<TH>` tags that affect the contents of individual cells in a table. Here's the only hitch with these attributes: You have to add them to *every single* cell separately. If you're programming in regular ol' HTML, there's no way to type in the code once and let your browser know that you want to add the same formatting to every single cell in your table. Some programs, like Adobe PageMill, apply these codes for you. But if you want to do it on your own, you're going to get really friendly with the cutting and pasting functions of your word processor and turn into your own personal macro.

Here are some attributes you can add:

♦ **NOWRAP.** Normally, if you type in text that extends beyond the width of a table cell, the text wraps down to a new line, much like in your word processor. However, if you add this NOWRAP attribute to a cell tag, the cell just keeps getting wider and wider, and everything you type stays on a single line. You just type it in like this:

```
NOWRAP
```

Remember, you can add this attribute to either the `<TD>` or the `<TH>` tag. Just add a space and type **NOWRAP**. Remember, too, that you have to add it to every single cell.

♦ **ALIGN.** This attribute lets you control whether the contents of an individual cell are left-justified, centered, or right-justified. Your choices are *left, right,* and *center.* For example, to center the cell contents, you would type:

Notes:

```
ALIGN=center
```

◆ **VALIGN.** This attribute controls the vertical alignment in the cell. In other words, whether the contents are pushed up toward the top of the cell, set right in the middle, or pushed down toward the bottom of the cell. Your choices are *top, middle,* or *bottom.* For example, a middle vertical alignment would look like this

```
VALIGN=middle
```

Remember, you can add any of these alignment tags to either the <TD> or the <TH> tag. Just add a space and type in the alignment code of your choice. Remember, too, that if you want all the cells formatted the same way, you have to add the tag to every single cell.

◆ **WIDTH** and **HEIGHT.** Normally, the size of a table cell adjusts automatically according to what you put in it. However, if you want a cell to be a particular size, use either of these two attributes. The important thing to keep in mind is that if you use the WIDTH attribute, it affects the width of the entire column. Likewise, the HEIGHT attribute affects the entire row. Both WIDTH and HEIGHT are expressed in number of pixels or as a percentage. I like to use the number of pixels because it provides a more precise measurement. But if you don't know the number of pixels or aren't that picky, use a percentage measurement that is based on the size of the screen. If you added both of these to either your <TD> or <TH> tag, it may look something like this:

```
<TD WIDTH=50 HEIGHT=10>
```

or

```
<TH WIDTH=50 HEIGHT=10>
```

◆ **COLSPAN** and **ROWSPAN.** (No, it's not another law firm.) Say you want to split your phone directory into two different departments. The best way to do this is to have the department names serve as dividers in the table. To do this, you'd use the COLSPAN attribute. That attribute lets you add a row that spans more than one column and acts as a type of heading. ROWSPAN lets you add a column that spans more than one row. Here's the code for the table you created above, with the new COLSPAN additions in bold type.

```
<TABLE >
<CAPTION>Employee Phone Directory</CAPTION>
<TR><TH>Employee Name</TH><TH>Telephone Number</
        TH></TR>
<TR><TH COLSPAN=2>Administrative</TH></TR>
<TR><TD>Joe Blow</TD><TD>555-1201</TD></TR>
<TR><TD>Jane Doe</TD><TD>555-1202</TD></TR>
<TR><TH COLSPAN=2>Sales</TH></TR>
<TR><TD>Fluffy Snow</TD><TD>555-1203</TD></TR>
<TR><TD>Edgar Poe</TD><TD>555-1204</TD></TR>
<TR><TD>To and Fro</TD><TD>555-1205</TD></TR>
</TABLE>
```

☑ **Progress Check**

If you can do the following, you've mastered this lesson:

❑ Create a basic HTML table.

❑ Customize the cells, rows, and columns of the table so it looks the way you want it to.

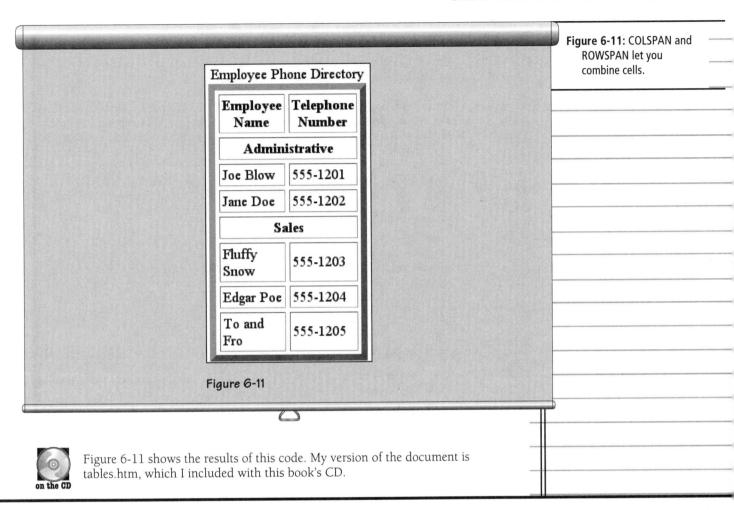

Figure 6-11: COLSPAN and ROWSPAN let you combine cells.

Figure 6-11 shows the results of this code. My version of the document is tables.htm, which I included with this book's CD.

You've Been Framed

Lesson 6-4

HTML *frames* are a way for you to split up your Web page into two or more separate sub-windows that can function independently of whatever is in any other frame. You've probably seen this all over the Web. (It has spread faster than a rumor in Hollywood.) It's particularly handy if you want to have a table of contents in one frame and the actual content in the other frame.

Adding frames can be a little tricky, but not quite as bad as it sounds. You see, the content of each frame is simply a separate HTML document. Let's say, for example, that your Web page has two frames. This actually requires three HTML documents.

Why three? Let me give you an example. Remember that *index.html* document that always acts as the opening page to your Web site? Well, say you want to split that page into two frames. The actual *index.html* document just acts as a pointer to the two other documents, each of which serves as one of the frames. In other words, all the *index.html* document really does is specify which HTML document is to be displayed in the two frames. Then the two documents specified in the main document actually serve as the content for the two frames. Together, this group of HTML documents is a *frameset*.

Notes:

Let's create a Web page using frames, and I guarantee you'll understand what's going on by the time you finish.

Before you begin, you need to create two HTML documents that will serve as the content for the two frames you're about to create. They can have as little or as much in them as you want. If you're feeling really lazy, you can even leave them blank. The only problem with doing that is that you'll have two frames that look exactly the same and you won't be able to tell the difference between them. So go ahead and take a minute to create two different HTML documents. Just put a line or two of text in each. Call one of them *test1.htm* and the other one *test2.htm*. And if you're really lazy, use *t1.htm* and *t2.htm*.

Now, you also need to create the third, or pointer, HTML document. You're probably best off calling this one *index.htm* or *index.html*. This document should be blank, except for a title bar. Remember, this is a document you're going to work in: This pointer document points your browser to the two other documents that serve as the frames.

Now it's time to get started. (As if you've been wasting time!)

1 Open the pointer document.

If you followed my advice, you should have called the document *index.htm*. The document should be blank, except for the tags for the title bar.

2 Now type the following line of code:

```
<FRAMESET COLS="*,*" >
```

This tells your Web browser to display two vertical frames that are right next to each other. If you want the frames to be horizontal (on top of each other), you can substitute `ROWS` for `COLS`. The two asterisks tell your Web browser that the space in the browser window should be split evenly between the two frames.

3 Press Enter. On the next line of your HTML document, type:

```
<FRAME NAME="frame1" SRC="test1.htm">
<FRAME NAME="frame2" SRC="test2.htm">
```

This coding gives each frame in your document a name and also tells your Web browser which document to display in each frame. Remember that `test1.htm` and `test2.htm` both need to be in the same folder as the pointer HTML document that you're working in right now. Otherwise, your browser won't be able to find them. Same story, different chapter.

4 To wrap it all up, type:

```
</FRAMESET>
```

5 Save your document and now open it in your Web browser.

You see two separate sides of the page. Your new page should look something like the one in Figure 6-12. Test it out: You should be able to scroll the two sides separately. If you want to experiment some more, go ahead and change the `COLS` in the `<FRAMESET>` tag to `ROWS`. Then, save the document again and view your horizontal frames in your browser.

I included my version of index.htm, test1.htm, and test2.htm on this book's CD.

on the CD

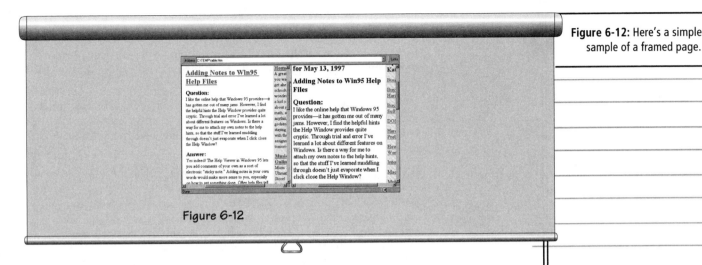

Figure 6-12

Figure 6-12: Here's a simple sample of a framed page.

Frame attributes

As you may have already suspected, there are a few attributes that you can use to modify the appearance of your frames. Here they are:

- **COLS and ROWS.** Remember a few minutes ago when you typed in this code?

```
<FRAMESET COLS="*,*" >
```

The two asterisks indicate that there are two frames and that each frame gets the same amount of space in the browser window. If you are a controlling type of person and want to control the exact or relative size of a frame, you can replace either of the asterisks with a number value or a percentage value. If you use the COLS attribute, this value affects the width of the column. If you use the ROWS attribute, that means you're splitting the page horizontally and this value then affects the height of the row. If you express the value as a percentage, just remember to include the percent sign. Finally, if you use a percentage value to define each and every frame in the document, make sure the numbers you use all add up to 100 percent.

Say you want one of your vertical frames to act as a table of contents, one that doesn't need a lot of room — maybe only 30 percent of your screen. The code may look something like this:

```
<FRAMESET COLS="30%,70%">
```

Now say that you want that same table of contents to be only 150 pixels wide and you want the other frame to take up the rest of the screen. Then, you would just leave an asterisk, instead of filling in a second number. The code would look like this:

```
<FRAMESET COLS="150,*">
```

- **SCROLLING.** Depending on how much information you put on a page and how big a monitor you use, you may not be able to see the entire

Notes:

contents of a frame at the same time. On a normal HTML page, this isn't a problem; you just use the scroll bar on the right side of the window to scroll down.

By default, most browsers add a scroll bar to the right side of each frame in a framed document. However, if you want, you can turn the scroll bar off for any given frame by using this attribute and giving it a value of *no*. The code looks like this:

```
<FRAME NAME="frame1" SRC="test1.htm" SCROLLING="no">
```

▶ **MARGINHEIGHT** and **MARGINWIDTH**. You can use these two attributes to add margins to your frames. Together, these attributes work just like cell padding does in HTML tables. MARGINHEIGHT controls the margin along the top and bottom of the frame; MARGINWIDTH controls the margin on the sides. To add a margin of 3 pixels all the way around, you add this code to a FRAME tag:

```
<FRAME NAME="frame1" SRC="test1.htm" MARGINHEIGHT=3
        MARGINWIDTH=3>
```

Frames and links

Normally, if you create a link within a frame and then click on that link in your Web browser, the document you link to replaces the document that contains the link. In other words, the linked-to document displays in the same frame as the original document. But with frames you have a little more control — again, perfect for people who love control.

You can control where the linked-to document displays by using the TARGET attribute within the link itself. You can have the new document display in one of the other frames, or you can have the new document take up the entire browser window with no frames at all.

In the previous example, you created two frames. One frame held *test1.htm* and was named *frame1*; the other held *test2.htm* and was called *frame2*. Now let's suppose that in *test1.htm* you want to create a link to another document called *test3.htm*. If you want *test3.htm* to display in frame2, your link looks something like this:

```
<A HREF=test3.htm TARGET="frame2"> Click here for
        TEST3.HTM</A>
```

If you want *test3.htm* to occupy the entire browser window with no frames, you'd type the link something like this:

```
<A HREF=test3.htm TARGET=_top> Click here for TEST3.HTM
        </A>
```

If you use this tag, *test3.htm* replaces the frames that are on the page.

☑ **Progress Check**

If you can do the following, you've mastered this lesson:

❏ Create frames on an HTML page.

❏ Modify frames to get the look you want on your page.

❏ Create links that either are displayed in a particular frame or over the frames of your page.

Getting There with Image Maps   Lesson 6-5

If you've already done some exploring on the World Wide Web (a good way to procrastinate instead of working on your Web page), chances are you've come across a graphic where you can click on different parts of the image to get to a bunch of different locations. This type of graphic is called an *image map*.

The idea behind an image map is very simple. First, you identify in your HTML code which graphic you want to use for the image map. It can be any *still* graphic you want. Animations won't work, so don't even bother to try it. Then you indicate coordinates that define the various *hotspots* on the image map. Finally, you specify links that correspond to each of the hotspots.

on the test

The hard part is determining the coordinates for the various hotspots. Even in this image map where all the hotspots are rectangular (the code looks like SHAPE="rect"), figuring out the coordinates can take forever. Besides that, hotspots can also be shaped like a circle (SHAPE="circle") or a polygon (SHAPE="polygon"), confusing the matter even further.

If you want to, you can spend the next year trying to manually figure out the right coordinates for your image map. (But that's a pretty low-tech solution, not to mention a big waste of time.) What you need is a computer program that can figure out this stuff for you.

on the CD

Many of the Web page editors covered earlier in this book include tools for creating image maps. However, if you don't happen to have one of those programs, you're still in luck. The CD-ROM at the back of this book includes a shareware program called LiveImage (for Windows) or ImageMapper (for Macs) that makes all of this as easy as can be. When you get ready to create some image maps, give these programs a try. You're welcome. Thank me with a link.

Unit 6 Quiz

Sit up and take a quiz. Circle the best answer to each question.

1. **A mailto link creates . . .**

    A. A link to an FTP site

    B. A link to a Gopher hole

    C. A new, pre-addressed e-mail message window

    D. A wrapped and tied Christmas present

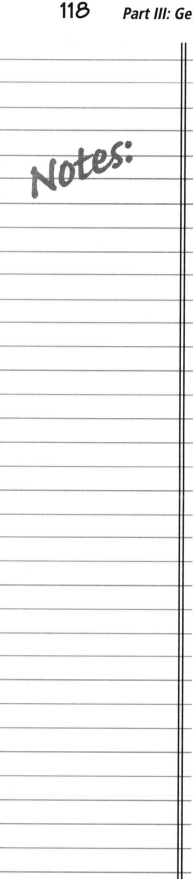

2. **Gopher is . . .**

   A. A character on *The Love Boat*

   B. A search engine on the World Wide Web

   C. A small, furry animal

   D. A way to archive text-based information

3. **FTP stands for . . .**

   A. File Transfer Protocol

   B. File Transfer Plan

   C. File Transport Protocol

   D. File Transport Priority

4. **Usenet newsgroups . . .**

   A. Exclusively report national news

   B. Are owned by The Associated Press

   C. Allow people to exchange messages on thousands of topics

   D. Are not part of the Internet

5. **An online form requires . . .**

   A. A CGI script to handle form input

   B. Two megabytes of disk space on your ISP's server

   C. Special permission from your ISP

   D. The use of HTML frames

6. **Forms allow the user to . . .**

   A. Type text into a field

   B. Make selections from a list

   C. Clear the screen and start over

   D. Contact their local government office to lodge a complaint

7. **HTML tables are a great way to format . . .**

   A. Multiple paragraphs

   B. Section headings

   C. Rows and columns of information

   D. Your résumé

8. **Table width can be specified as . . .**

   A. A percentage

   B. The number of folks you're inviting for dinner

   C. How many people are sitting there

   D. A set number of pixels

9. **To create a Web page with two frames, you need how many HTML documents?**

    A. Two

    B. Three

    C. Four

    D. Five

10. **A frameset is . . .**

    A. The group of HTML documents that makes up a framed Web page

    B. All the fields in an online form

    C. The location of a particular frame

    D. The settings for a particular frame

11. **When you create a link in a framed document, you can have the link-to document . . .**

    A. Appear in the same frame

    B. Erase all the other documents that came before it

    C. Occupy the entire browser window

    D. Appear in a different frame

12. **An image map lets you . . .**

    A. Locate any image on your Web site

    B. Create a clickable graphic with multiple hotspots

    C. Find online maps of your city

    D. Plan out your Web publishing strategy

13. **Hotspots are shaped like . . .**

    A. Circles

    B. Rectangles

    C. Polygons

    D. Hearts and flowers

Unit 6 Exercise

1. Add a mailto link to your home page. Although you may not ever use some of the other links described in this chapter, a mailto link is important for every Web site.

Notes:

2. Using the skills you learned in this unit, create your own online form. If possible, locate a CGI script that you can use to process the information gathered by your form. Remember to check with your ISP first, because they may have some CGI scripts already available for your use. If your ISP doesn't offer any, do a search on one of the big search engines (like Yahoo! or AltaVista) for CGI scripts.

3. Take a few entries out of your address book and create a table out of them. You can have fields for name, address, phone number, and whatever else you want. Use COLSPAN to divide the entries alphabetically.

4. Create a framed document that includes some sort of hypertext link. Make sure to use the TARGET attribute in the link.

5. Install LiveImage or ImageMapper on your system and create an image map. Test it out in your Web browser.

The Pages are Alive with Multimedia

Prerequisites
▶ A firm understanding of HTML basics
▶ Know what constitutes of a good Web page and not an overdone Web page
▶ Know how to work with graphics on the Web
▶ The ability to carry a tune without a paper bag (no, not really)

Objectives for This Unit

✓ Adding sound to your Web pages

✓ Adding animation and video to your Web pages

✓ Creating a Web-based slide show

on the CD

▶ sound.wav
▶ qt.mov
▶ quicktime.htm
▶ slide1.htm
▶ slide1.gif
▶ slide2.htm
▶ slide2.gif
▶ slide3.htm
▶ slide3.gif
▶ slide.wav

on the test

What exactly is multimedia anyway? In terms of the World Wide Web, multimedia is simply the incorporation of sound, animation, movies, and so on, into your Web pages to make the pages a little more lively and compelling. After all, which do you think would have the most impact: Reading U.S. President John F. Kennedy's famous quote: "Ask not what your country can do for you, but what you can do for your country," or seeing a video clip of the late president actually delivering those immortal words? Better still, would you rather read about his affair with Marilyn Monroe or see it. You get my point. Yep, multimedia can put a giant exclamation point on your Web pages. But just like anything else, too much multimedia can bog down your site and encourage people to do their Web surfing in other cyberwaters.

Before you get started, I'm going to play devil's advocate and give you both the pros and cons of adding multimedia to your Web site.

Lesson 7-1

Why Multimedia? Why Not?

Notes:

The advantages of multimedia are obvious. Instead of risking rain or snow or other unpleasant atmospheric conditions to make it to the local library, students have to make it only as far as the family computer to do research for a report. Once at the computer, instead of thumbing through volume after volume of printed material, today's kids just plop their copy of *Encarta* or *Compton's* or *Grolier's* into the CD-ROM drive. In just a matter of moments, all the information they need is right there on the computer screen.

Multimedia doesn't just make information easier to get at; it also makes getting that information more enjoyable and interesting. Instead of mind-numbing pages of text, multimedia brings information to life, or is that life to information? Research suddenly goes from boring to fun. Information takes on a new context. Like magic, the world becomes a wonderful and richly textured place.

Okay, okay. I guess I'm getting a little carried away here, but you get my point. Multimedia can add a new and exciting dimension to even the most tedious topics. Well, the same holds true for your Web pages. The right dose of multimedia can push your Web site from merely a good one to a great one that people will want to visit and revisit. And that's really the whole point, isn't it?

Sounds great, right? So why in the world would you *not* want to add multimedia to your Web pages. I'll give you a bunch of reasons.

Playing devil's advocate

on the test

Let's start with the cost of multimedia to you, in terms of both time and money. For this, I'm going to give you an example.

If you own any multimedia titles on CD-ROM, there's a pretty good chance that at least a few of the titles were created with a program called Director, made by a company called Macromedia. Director is probably the top program that professional multimedia developers use to create their works of cyberart.

on the test

After the World Wide Web started taking off, the folks at Macromedia decided it would be cool to take the type of high-impact multimedia that Director makes possible to the Web. So the folks at Macromedia created an add-on technology for Director called *Shockwave* and are making some cool cash with it. With the various Shockwave components, you can convert Director multimedia into a format that you can use on the Web.

Well, in concept, Director is great. However, Director also costs a few hundred bucks, well worth it for professional multimedia developers who plan to mass-market their creations and make substantial money doing so, but a major drawback to many others.

Suppose for a moment that you have a fat bankroll and don't mind spending the money. (But in which case you'd probably be paying someone else to create your Web page.) Programs like Director are very sophisticated, and if you plan to produce top-quality multimedia for your Web site, you have to be willing to spend the time it takes to master such a program. *Macromedia Director 5 For Dummies,* by Lauren Steinhauer (IDG Books Worldwide, Inc.) can help, but even this is no "learn it overnight" proposition.

I don't mean to sound like I'm picking on Director. It's a great program and, like I said, worth its weight in gold if it offers the tools you need to create the multimedia you want. Plenty of other ways to create multimedia exist.

How about live-action video, like the video clip of President Kennedy? Stock footage like that may be easy to come by, but suppose you want to add some original video to your Web site?

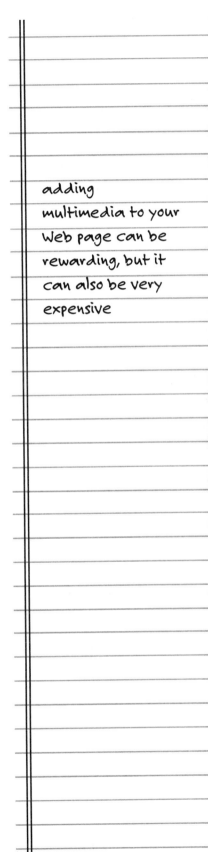

adding multimedia to your Web page can be rewarding, but it can also be very expensive

First, you need a video camera. Depending on the quality you want, you may be able to get by with a consumer camcorder that costs a few hundred dollars. On the other hand, you may need to rent an entire video studio to get the results you want. I've been involved with enough television productions to be able to tell you that studio time ain't cheap. It costs more than Director.

After you get your footage committed to tape, you need video-capture equipment to get that footage from the tape to your PC. Next, you need video-editing software to tweak your footage to perfection. Graphics cards are available that let you do this — and it may not even cost more than about $500. Even if creating original video doesn't cost you a bundle, the process is still going to add up to a lot of your time.

If you do a lot of graphics, look for a video accelerator card. It has special built-in circuitry that speeds up the screen display in Windows. The card is tailored for Windows because everything in Windows (including words, menus, and buttons) is a graphic or a picture. Working with Windows is a lot like ordering food at Denny's — everything on the menu is shown with a picture. A computer takes longer to draw a picture on-screen in Windows than it does to display text on-screen in DOS.

The 2MB of RAM on the accelerator card speeds up the video display. With the extra RAM, you can increase the number of colors that appear on-screen at once and adjust the size of the video display (VGA mode: 640 x 480 pixels or SVGA mode: 800 x 600 pixels). Some cards help draw fonts on-screen, too.

The standard Windows VGA display shows 16 colors, and enhanced Windows modes let you see over 24 million colors. But colors take juice: the more colors, the slower the screen display. Unless you're doing high-end graphics work, a 256-color display should suit you just fine and won't slow down the system very much.

The 14- or 15-inch monitors that are sold with computer systems have a screen size of 800 x 600 pixels. Although the video card can display 1024 x 786 pixels, the size of icons and text on-screen is so small that it's not practical for most people to use. You need a magnifying glass to see anything.

heads up

Multimedia can be tough on the people who visit your site, too. Let's go back to Director and Shockwave for a minute. To view Shockwave multimedia through your Web browser, you need to have the Shockwave *plug-in* installed on your system. A plug-in is a little bit of add-on software that allows your

a plug-in is add-on software that allows your Web browser to display files that it can't handle on its own

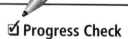

☑ **Progress Check**

If you can do the following, you've mastered this lesson:

❏ Argue both sides of the multimedia issue.

❏ Understand that arguing this issue turns you into a true techie nerd.

❏ Realize that you don't want to be a techie nerd.

❏ Move onto the next lesson, putting your nerd phase behind you.

Web browser to display files that it can't handle on its own. If visitors stop by your site and they don't have the right plug-in for whatever type of multimedia you've included on your site, they're out of luck. Your cybervisitors will have to find the plug-in at Macromedia's Web site, download the plug-in, and then return to your site to view your multimedia. If you use any other plug-ins, visitors have to go to the site of the company that created the plug-ins. And you may never see them again.

One way to minimize this problem is to provide a link from your site to the appropriate plug-in; people can download the plug-in on the spot and enjoy the full impact of your site. Even those couple of extra steps can be enough to discourage some people from hanging around your site very long. It's the old case of "Plug-in, Turn-off, Drop Out."

That's not all. Why do you think multimedia titles come on CD-ROM and not floppy disks? It's because multimedia files are big — very, very big. A simple little animation file of 200K or so may not seem like any big deal on your 2GB hard drive. However, when you have to download that file over a standard modem connection, the couple of minutes it takes waiting for that file can seem like an eternity. If your multimedia files are too big, people who surf by modem won't even bother waiting for the download.

I scream for multimedia

Does this all mean you should skip multimedia altogether? No way! I love multimedia. Like I said earlier, I just wanted to play devil's advocate and make sure you knew exactly what you may be getting yourself into. There are ways around all of the obstacles I presented.

For example, if you're not out to win any major multimedia award for your Web site, and remember you can give yourself your own rewards — you don't have to use an expensive program like Director to create your multimedia. Heck, even an animated GIF (which you read about in Unit 5) qualifies as multimedia.

If originality isn't a major concern, you can find plenty of *public domain* multimedia elements on the Web that you can easily add to your own Web pages. (Public domain refers to anything released by its creator for use by anyone who wants it.) Likewise, you can also buy collections of multimedia on CD-ROM designed specifically for you to add to your Web pages.

Making sure people have the right plug-ins can be a problem, but it's one that I see going away eventually. Every multimedia company on the planet seems to have created a special plug-in for its products. As time goes by, I believe that a certain small set of plug-ins will become standard. When that happens, companies like Netscape and Microsoft will start building support for those types of files directly into your Web browser, so you won't even need a separate plug-in.

What about those huge multimedia files? As I write this, Time Warner has already introduced its RoadRunner cable modem services in several major cities around the country. RoadRunner uses cable television lines to deliver Internet access to your home as quickly as some of the office systems set up in fancy-schmancy corporations — and for a fraction of the cost.

In the meantime, one option that I see more often is to offer two versions of your site, one for people with high-speed connections and another for people with regular modem connections. Offering both means some extra work on your part, but by doing this you can offer both types for users to get the most bang for their buck.

Let's Add Some Sound

Lesson 7-2

on the CD

Because sound files are generally smaller than animation and video files, this seems like a good place to start. Let's get one thing straight, though. Exactly how to create or acquire multimedia files is way beyond the scope of this book. So for this lesson, you can use a sound file that's on the CD-ROM at the back of this book. The name of the file is *sound.wav*.

The most common sound file formats on the Web are AU (with file extension *.au*), Audio Interchange File Format (with file extension *.aiff* or *.aifc*), and WAVE (with file extension *.wav*). Most Web browsers support these formats without requiring an extra plug-in. You can use any format you want, but you have to make sure you use standard HTML naming conventions (which you covered previously in Unit 4), including the correct file extension. Remember, using the right file extension is the only way your Web browser knows what kind of file it's dealing with.

on the test

You can handle sound files on your Web page in two ways. First, you can create a link to the sound file so that when someone clicks on the link, they hear the sound. The other option is to embed the sound file so that the sound plays automatically when your Web page loads. This lesson covers both options.

The simple linked sound

Adding a sound link is just like creating any other link. Here are the steps to follow:

1 **Copy the *sound.wav* file from the files that came with this book's CD-ROM to the same folder that holds your Web page.**

See Appendix C for more details.

2 **Use your text editor or word processor to open the Web page into which you want to place the sound file.**

If you don't want to foul up one of your existing files with this exercise, you're welcome to create a new one, too. However, if you do, remember to save the file in the same folder as sound.wav so that the relative link you're about to create works correctly.

Notes:

Figure 7-1: A link to a sound file looks just like any other link.

Notes:

Figure 7-1

3 **Position the cursor where you want to create the link to the sound file.**

4 **Type in the following line of HTML code:**

```
<A HREF="sound.wav">Click here to listen to the
            sound.</A>
```

Now it's time to test the sound.

5 **Save and close the file.**

Don't forget: If you created a new file in your word processor, you have to save the file as plain text. No matter what program you used to create the file, it needs to have the *.htm* or *.html* extension.

6 **Launch your Web browser.**

7 **Using your Web browser's Open File command, open the file you just created.**

You can see the link you just created, looking something like the one shown in Figure 7-1.

8 **Click on the link.**

If you followed my instructions to a T, you should hear my little surprise message to you.

How about some mood music?

Having a clickable link is all fine and dandy, but suppose you want the sound to play in the background any time your page loads — a little tune or a drum roll, for example. Obviously, the little sound file you used in the first part of this lesson isn't much in terms of mood music, but it works for helping you figure out how to do this. I'm going to assume that you've already copied sound.wav to the right folder. Now let me show you how to get sound to play when your page loads.

1 **Use your text editor or word processor to open the Web page where you're going to place the sound file.**

Just as in the first part of this lesson, you can create a new file if you want to. Just remember to save it in the same folder as sound.wav.

2 **Position the cursor at the very end of the file.**

This is important, because you don't want the whole process of the sound loading to interfere with the loading of the rest of your page.

3 **Type in the following lines of HTML code:**

```
<BGSOUND SRC="sound.wav">
<EMBED SRC="sound.wav" autostart="true"
          hidden="true" >
</EMBED>
```

Take particular note of the <EMBED> tag. This is a tag I haven't discussed yet. <EMBED> is also the tag you'll use to embed animation/video files in the next lesson. For right now let's finish with sound.

Let's test this out.

4 **Save and close the file.**

Don't forget all of the format and file extension stuff associated with saving a new file. See Unit 3 if you need a refresher.

5 **Launch your Web browser.**

6 **Using your Web browser's Open File command, open the file you just created.**

Pretty cool, eh? Your page may not look any different than before you started, but it sure sounds different, doesn't it?

☑ **Progress Check**

If you can do the following, you've mastered this lesson:

❏ Add a simple sound file to a Web page.

❏ Add a sound to your Web page that opens as you open the page.

❏ Sing along with your sound file.

Time for Some Action

Lesson 7-3

on the test

Animation and live-action video come in all shapes and sizes, and in a wide variety of formats. With the single exception of the animated GIF, which you already learned about earlier in Unit 5 (and which your browser really thinks of as a still graphic), each one of these file formats requires a separate browser plug-in in order for visitors to properly view the file. The good news is that the browser is the only variable. When you create your Web page, you can use the same basic technique for adding these multimedia files, no matter what type of file it is you're working with.

The secret to all this is that handy <EMBED> tag. This tag simply tells your Web browser that some sort of multimedia file is embedded into your Web page. As long as the multimedia file has the right file extension and you have the right plug-in, the multimedia appears as part of the Web page. Again, the key at your end as the creator of the Web page is to make sure that your

Notes:

multimedia files have the right file extensions. That's the only way your Web browser knows which plug-in to call on to make your page work correctly.

Here are a few of the more common multimedia file formats and their corresponding extensions:

Table 7-1:	Common Multimedia Types
File Type	Extension
QuickTime movies	.mov
MPEG movies	.mpeg or .mpg
AVI movies	.avi
Shockwave multimedia	.dcr

on the CD

For this lesson, you're going to add to your Web page a QuickTime movie that I've included with the files on this book's CD-ROM. Like I said before, the procedure is the same no matter what type of multimedia file you actually use later on. The name of the QuickTime file is *qt.mov*.

You can download the most recent version of the QuickTime plug-in at http://www.quicktime.apple.com. Simply follow the installation instructions for your operating system. Before you get started, make sure you install the QuickTime plug-in on your system. For most major Web browsers like Netscape Navigator and Microsoft Internet Explorer, this simply means copying the plug-in to the Plug-Ins folder located in the folder where your Web browser resides. When the plug-in is the Plug-Ins folder, the browser automatically locates and launches it, as long as the browser recognizes the extension you've used on your file.

Now that you have the QuickTime plug-in installed, here's how to add a QuickTime movie to your Web page.

1 **Copy the qt.mov file from the CD-ROM to the same folder that holds your Web page.**

2 **Use your text editor or word processor to open the Web page into which you want to place the sound file.**

Once again, I invite you to create a brand-new Web page for this exercise if you so desire. However, don't forget to save it in the same folder as qt.mov.

3 **Position the cursor where you want the QuickTime movie to appear on your Web page.**

4 **Type in the following line of HTML code:**

```
<EMBED SRC="qt.mov">
```

That was pretty simple, wasn't it?

5 **Save and close the file.**

Don't forget, if you created a new file in your word processor, you have to save the file as plain text, and you have to save it in the same folder where you copied qt.mov.

Now, let's check it out.

6 **Launch your Web browser.**

7 **Using your Web browser's Open File command, open the file you just created.**

FYI, my version of the document is quicktime.htm and came on this book's CD. You should see a little box that looks something like the one shown in the margin. And there you have it — live-action video on your Web page.

☑ **Progress Check**

If you can do the following, you've mastered this lesson:

❏ Add a video clip to your Web page.

❏ Consider writing to George Lucas to ask for a job as his webmaster.

A movie with this QuickTime box is ready for action.

Macintosh and QuickTime movies

If you're a Macintosh user, you may already be familiar with QuickTime movies; Apple Computer originally developed QuickTime for the Macintosh platform. And perhaps you have some QuickTime movies of your own that you want to add to your Web page. You can do it, but there's just one problem.

Macintosh files differ from files on other computer platforms in that Macintosh files come in two parts. The data fork stores the main part of the file; however, the resource fork also stores information, albeit a small amount. That small amount includes information about the type of file and what application program created it.

When you create a QuickTime movie on a Macintosh, some important information gets stored in the resource fork. The problem is that when you transfer a Macintosh file by modem, the resource fork gets stripped away — and even if it didn't, non-Macintosh computers wouldn't know what to do with the information in the resource fork anyway. That's known as being *forked* in computer lingo.

To get a Macintosh QuickTime movie ready for presentation on the Web, you must first flatten it. No, I'm not talking about some new-fangled movie star diet. *Flattening* the movie means taking the important information out of the resource fork and packing it into the data fork so that other types of computers have access to all the right information.

Many Macintosh programs that create QuickTime movies have built-in utilities for flattening the movies. However, if you already have a QuickTime movie that you want to use, you can flatten it by using a freeware program called flattenmoov. You can find this program in plenty of Macintosh archives on the Internet. One such location is at

```
ftp://ftp.the.net/mirrors/_
   ftp.utexas.edu/graphics/_
   flattenmoov.hqx.
```

Just use that address in your Web browser and it should start downloading the file automatically.

Lesson 7-4

Creating an Online Slide Show

Notes:

Back when I was in grade school — in the good, old days when the simplest computer still took up an entire room and the Enter key was the size of a desk — multimedia usually just meant a slide show synchronized with some sort of music. That may seem pretty low-tech now, but these presentations were actually quite powerful. Well, at least they got a bunch of fourth graders to sit quietly during health class. In this lesson, you learn how to create an online version of one of these old-fashioned slide shows.

This Web recipe is a little complicated, so you have to make sure you have all your ingredients lined up ahead of time. To create an online slide show, you need the following items:

▶ A series of Web pages that you want to use as the individual "slides" in your slide show. You probably shouldn't include any animations or video on these pages because you want your slides to load as quickly as possible.

▶ A sound file that you want to use for the background music on each slide. You can use the same file for all slides, or a different one for each slide.

on the CD

To make this all easier on you, I include a folder called SLIDES on this book's CD-ROM. This folder contains three HTML files (slide1.htm, slide2.htm, and slide3.htm), a sound file (slide.wav), and three GIF images (slide1.gif, slide2.gif, and slide3.gif). These files include everything you need to create a simple slide show. The only thing missing in each HTML file is the code to enable the background music and the code to auto-advance the slide show. By *auto-advance*, I mean that you add HTML code that actually makes your Web browser move from one slide to the next without any input from the person doing the browsing. If you try to link a slide show from your main Web page, the best bet is to create an interim page that directs visitors to the slide show. On the last page of the slide show, add the HTML code to advance visitors back to your home page so they can browse around some more.

Before we get started, copy the entire SLIDES folder from the CD-ROM to your hard drive.

1 Use your text editor or word processor to open slide1.htm.

2 Position the text cursor on the blank line directly after the opening `<BODY>` tag.

3 Type in the following HTML code:

```
<META HTTP-EQUIV="REFRESH"
        CONTENT="10;URL=slide2.htm">
```

Let's take a minute to discuss the HTML code you just typed. Several `<META>` tags are used on the Web. Basically, this `<META>` tag tells the Web browser to refresh the contents of the browser window after 10 seconds with slide2.htm. If you want to change the time, change the number associated after the CONTENT=. Now, it is set to 10 seconds. If you want it to be 15 seconds, change the 10 to 15, and you've got it.

4 Position the cursor right before the final </HTML> **tag.**

5 Type in the following lines of HTML code:

```
<BGSOUND SRC="slide.wav">
<EMBED SRC="sound.wav" autostart="true"
             hidden="true" >
</EMBED>
```

This should seem familiar from Lesson 7-2.

6 Save and close the file.

7 Use your text editor or word processor to open slide2.htm.

8 Position the text cursor on the blank line directly after the opening <BODY> **tag.**

9 Type in the following HTML code.

```
<META HTTP-EQUIV="REFRESH"
           CONTENT="10;URL=slide3.htm">
```

I'll bet you know what this means by now. You guessed it: After 10 seconds, your browser advances to slide3.

10 Position the cursor at the very end of the file.

11 Type in the following lines of HTML code:

```
<BGSOUND SRC="slide.wav">
<EMBED SRC="sound.wav" autostart="true"
             hidden="true" >
</EMBED>
```

12 Save and close the file.

13 Now use your text editor or word processor to open slide3.htm.

This should seem like second nature now.

14 Position the text cursor on the blank line directly after the opening <BODY> **tag.**

15 Type in the following HTML code.

```
<META HTTP-EQUIV="REFRESH"
           CONTENT="10;URL=slide1.htm">
```

Now your browser loops back around to the first slide of the show.

16 Position the cursor at the very end of the file.

17 Type in the following lines of HTML code:

```
<BGSOUND SRC="slide.wav">
<EMBED SRC="sound.wav" autostart="true"
             hidden="true" >
</EMBED>
```

Progress Check

If you can do the following, you've mastered this lesson:

❑ Post a multimedia slide show on a Web page.

❑ Recall all the slide shows that you were subjected to in fourth-grade health class.

18 **Save and close the file.**

19 **Now use your Web browser to open slide1.htm.**

Don't do anything else. In about 10 seconds, your Web browser automatically switches to the second slide. Ten or so seconds after that, it switches to the third slide, and then starts all over again. To stop this continuous loop, just close the browser window.

heads up

If you create an online slide show using the techniques from this lesson, chances are that you may want the background music to play the entire time that each slide displays. The trick is to time the sound file and then make sure the delay between slides is shorter than the length of the sound file. For example, suppose the sound file takes 15 seconds to play. If you make the delay between slides 10 seconds, you can be sure that the slide show advances before the music stops.

Recess

Do you want to see a throbber? Hey, get your mind out of the gutter. A throbber is an animated graphic you can use on your Web page, and there are tons of resources available to help you. Point your browser in any of these directions for some play time on the Web, um, I mean, for some research time for your Web page.

▶ **Animated Gif Gallery.** How about some animation to spruce up your Web site? The animated gif gallery has nearly 900 gifs for your use . . . *free!* If you'd like to share, you can also submit your own gifs to be listed in the gallery. Get animated at `http://www.vr-mall.com/anigifpd/anigifpd.html`.

▶ **Image Finder on the Web.** While search engines allow you to locate Web sites using keywords, Image Surfer lets you search for . . . images. Search for cartoons, comics, cars, computer games, photography, sports, and more at `http://isurf.interpix.com`.

▶ **My Shareware Page.** Looking for some downloads? Pay a visit to the My Shareware Page and see what tools you'd like to download. This site has audio/sound utilities, communication clients, conferencing tools, ftp and gopher clients, HTML editors, multimedia tools, networking tools, and more. Mosey on down to `http://www.mysharewarepage.com`.

▶ **Tucows.** Known for one of the best collections of Internet software, Tucows offers up to 140 access locations worldwide. You find a wide array of Internet software as well as plug-ins for your computer and more at `http://www.tucows.com`.

Unit 7 Quiz

Choose the best answer for each of the following questions.

1. **Multimedia incorporates . . .**

   A. sound

   B. video

   C. animation

   D. any or all of the above

2. **You should be careful when you add multimedia to your Web page because . . .**

   A. multimedia files can take a long time to download over a modem connection

   B. the person viewing your page may not have the right plug-in

   C. multimedia can increase the amount of time and money necessary to create your Web page

   D. nobody wants to see your silly home videos anyway

3. **Sound files are generally . . .**

   A. smaller than video files

   B. larger than video files

   C. the same size as video files

   D. incorporated into video files

4. **Shockwave is a technology that lets you . . .**

   A. add bright neon colors to your Web page

   B. measure seismic activity on your Web page

   C. display Director multimedia on your Web page

   D. flatten QuickTime movies

5. **You can add a sound file to your Web page . . .**

   A. as a clickable link

   B. as an attached, but separate Web page

   C. as background music

   D. by turning on the radio while you're designing your page

6. **To add a video or animation file to your Web page, you use which tag?**

   A. `<MM>`

   B. `<ANIM>`

   C. `<META>`

   D. `<EMBED>`

7. **When you create a slide show using the procedures described in this unit, you use the _____ tag to control the delay between slides and the _____ tag to add the background music.**

   A. `<EMBED>, <META>`

   B. `<META>, <EMBED>`

   C. `<EMBED>, <EMBED>`

   D. `<META>, <META>`

8. **In your slide show, the sound file should be _____ the delay between slides.**

   A. longer than

   B. shorter than

   C. the same length as

   D. more interesting than

Unit 7 Exercise

You can find plenty of multimedia files on the World Wide Web. Your mission, should you choose to accept it, is to track down some of these files using your finely-honed Web searching skills. After you find them, experiment with adding these multimedia elements to your own Web pages.

Part III Review

Unit 5 Summary

▶ **Graphics formats:** If you want to put image files on your Web page, they need to be in one of two formats — GIF or JPEG. If images are in a different format, you have to convert them into one of these two formats. JPEG images are higher quality, so this format is better for photorealistic images. GIF images have less color, so they are smaller and download faster than JPEG images.

▶ **Finding images:** Several different ways exist to get images that you can add to your Web page. You can use images that you already have. If these are photos, you have to either scan them into the computer or have them digitized on a Photo CD. You can also create your own digital images to use. If you want to get art from someone else, you need to be sure that it's royalty-free. Many companies offer collections of royalty-free art, and some is also available on the Web. However, you cannot take any old graphic off the Web and use it on your page.

▶ **Graphics on your page:** When you put a graphic on your page, you can align it with your text or have it by itself. Graphics can also act as links, both to other Web sites or to other locations on your page. You can do some fun things with GIF images: You can make parts of them transparent (this is good for logos) or you can take several of them, join them in one file, and create an animation.

▶ **Background images:** Backgrounds of Web pages can either be a solid color or an image, not both. If you specify both, the viewer does not see the color until the image is done loading.

Unit 6 Summary

▶ **Advanced HTML:** In this unit, you learned about more advanced HTML tags. The unit covers the steps of creating mailto links, FTP downloads, gopher downloads, and links to Usenet newsgroups. Unit 6 also covers the creation of forms, tables, frames, and image maps.

Unit 7 Summary

▶ **Multimedia:** There are pros and cons to having multimedia elements on your Web page. While such elements are a lot of fun and add a great deal of excitement, they also can be hard to create. Also, cybervisitors need the right browser plug-ins to be able to view your multimedia elements. Getting the plug-ins is often a hassle for visitors. Be sure to think through multimedia elements carefully before adding them to your page.

▶ **Sound:** Your Web page can attach sound files in two different ways. You can either create a link to the sound file, or you can program the page so the sound plays automatically when the page loads.

▶ **Animation and Video:** Using the <EMBED> tag, you can add QuickTime movies, MPEG movies, AVI movies, or Shockwave multimedia to your Web page. If you're interested in animated graphics, you can either create them yourself or you can find ones that are available for free on the Web.

▶ **Online slide shows:** If you have several images, you can link them all together into a slide show. By adding background music to this, you create a true multimedia experience.

Part III Test

The questions on this test cover all the material presented in Part III (Units 5,6, and 7).

True   False

T   F   1. GIF is just another name for the peanut butter Moms love best.

T   F   2. Paint Shop Pro is a program that will help you convert your images into GIF and JPEG formats.

T   F   3. If you see art you like on someone else's Web page, you can take it and add it to your own.

T   F   4. The HTML tag `<IMG SRC="image .gif" ALIGN=BOTTOM>` will align the top edge of a graphic with the line of text in which it appears.

T   F   5. To create a GIF transparency, you have to be sure that the background of the original image is white.

T   F   6. The main graphic on your page should be smaller than 60K.

T   F   7. A mailto link is important so your visitors can give you comments and feedback.

T   F   8. After you've created a form on your Web page, it's easy to collect the data that people give you.

T   F   9. If you add the NOWRAP attribute to one table cell, it's like you added it to all the cells of the table.

T   F   10. Frames add an attractive border around the outside of your Web page.

T   F   11. A image map can have several different hotspots.

T   F   12. Adding multimedia to your Web page is easier, cheap, and always good for your visitors.

T   F   13. A WAVE file makes an image of the ocean on your Web page.

T   F   14. If you're adding a lot of multimedia to your page, you'll use the `<EMBED>` tag a lot.

Multiple Choice

For each of the following questions, circle the correct answer or answers. Some questions may have more than one right answer, so read all the answers carefully.

15. **If you flatten your QuickTime movie, you**

   A. Run over the disk with your car so you're sure it's really thin

   B. Take the data from the resource fork and add it to the data fork

   C. May be using a freeware program called flattenmoov

   D. Are working on the Macintosh

16. **A plug-in is**

   A. A kind of electrical circuit in your computer

   B. A special kind of program that's beyond the scope of this book

   C. Add-on software that allows your Web browser to display files that it can't handle on its own

   D. Often difficult for your viewers to load and use

Part III Test

17. JPEG images are

   A. Bitmapped images

   B. Raster images

   C. In a 24-bit color format

   D. Photorealistic

18. Which of the following are acceptable methods of getting art for your Web page?

   A. Scanning an image of your kids' birthday party

   B. Buying a CD-ROM with royalty-free art

   C. Borrowing an image from someone else's page

   D. Taking an image from a royalty-free art collection on the Web

19. A link to a Usenet newsgroup can be helpful because

   A. The newsgroup can offer more information about a topic that your Web page focuses on

   B. People need encouragement to socialize

   C. People should be reading news daily

   D. Newsgroups are hard to find unless you give people directions

20. A CGI script

   A. Is often available from your ISP

   B. Is a service provided by the CIA

   C. Allows you to collect information from forms posted on your Web page

   D. Requires the `<METHOD>` and `<ACTION>` tags

Matching

21. Match the tags to their tasks:

   A. `<TR>`   1. FTP download

   B. `<A HREF=ftp://ftpaddress> </A>`   2. Alignment for a table cell

   C. `<EMBED SRC="qt.mov">`   3. Row of a table

   D. `<ALIGN=center>`   4. Add multimedia element

22. Match the extension with the type of file:

   A. .jpg   1. multimedia

   B. .au   2. sound

   C. .avi   3. image

   D. .dcr   4. Movie

23. Match the term to its definition:

   A. Transparency   1. A graphic which has several hot spots or links

   B. Image map   2. A way of dividing a Web page into several viewable areas

   C. Frames   3. A graphic in which one color is invisible

   D. Form   4. A method of gathering information from Web visitors

Part III Lab Assignment

In this exercise, you dig deeper into the same code that you explored in the Part II Lab Assignment.

Step 1: Return to that good-looking Web page

Fire up your Web browser and call up the same Web page you used for the Part II Lab Assignment.

Step 2: Identify more coded elements

Identify the elements on that Web page whose coding was discussed in Part III.

Step 3: Try to re-create that HTML code

Write down the HTML you think that Web page designer used to create those elements.

Step 4: Grade yourself

Double-check your HTML estimates by using the View⇨Source function on your browser.

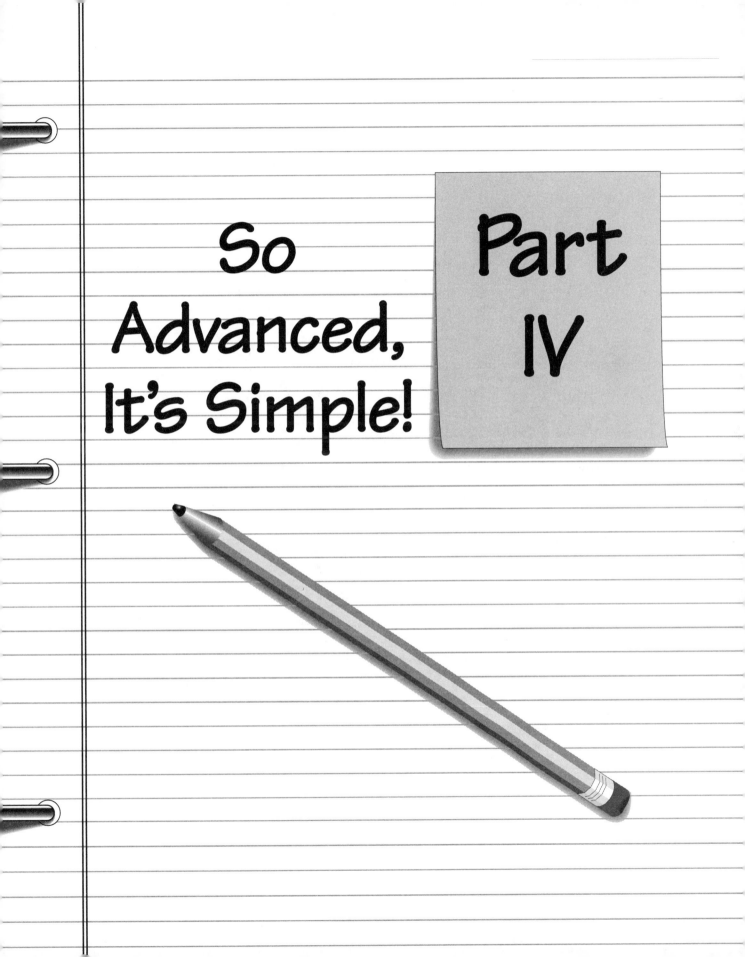

So Advanced, It's Simple!

Part IV

In this part . . .

I decided to join the latest rage and plunk down a hundred and twenty bucks for a bread machine. Using this machine is the way homemade bread should have been done all along. You throw in some flour, a little water, just the right amount of yeast, and maybe a couple of other ingredients, depending on what kind of bread you're baking. Then you just turn the thing on and go back to perfecting your Web page.

The machine mixes the ingredients, kneads the dough, lets it rise, and finally bakes the bread to perfection. Aside from tossing in the ingredients, your only job is to make a pig of yourself by downing the whole loaf before anyone else in the house gets a shot at it. This may not make you the most popular person at home, but being popular will seem less important than ever before.

So what do all these excess carbohydrates have to do with creating Web pages? Well, if you have ever baked bread from scratch, maybe you felt a real sense of accomplishment the first time you did it. Maybe even the first few times. But sooner or later, you probably said to yourself, "There's got to be a better way." Then along came bread machines. I figured out that I have to bake bread with my bread machine 137 times before I break even.

Web pages are the same. You probably got a real kick out of hammering out that first page of HTML code and watching your Web browser convert all that gibberish into a beautiful work of cyberart. Take my word for it: After a while, all that manual coding really gets to be a pain in the digital derriere. Sooner or later, you're going to say to yourself, "There's got to be a better way." Then you'll discover Web page editors — programs designed specifically to make easy work of creating complicated Web pages.

Creating complicated Web pages with little effort is what this part is all about. You're going to take a look at a few of the more popular Web editing programs. Hopefully, when the time comes for you to purchase and/or use such a program — and believe me, the time will come — the information you've tackled in these units will help you decide which program is best for you. I even include instructions at the end of Unit 9 on using my own software, which I also tell you how to access. Isn't that nice of me?

(Got a Good Reason for) Taking the Easy Way Out

Prerequisites
▶ An idea of what you want on your Web page (Unit 2)
▶ Basic knowledge of HTML (Units 3-5)

Objectives for This Unit

✓ Checking out the following programs and learning how to build a simple Web page in each of the programs:

Adobe PageMill

Claris Home Page

Corel Web.Graphics Suite

Microsoft FrontPad

Microsoft FrontPage

MySoftware MyInternetBusinessPage

NetObjects Fusion

Netscape Composer

Sausage Software HotDog Pro

✓ Seeing how the world's two most popular word processors, Microsoft Word and WordPerfect, can help you along the road to a better Web page.

on the CD

▶ HotDog Pro
▶ HotDog 16

A ll right, I believe you — you read through those units on HTML. I bet you even tested every single piece of code. (Don't tell me that you didn't — I'll be crushed.) By now you may be tired of fussing over every single end bracket and every punctuation mark. Well, here's the best news: There's an easier way. You can buy lots of programs to do the job with less fuss and muss. In this unit, I take you on a walk through different programs. You can pick the one that best meets your needs, after you're ready to give up the do-it-yourself attitude.

Lesson 8-1

What the Heck Is in This Lesson? (WTHIITL)

on the test

When it comes to designing Web page editors, programmers can take one of two basic approaches. They can create what is called a *WYSIWYG* program. This jumble stands for What You See Is What You Get, and it's pronounced wizzy-wig. I dated a guy like that once, but that's another story.

With a WYSIWYG program, you never have to see the HTML code itself. Instead, you visually lay out the page to look the way you want it to look, and the program generates the appropriate HTML code based on your instructions.

I suppose you can call the other method WYSIABOCTYHWR. Now, I don't have the slightest idea how to pronounce this (even though I just made it up), but I can tell you that it stands for What You See Is a Bunch of Code That You Hope Works Right. With this type of program, the program still generates the HTML code for you, but that's exactly what you see on the screen — lines and lines of HTML code.

For example, suppose your document contains the word *wow,* and you want to make it bold. In a WYSIABOCTYHWR program, you select the word *wow* and then click on the Bold option. The program automatically fills in the correct code, so you see `<B>wow</B>` right on your screen.

Why would you want such a program? I'll be honest with you. At this point in my career (and I've been on a computer since I was 9 years old and, no, it wasn't the UNIVAC), I much prefer a WYSIWYG program. However, I did use a WYSIABOCTYHWR program for quite some time when I first started out. And by doing that I actually learned HTML code. The reason WYSIABOCTYHWR makes such a good learning tool is that you tell the program what to do, and you get to see the exact code required to produce that result. Only a very dimwitted person can use a WYSIABOCTYHWR program for very long and not pick up some good information. Of course, I know that none of my readers falls into that category.

Let me give you the heads-up on what to expect in the rest of this unit. Hold on to your hats and your shorts. I'm going to tell you about the strengths and weaknesses of each of these Web page editing programs. I'm also going to give you a simple way to compare them head-to-head. I've come up with a simple Web page, as shown in Figure 8-1, that consists of a few basic Web page elements. Specifically, this sample page has:

- ◗ A white background
- ◗ A header graphic
- ◗ A single line of regular text
- ◗ A table, including a caption
- ◗ An image map that includes links to the *...For Dummies* Web site (*http://www.dummies.com*) and to my Komputer Klinic (*http://www.komando.com*)

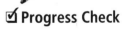

My Personal Home Page

This test page will help us compare different Web editing programs.

Some of My Favorite Computer Books

Book Title	Author
1,001 Computer Answers	Komando
CyberBuck\$: Making Money Online	Komando
PageMill 2 for Dummies	McClelland and San Filippo
Windows 95 for Dummies	Rathbone

...for Dummies Press   The Komputer Klinic

Figure 8-1

Figure 8-1: Here is your test page.

I'll describe for you the steps required to create this same exact page in each one of these programs. This way, you can get at least a little glimpse of how they stack up against each other. However, I want to make one thing perfectly clear. While some programs may seem more complicated than other programs, that doesn't necessarily mean the more complicated programs are less desirable. In many cases, it simply means that the more complicated program is also more powerful, and can do more for you than what this little test may reveal. I'm just wetting your digital whistle, so to speak. It's the same with people — just because they're complicated doesn't necessarily mean they are less desirable. Are complicated people more powerful? I can't go into that here.

more complicated doesn't necessarily mean worse when it comes to Web page creation programs; sometimes it just means more powerful

In creating these pages, I try to use as many program default settings as possible to make the whole promise as simple as possible. That means that each page looks a little different than the others. For example, the table in one may be wider than the table in the next. As long as the program in question supports tables, you can be assured that it likely offers a way to customize the look of that table. My point is that just because you happen to like the layout created by one program a little better than the layout created by another, that's not necessarily a good criterion to base a decision on.

heads up

Also, there's more than one way to skin a cat. Actually, I hate that phrase. I should point out that many of these programs offer many different ways to accomplish the same result. I always use the taskbar button if one's available, and the menu option if not. Just keep in mind that there may be other ways to do the same thing.

Finally, you may be wondering what kind of computer you need to run all this. Most of these programs run on a minimally configured Windows 95 system — and minimal isn't what it used to be. By minimally configured, I mean a 486 computer with at least 8MB of RAM. The one exception to this rule is NetObjects Fusion, which requires you to have 16MB of RAM. For Mac users, any system running system 7.5 or later will get you by, but because creating Web pages is an exercise in graphics, your best bet is a Power Mac. All of these programs come on CD-ROM. The amount of hard drive space the programs take up varies greatly depending on the program and how much of the program you plan to install on your system. While Adobe PageMill uses up only about 10MB of disk space, for example, Corel Web.Graphics Suite can take up well over 100MB if you decide to pull all of its clip art onto your hard drive. Many of these programs have Macintosh versions, too; I'll be sure to indicate the ones that do.

Enough with the rules and regulations. Let's get started.

☑ Progress Check

If you can do the following, you've mastered this lesson:

❑ Identify the differences between a WYSIWYG and WYSIABOCTYHWR program.

❑ Understand how I've structured the rest of this chapter.

Figure 8-2. This is what you see when you start PageMill.

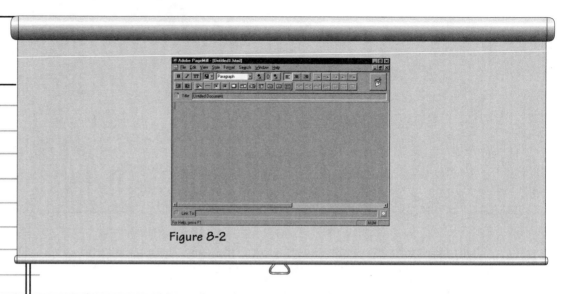

Figure 8-2

Lesson 8-2   Adobe PageMill

Although I'm not really putting these programs in any particular order of importance, putting PageMill at the head of the pack is appropriate. Not that PageMill is necessarily the best program, but it was the first WYSIWYG Web page editor on the market. Even though version 1.0 was a little lackluster, the program sold like hot cakes to a world that was hungry to create Web pages but did not want to fiddle with HTML code. PageMill version 2.0 offers improvements and refinements so now the program sells like hamburgers. The tremendous success of this program is particularly surprising when you consider that until recently, PageMill was available only for Macintosh systems. Like all great Mac programs invariably do, PageMill has now migrated over into the Windows camp as well. Yea!

PageMill: What's hot and what's not

PageMill is available for both Windows and Mac systems

Out of all the programs I looked at for this unit, I think PageMill is probably the easiest to use. You can do just about everything by clicking on some button on the program's taskbar. You don't often have to go into the menu structure, unless of course you prefer that to pointing and clicking. You can have it either way here. Figure 8-2 shows PageMill ready to go with a new, untitled document.

About the only downside to PageMill is that when version 2.0 started shipping, that's about all you got. Some of the other programs you encounter in this unit come with gigantic clip art collections, but not PageMill. Adobe finally saw the light when it started shipping the Windows version, and packed the CD with over 1,000 graphic and multimedia elements, plus a slightly scaled-down version of Photoshop, arguably the best image-editing software on the market.

extra credit

What's a taskbar?

taskbar (taskbar) n. 1. a candy bar, 2. an establishment for tasks to meet and drink, 3. a row of function buttons at the top of the screen.

You're going to see the term *taskbar* used quite a bit throughout this lesson. What I'm referring to is the row of function buttons that most programs display across the tops of their viewing windows.

Now don't confuse a program taskbar with the Windows 95 taskbar. The taskbar is an area of the Windows 95 screen that provides the Start button (which enables you to start up all the programs on the computer) and shows which programs are currently running. When Windows 95 is installed, the taskbar appears on the bottom of the screen, but you can drag and drop it anywhere on-screen.

Other programs come with utilities that help you to manage an entire Web site, but not PageMill. Not here. However, on this last point, I would be remiss if I didn't also mention PageMill's sister application, SiteMill. SiteMill offers all of the site management features that Adobe left out of PageMill. For full functionality, you have to buy two programs instead of one. The good news is that both products are reasonably priced. Also, although the whole idea behind SiteMill is to serve as a companion to PageMill, in truth you can use SiteMill with any Web editor you want.

What's all this site management stuff anyway?

Site management means taking control of your Web site to make sure it functions properly as a whole.

For example, say you have a page with a file name *info.htm* and that several other pages around your site are linked to that page. Now, for whatever reason, you want to change the name of the file to *background.htm*.

Without a site management program, you have to search manually through every other page on your site to figure which ones contain links to that page. Then you have to manually fix all those links. Doing all that work is a real drag.

A good site management program such as SiteMill automatically identifies all the broken links on your site and then fixes them according to your instructions. This can save you hours of work. Many site management programs, including SiteMill, can even check your external links (links to other pages outside your own site) to make sure they're still there. If the external site has moved, the site management program can sometimes even figure out the new URL and fix your link accordingly. That's pretty cool.

The bottom line on site management programs is this: You may not need one now, but the more complicated your site gets and the more external links you add, the more a good site management program can make your life easier.

Notes:

Notes:

PageMill has one more spiffy thing — its translation capability. In 1996, Adobe purchased a company called MasterSoft, whose only real claim to fame was an excellent file translation program called Word for Word (one that I use myself) that allows you to convert files in just about any known format to just about any other format. For example, you can convert a Macwrite file (a Macintosh word-processing format) to a Word for Windows file with just a couple of mouse clicks.

The reason this is so important is that Adobe has included some of the MasterSoft translators with PageMill. For example, if you have a Microsoft Word file that you want to turn into a Web page, you can open the file using PageMill's standard Open dialog, and the MasterSoft software automatically translates your document into HTML. MasterSoft preserves, as best it can, all of the bold, italic, and other formatting from your original Word file. That can be a real time saver.

PageMill: The sample page

For the sample page, I created two graphics in Adobe Photoshop and saved them in GIF format on my hard drive. Here are the steps I followed in PageMill to create the sample page:

1 Start the PageMill program.

This is a pretty obvious step, but I don't want to leave anything out. When you launch PageMill, the program automatically opens to a new, untitled document.

2 Save the document.

heads up

Whenever I use one of these Web page editors, I *always* save the page as my very first step (after launching the program). The reason is that when you add graphics and stuff like that, these programs generate HTML code for relative links, as you learned about earlier in this book. If you haven't saved the document in any particular place on your hard drive, how can the program create a relative link? Relative to what? As you know, saving your HTML documents and your graphics in the same folder ensures that all your relative links really work. In the case of this sample page, I saved all the pages created by all the programs in the same folder as my two sample graphics. You should save yours in the same folder, too.

3 Enter the page's title.

Many of the programs I discuss in this unit force you to go to a pull-down menu just to indicate the title for your page. Not so with PageMill. The program provides a field for this purpose near the top of the window, as shown in Figure 8-3. You just click on that field and start typing.

4 Change the background color to white.

When you first start PageMill, a little window full of buttons and other doodads appear off to the right of the screen, as shown in Figure 8-4. This window is the Inspector palette (named after the famous French detective) and offers all sorts of controls for your page and its various elements.

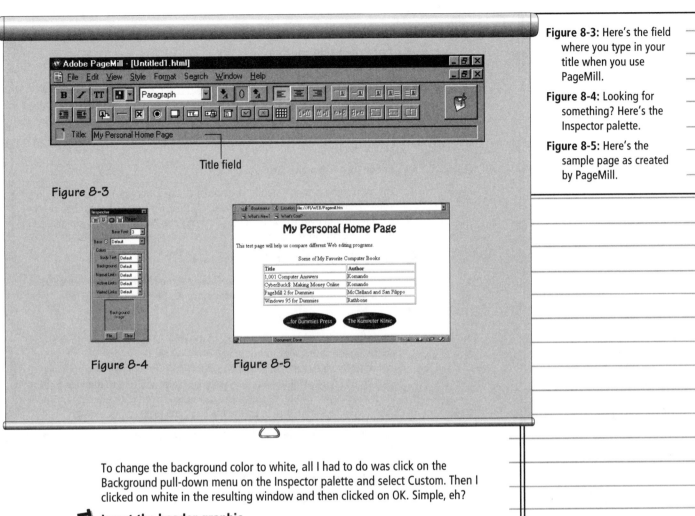

Title field

Figure 8-3

Figure 8-4   Figure 8-5

Figure 8-3: Here's the field where you type in your title when you use PageMill.

Figure 8-4: Looking for something? Here's the Inspector palette.

Figure 8-5: Here's the sample page as created by PageMill.

To change the background color to white, all I had to do was click on the Background pull-down menu on the Inspector palette and select Custom. Then I clicked on white in the resulting window and then clicked on OK. Simple, eh?

5 Insert the header graphic.

Insert Graphic is one of the buttons in PageMill's taskbar. To drop the header graphic into this page, click on the Insert Graphic button and then select the appropriate file from your hard drive in the Open dialog box.

To center the graphic, I just had to click on the graphic and then click on the Center button in the taskbar.

6 Type in the line of text.

Don't expect this particular step to be too complicated in most of these programs.

7 Create the table.

PageMill offers an Insert Table button in its taskbar. The cool part is that if you click and hold on that button (don't let up on the mouse button), you can drag the mouse down and to the right in order to specify the size table you want. Skinning cats, dragging mice. It's terrible. PageMill lets you create tables up to 10 rows by 10 columns in this manner. This simple step saves you from fuddling around through a cumbersome dialog box. The table I created was two columns by five rows, as shown in Figure 8-5.

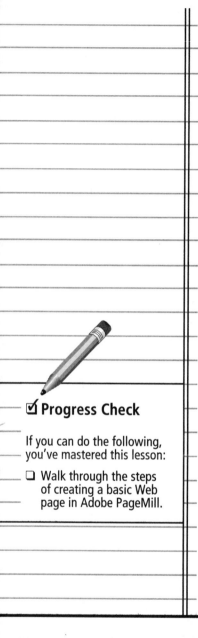

☑ Progress Check

If you can do the following, you've mastered this lesson:

❏ Walk through the steps of creating a basic Web page in Adobe PageMill.

8 **Type the table caption.**

When you select the table by clicking on it, PageMill's Inspector palette automatically switches to the appropriate tab, which includes an option to specify the placement of the table's caption (above or below the table). Once you specify the location, a spot for the caption automatically appears in the appropriate place. Then, you just click the mouse there and type your caption. Easy breezy.

9 **Enter data into the table.**

This procedure is pretty standard for most of the programs I cover in this unit. You simply click into the first table cell, type the information, and then use the Tab key to hop over to the next cell. To make the first row bold, I simply used the Bold button in the taskbar.

10 **Insert the graphic for the image map.**

This follows the same exact steps as inserting the header graphic. What's different is what you do to the graphic once it's already been inserted.

11 **Create the image map.**

To go into *image map mode*, for lack of a better term, you simply double-click on the image you want to turn into an image map. Doing so magically displays a group of image maps tools in the taskbar, tools for creating rectangular, circular and polygonal hotspots, as well as a selection tool to move and resize the hotspots you create. Because you can make circular but not oval hotspots, I used to the rectangle tool to create the hotspots for this image map.

To create the hotspot, you just select the desired tool, click and hold the mouse in one corner of the hotspot, and then drag to the opposite corner. After you mark off a hotspot, you simply type the URL into the Link To field that appears at the bottom of PageMill's main application window.

12 **Save and close the document.**

This works pretty much the same as most programs. You select the Save option from the File menu and follow the dialog boxes.

That's it. If you're using PageMill, you're done. As for me, I've got to create this Web page seven more times. Ah, but don't pity me; I'll get through it. Figure 8-5 shows the results of this effort.

Lesson 8-3	# Claris Home Page

Claris is the software subsidiary of Apple Computer, Inc. Windows programs from Claris have always been top-notch (FileMaker Pro, a relational database program is an excellent example), but Claris programs have never seemed to catch on in a big way on the Windows side of the world. I think it's been more of a matter of less-than-effective marketing than any deficiencies in its applications. Ah, but that's Apple. In any event, Home Page is certainly worth your consideration.

Home Page: What's hot and what's not

In terms of simplicity, Home Page reminds me a lot of PageMill. Home Page is another very-easy-to-use program that's great for generating attractive and effective Web pages. It does, however, have an edge over PageMill in a couple of areas.

For one thing, if you happen to act contrary to my rule of relative links and save your HTML documents and graphics in different folders (either accidentally or because you're just stubborn), Home Page can automatically copy your graphics over to where they need to be for uploading to your ISP. When you are ready to upload those files, Home Page comes with built-in FTP functionality. If the only thing you need FTP for is to upload your Web pages, there's no point tracking down an FTP program and learning its intricacies. You can just tell Home Page the same information you'd tell any ol' FTP program, and Home Page handles the rest for you. To get these same built-in FTP capabilities from Adobe, you'd have to buy SiteMill.

One other nice feature is that Claris ships Home Page on a hybrid CD. By hybrid, I mean that the CD itself is partitioned, or split, into a Windows section and a Macintosh section. When you put the CD in on a Windows system, you can install the Windows version of Home Page; when you put the CD in on a Macintosh system, you can install the Macintosh version.

This is handy if, for example, you have a Windows PC and a Macintosh PowerBook laptop, and want to work on your Web pages on both systems. Just make sure you don't interpret the software license agreement too liberally and think it's OK to put Home Page on your PC and your neighbor's Macintosh. Most likely, that's a violation of the license agreement and any applicable copyright laws. Not only that, but the Software Fairy will put a curse on your computer.

Home Page: The sample page

Here are the steps I followed to create the sample page using Home Page. Figure 8-6 shows what you start with in Home Page; Figure 8-7 shows the finished product.

1 Start the Home Page program.

Yes, I know, an obvious first step, but you just never know. But we've already been through that. As with PageMill, starting Home Page creates a new, untitled document like the one in Figure 8-6.

2 Save the document.

If you save your document in Home Page before you've given it a title, Home Page forces you to supply one. That's a very nice feature, because the title is very easy to forget in one of these programs. I've come across commercial sites where the webmaster forgot to add a page title. Because I was forced to name the page when I saved it, I didn't have to add a title as a separate step.

Notes:

Claris Home Page comes on one CD-ROM that can load either a Macintosh or Windows version of the program

Figure 8-6: This is what you see when you start Home Page.

Figure 8-7: Here's the sample page as created in Home Page.

Notes:

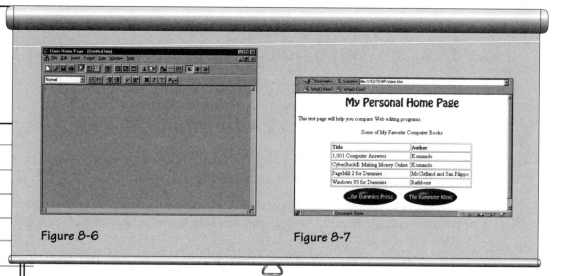

Figure 8-6   Figure 8-7

3 Change the background color to white.

Click on the Edit menu and then select Document Options. This pops up a window that allows you to change a variety of document characteristics, including the background color. Changing the color took 2.5 seconds longer than PageMill, which may matter during critical deadlines. This window also contains the document title, should you want to change it later.

4 Insert the header graphic.

Just as in PageMill, you click on the Insert Image button in the taskbar, and then select the graphic using the resulting dialog box. Once the graphic appeared, I was able to center it by clicking on the Center button in the taskbar.

5 Type in the line of text.

6 Create the table.

Like PageMill, Home Page offers an Insert Table button in the taskbar. Unlike PageMill, the result of doing this is a Table Setup dialog box in which you specify the various characteristics for your table. Aside from telling Home Page I wanted my table to be two columns by six rows, I accepted all the default options.

7 Type the table caption.

Oddly enough, Home Page doesn't include a way to automatically create a caption for your table. Instead, you have to center some regular text wherever you want the caption and then type it in, which is exactly what I did in this case. Clock that at an additional 6 seconds.

8 Enter data into the table.

As with PageMill, you just click your mouse pointer into the first table cell, type whatever information you need to type, and then use the Tab key to move on to the next cell. Also, like in PageMill, I used the Bold button in the taskbar to make the first row bold.

9 Insert the graphic for the image map.

Once again, inserting this graphic is just like inserting the header graphic.

10 **Create the image map.**

To do this, you double-click on the image. This pops up an Image window that offers several buttons, among them one marked Client-Side Image Map: Edit. When you click on this button, a copy of the graphic appears in a little editing window. This window includes the tools you need to create your image. Strangely, it only includes tools for round and rectangular hotspots — no options for polygons. Speaking of shapes, I have a shape joke.

> *Clever Math Boy: You're father is a square!*

> *Clever Math Girl: You're close. He's never a round.*

All right, I didn't say it was a good shape joke.

At the same time the editing window appears, a separate Link window also appears. When you create a new hotspot, the Link window automatically becomes active so you can type in the URL associated with that hotspot. Close these two windows to finish up the image map.

Again, Figure 8-7 shows the completed sample page á la Home Page.

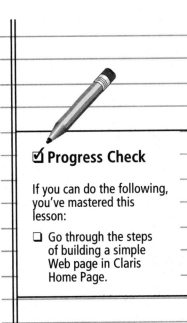

☑ Progress Check

If you can do the following, you've mastered this lesson:

❑ Go through the steps of building a simple Web page in Claris Home Page.

Microsoft FrontPage

Lesson 8-4

FrontPage is the first program we're going to look at that offers extensive built-in site management features. To tell you the truth, the entire program focuses more on site management than it does on creating individual Web pages.

FrontPage: What's hot and what's not

The true focus of FrontPage is more site management than Web page creation. This can be a good or bad thing. If you have a large, complicated site, you may appreciate all of these site management features. However, if you just want to fire up the program and churn out a fast Web page, FrontPage takes you through plenty of extra steps that you may find frustrating.

Another minor problem is that FrontPage suffers from some non-standard terminology that can be a little confusing. For example, FrontPage calls your Web site simply a *web*. While I suppose that's not entirely unreasonable, I've never heard the term *web* used quite that way before, and I can't help but wonder why Microsoft didn't just stick with the standard *Web site* or simply *site*. However, when you are Mighty Microsoft, it seems that you can do just about anything you want . . . or at least you can try.

One thing that FrontPage does have going for it is its so-called *FrontPage extensions*, little bits of programming code that Microsoft developed as enhancements for your garden-variety Web pages. For you to use these extensions on your Web page, your ISP must also have them installed and available to you. You need to check with your ISP to see if they do have them. However, the extra effort may be worth it, because FrontPage extensions can make easy work of some otherwise complicated tasks.

Notes:

For example, remember when you learned about forms in Unit 6? Forms are easy enough to create, but fiddling around with the CGI programming to actually make forms work is another story. However, using FrontPage extensions, you can develop handlers for your forms that let you bypass the CGI baloney altogether. Instead, the FrontPage extensions handle the forms processing. That right there may be worth the price of admission if your site (or *Web*) is long on forms, but you're short on CGI programmers.

FrontPage: The sample page

This is what it takes to create our sample page using FrontPage: Figure 8-8 shows an empty Web document in FrontPage; Figure 8-9 shows our finished product.

1 Start the program.

Maybe you're expecting this to be another simple step. If so, the joke's on you. To get from this point to Step 2, you need to do plenty of work.

When you start FrontPage, a dialog box appears that asks you if you want to open an existing web (sorry, I'm switching into Microsoft lingo) or if you want to create a new one. If you elect to create a new one, you have the option to use one of several templates or create a blank one. I opted for the blank one.

So now you're ready to get going with your Web page masterpiece, right? Wrong. Next, another dialog box appears that asks you for the File Location and Name of Web. If you're actually working on a Web server or have a direct, permanent connection to one, you can specify the server for the File Location. If not, you just specify a folder on your hard drive. The Name of Web field is really just the name of your Web site. Fill that in too.

After you fill in the Name of Web field and click on OK, FrontPage creates a new folder inside the folder you specified in the File Location field. FrontPage gives that folder the name you typed in the Name of Web field. In other words, if you type the File Location as `c:\Web Files` and type `My Site` as the Name of Web, FrontPage creates your new site at *c:\WebFiles\My Site*.

We're almost there. After FrontPage creates all the necessary folders, it displays a large window that represents your entire site. An icon marked Home Page appears in the middle of the window. The icon is a file that FrontPage already has created and named index.htm.

Now, to actually edit this document, you double-click on it, which finally results in an empty Web document like the one shown in Figure 8-8. Because FrontPage was kind enough to save our document for us already, we can skip that step and move on to the next.

2 Enter the page's title.

To do this, I had to click on the File menu and then select the Page Properties option. This popped up a dialog box where I entered the document title. There was also a tab marked Background that I could have clicked on to change the background color. However, FrontPage defaulted to a white background, so I didn't have to fiddle with it. Had I wanted to change the background color later, I could have taken this same route back, or I could have clicked on the Format menu and selected the Background option.

At any rate, I was able to skip the "change the background color" step.

starting with a "blank page" in FrontPage takes a few more steps than in most of the other programs

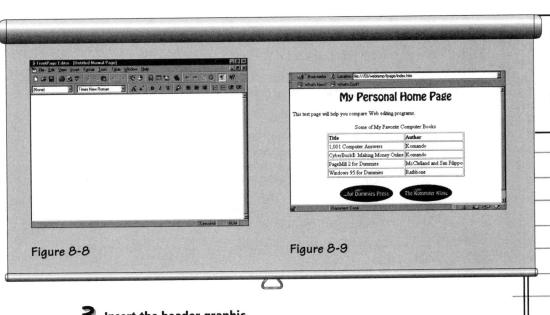

Figure 8-8

Figure 8-9

Figure 8-8. When you finally get there, this is what a blank document looks like in FrontPage.

Figure 8-9: Here's the FrontPage version.

3 Insert the header graphic.

This takes one more step than I think it should. Like all the other programs, FrontPage has an Insert Image button in its taskbar. When you click on the button, you get a little dialog box. However, if the graphic doesn't happen to be in the folder where your Web page resides, you have to click on the Other Location tab and then on the Browse button before you can actually browse your system for the desired graphics. As with all the other programs, centering the graphic is as easy as clicking on a button in the taskbar.

4 Type in the line of text.

5 Create the table.

The Insert Table button in the FrontPage taskbar works a lot like the one in PageMill; you can click and drag on the button to indicate the size of the table.

The odd thing is that when you insert the table, it appears as very skinny, with columns that are only about one character wide. There's no need to worry, though. The cells expand as you start typing in them.

FrontPage has one other oddity worth noting. In the previous programs, I never mentioned the step where I centered the table on the page. It didn't seem too important, because it was just like centering the header graphic.

Unfortunately, it's not quite that easy in FrontPage. First you have to click on the table itself. Then you have to click on the Table menu and select the Table Properties option. From there you can have FrontPage center your table.

6 Type the table caption.

To create a spot for your caption, you click on the Table menu and select Insert Caption. This automatically centers the text cursor above your table, ready for you to type your caption. If you should decide later that you want the caption at the bottom of the table instead, you need to click on the Table menu again, select Caption Properties and indicate your preference there.

7 Enter data into the table.

Nothing tricky here. FrontPage works like the others in this respect — just hit that Tab key and keep the fingers going on the keyboard.

☑ **Progress Check**

If you can do the following, you've mastered this lesson:

❑ Go through the steps of creating a basic Web page in FrontPage.

8 **Insert the graphic for the image map.**

Again, nothing special about the procedure here, except that you have to make that extra mouse click, as described in Step 3.

9 **Create the image map.**

This is another area where FrontPage seems to be a little more complicated that it needs to be. When you click on the image, a small palette of hotspot-creation tools automatically displays. When you create a hotspot, a big Create Hyperlink dialog box appears on your screen. To indicate the URL I wanted to use for the link, I had to click on the World Wide Web tab in this dialog box, type in the URL and then close the dialog box. That seems like a little too much work to create a simple hypertext link.

Figure 8-9 shows the FrontPage interpretation of our sample page.

Recess

You may think I'm pretty smart after you read this book. Okay, you're right, I am. But there are some things in life that I just have never understood, such as:

- People's fear of ghosts when living is scarier

- The fact that only your nose keeps growing all your life

- The person who loves the least controls the relationship

- Sugar is bad for you but the inventor of Twinkies ate two everyday and lived to be eighty-five

Lesson 8-5

Corel Web.Graphics Suite

When you consider that CorelDraw is the leading illustration package on the Windows platform, it should come as no surprise that Corel has put together one impressive Web authoring tool kit. (*Web authoring* is another fancy term that means creating Web pages.) The Corel Web.Graphics Suite consists of six different applications, each one designed to help with a different aspect of Web page creation.

Web.Graphics Suite: What's hot and what's not

You get a lot for your money when you buy this package. Specifically, you get:

- **Web.Designer:** This is the main Web authoring tool in the suite. This tool is along the same lines of Claris HomePage or Adobe PageMill.

- **Web.Transit:** This is a conversion program that helps you turn your existing word processing documents into HTML documents. The program lets you set up templates so you have precise control over exactly how your documents get converted.

- **Web.Move:** This program lets you create animations for use on your Web pages. You have the option to save these animations as *Java applets* (mini programs that run on most current Web browsers), *AVI files* (a common PC animation format), or animated GIFs.

- **Web.Draw:** This is a good, basic drawing program for creating and manipulating the graphics for your Web page. While it's certainly no Photoshop in terms of functionality, it won't cost you $700 either.

- **Web.World:** Believe it or not, the suite also comes with a program that lets you create *VRML* environments for your Web pages. VRML stands for Virtual Reality Markup Language, and it's an offshoot of HTML that lets you create three-dimensional environments on your Web site.

- **Web.Gallery:** This is a graphic catalog program that helps you keep all your images organized into an electronic virtual photo album.

- **Guilt:** Because you've got so many tools, you'll feel terrible unless you use them all.

That's quite a lot of software to stuff into one package, but that's not all. (I think that I'm starting to sound like a salesperson.) The Corel Web.Graphics Suite also comes with 7,500 pieces of electronic clip art. The clip art ranges from backgrounds and buttons to silly cartoons and animations. I'm not usually too hot on using prepackaged art for your Web site. I feel you always run the risk of ending up with a Web site that looks just like somebody else's site. However, you get such a wide variety of artwork in this package, I think that risk is probably not very great. Plus, it makes it easier to get the art you need to get up and running.

Web.Graphics Suite: The sample page

Here are the steps for creating the sample pages using the Web.Graphics Suite. You start out with the document in Figure 8-10; the finished product is shown in Figure 8-11.

1 Ladies and gentlemen, start the program.

When you start Web.Designer, the program asks you to specify the folder or directory that you'll be working in. After you do so, the program asks you whether you want to open an existing document or create a new one. If you choose the latter, the program asks if you want to use a template or create a blank document. I opted for the blank document. The result was an empty Web page like the one shown in Figure 8-10.

2 Save the document.

This works as you'd expect. It's a lot like saving the rain forest, only instead of protesting evil manufacturers, you click on File menu and then click on Save.

Notes:

Figure 8-10: Starting out with Web.Designer.

Figure 8-11: Here's the sample page as created by Web.Designer.

Notes:

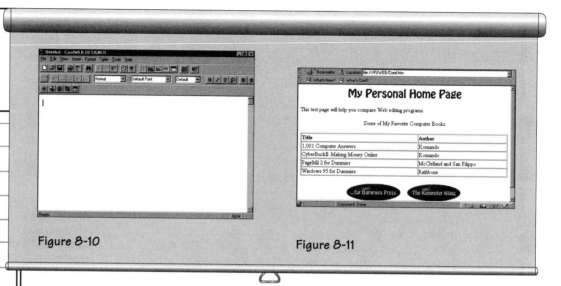

Figure 8-10   Figure 8-11

3 Enter the page's title.

Click on the File menu and then select the Page Properties option. This pops up a window that lets you type in the page title. You can also set the background color in this window, which I did, thereby eliminating the need for what would normally be the next step: Change the background color to white.

4 Insert the header graphic.

To start this process, you just click on the Insert Image button in the taskbar. This pops up an Image Properties window. From there, you have to click on the Browse button to actually poke through your system and locate the desired graphic. Quite frankly, I don't care for this extra step. I'd much rather click on the Insert Graphic button and be able to immediately select the graphic. While this Image Properties window does allow you to adjust certain options of the graphic, most of the time, you'll probably accept the defaults anyway. That means that most of the time you don't really need to see this window. I'm probably making more out of it than it's worth.

5 Type the line of text.

6 Create the table.

Like most other programs, Web.Designer has an Insert Table button in the taskbar. Clicking on this button pops up a Table Properties window. Here you specify the size of the table, as well as any other options.

7 Type the table caption.

Web.Designer doesn't offer an easy option for creating a true table caption. Instead, you are forced to type in a centered line of regular text above the table.

8 Enter data into the table.

Nothing unusual to report about this process — just type and tab.

9 Insert the graphic for the image map.

Just repeat Step 4.

10 Create the image map.

This works a little differently from the other programs. First, you click on the image to select it. Then you click on the Image Map Editor button in the taskbar. This pops up the Image Map Editor, a little sub-program that allows you to define the hotspots and type in the associated URLs. When you close the Image Map Editor, the program automatically saves a map file that you can use to create a server-side image map. What's that all about? Just read the sidebar, which is not to be confused with a taskbar.

That's all there is to creating the sample page with Web.Designer. Figure 8-11 shows the results.

Client-side versus server-side image maps

There are actually two types of image maps: *client-side image maps* and *server-side image maps*. The ones we've discussed so far have all been client-side image maps.

In a client-side image map, all the information about hotspot coordinates and their associated URLs are contained right in your HTML file. Because all the information is already in your computer when you load that particular Web page, your Web browser can figure out which Web page to ask for based on where you click on the image map. Your computer handles the image map by itself. Your computer is the *client* in this situation; therefore, these image maps are client-side image maps.

Client-side image maps are much newer than server-side image maps. In the old days of the World Wide Web (one or two years ago), server-side image maps were the only game in town.

With a server-side image map, you need an extra little text file on the Web server along with your other HTML files. This little text file is a *map file,* and it contains all of the coordinate and URL information to make the image map work. The actual HTML file contains only a pointer to this map file.

When you click on a server-side image map, the only information that your Web browser sends to the server is the coordinates that you clicked on. The Web server

then looks up those coordinates in the map file and from there, the Web server figures out what page to send back to your Web browser. As you can see, this method is much less efficient than a client-side image map, which is exactly why client-side image maps were invented.

With server-side image maps, if you move your mouse over a server-side image map, the status bar at the bottom of your Web browser displays only the map coordinates where the mouse is positioned, as shown in the following figure. At that point, your Web browser has no idea what Web page those coordinates represent.

On the other hand, with a client-side image map, your Web browser already has all that information. Therefore, when you move your mouse pointer over a client-side image map, the status bar at the bottom of the screen tells you exactly what Web page to expect by clicking on that point.

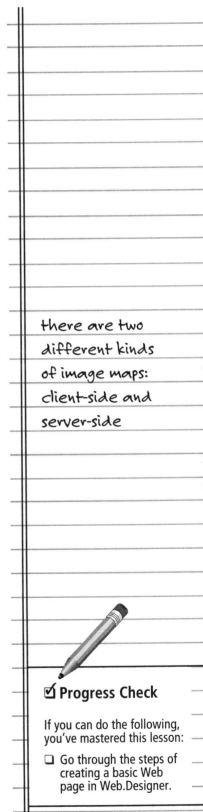

there are two different kinds of image maps: client-side and server-side

✓ **Progress Check**

If you can do the following, you've mastered this lesson:

❑ Go through the steps of creating a basic Web page in Web.Designer.

Lesson 8-6

Sausage Software HotDog Pro

I wanted to give you a look at at least one non-WYSIWYG (or WYSIABOCTYHWR, if you want) Web editor, and HotDog Pro is one of the most popular ones on the market. As I said earlier, these sorts of Web editors can make for very good learning tools.

HotDog Pro: What's hot dog and what's not

on the test

Despite how wonderful Windows is for personal computers, some people out there would still rather work in DOS (believe it or not). They seem to like being "closer" to the operating system, much like the guy who'd rather tinker with his own car than take it to a qualified mechanic.

I suppose the same holds true for Web page authors. As great as a WYSIWYG editor is, some people would still rather experience the "thrill" of diddling with raw HTML code. The big drawback to all this is that you're never quite sure what your Web page is going to look like until you check it out in your Web browser. HotDog Pro has a Preview button in its taskbar that automatically loads your page into whatever Web browser you specify, but that's still an extra, time-consuming step.

On the other hand, if you have your heart set on a WYSIABOCTYHWR Web editor, HotDog Pro is as good as any I've seen.

on the CD

If you'd like to give HotDog Pro a try, you'll find it among the files that came with this book's CD. (You're welcome.) And for you Windows 3.1 users, try HotDog 16, which is also among the CD files. The following section covers HotDog Pro, but HotDog 16 is similar.

HotDog Pro: The sample page

Figure 8-12 shows a new document in HotDog Pro; Figure 8-13 shows our finished product.

Here are the steps for creating the sample page with HotDog Pro:

1 Start the program.

When you start HotDog Pro, the program automatically opens to a new, untitled document, much like the one shown in Figure 8-12.

2 Save the document.

This is standard procedure. Save the file. You can do it!

3 Enter the page's title.

When you create a new page in HotDog Pro, some of the basic page tags get created automatically, including the TITLE tag. Just to make sure you don't miss it, HotDog Pro puts *type_Document_Title_here* between the TITLE tags. To add your own title, you just replace that text with whatever you want.

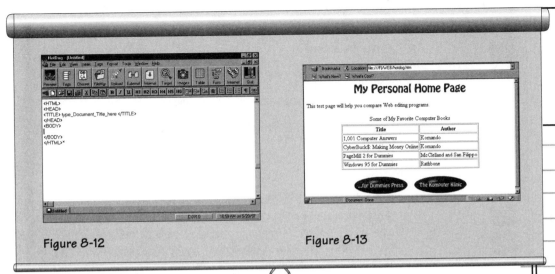

Figure 8-12: This is what you see when you start HotDog Pro.

Figure 8-13: HotDog Pro is a weenie in the image map department.

Figure 8-12

Figure 8-13

 Change the background color to white.

To do this, click on the Format menu and select the Document option. When the next window pops up, click on the Body Attributes button. From the resulting window, you can select the background color, as well as many other document attributes. After you OK your way out of this series of windows, and I use that term loosely, you'll see that HotDog Pro has automatically typed in the appropriate HTML code for you.

5 Insert the header graphic.

All this takes is a click on the little camera icon in the taskbar. Like so many other programs, doing so takes you to an Image Properties window. From there, you can browse through your system and locate the graphic you want. When you find the graphic, the program once again types in all the appropriate HTML code for you.

Up to this point, I've mostly left out the step where I center the graphic. With all the other programs, you just click on the graphic and then click on a Center button in the taskbar. Not really much worth mentioning but I thought I'd mention that anyway.

HotDog Pro works pretty much the same way, except you have to select the entire portion of HTML code that you want to center. That means you have to highlight the entire contents of the IMG tag before you click on the Center button. For example, if the code read:

```
<IMG SRC=header.gif>
```

. . . you'd have to highlight all of that and then click on the Center button.

6 Type the line of text.

Remember that in a program like HotDog Pro, you're responsible for making sure all of the right HTML code makes its way into your document. This means that when you press the Return key to drop down a line or two, you can't just start typing the line of text. Remember the <P> tag to specify a new paragraph? All of the other programs add it when you press the Return key. Not so with a WYSIABOCTYHWR program. You have to give it explicit instructions every step of the way. So before your start typing the line of text, you need to click on the Paragraph button in the taskbar. This automatically pops in the <P> tag.

HotDog Pro can't help you create image maps. If you can't live without one, you'll have to use a shareware program to help you instead

☑ **Progress Check**

If you can do the following, you've mastered this lesson:

❑ Go through the steps of creating a basic Web page in HotDog Pro.

7 Create the table.

This starts out just like the other programs; you just click on the Table button in the taskbar. This displays a Table window, in which you tell HotDog Pro the size and other characteristics of the table. When you're done, the program types in all the HTML code for the table, including the CAPTION tags.

8 Type the table caption.

Like I said, HotDog Pro automatically adds the CAPTION tags. You just add the caption between <CAPTION> and </CAPTION>.

9 Enter data into the table.

Since you're in a non-WYSIWYG mode, you can't just tab from one table cell to the next. Tabbing just creates a big, useless space in whatever table cell you happen to be in. HotDog Pro adds all the TH and TD tags for you. You just click your mouse into the middle of each pair of tags and type the information you want.

10 Insert the graphic for the image map.

Reread Step 5.

11 Create the image map.

Unfortunately, this is as far as you can go with HotDog Pro; it doesn't have any built-in tools for creating image maps. This shouldn't necessarily reflect badly on HotDog Pro, however. I don't know of any WYSIABOCTYHWR Web editors that offer such functionality. Since these are all text-based programs, it really does make sense that they don't offer much in terms of graphics. If you want all the bells and whistles, this isn't the program for you. If you're the do-it-yourself type, thank the stars for shareware programs like NRich WebMap2L (mentioned in the advanced HTML unit) that can help you fill in this big blank. Again, Figure 8-13 shows the HotDog Pro version of the sample page. Just keep in mind that the second graphic really isn't an image map in this one.

Lesson 8-7

MySoftware MyInternetBusinessPage

MySoftware has made a name for itself by creating economical business software that's typically "just enough" for the typical small-business owner. MyInternetBusinessPage brings this same philosophy of software design to the Web.

MyInternetBusinessPage: What's hot and what's not

This program definitely falls into the "for beginners" category. If you plan any long-term involvement with Web page creation, you'll probably want to skip this program altogether. For anyone serious about creating sophisticated Web pages, there's too much hand-holding and a serious lack of some popular features.

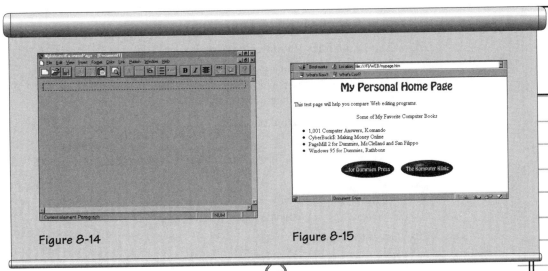

Figure 8-14

Figure 8-15

Figure 8-14: Getting started with MIBP.

Figure 8-15: MIBP came up short on the sample page.

Notes:

However, I can't dismiss this program completely. If you own a small business and you just want to get a reasonably nice page onto the Web without making a career of Web page design, this may be just the program for you. It's very easy to use, and if you're happy with a relatively conservative page, you may be perfectly happy with MyInternetBusinessPage. Your small business just better not be in technology, or you'll be laughed off the Internet.

MyInternetBusinessPage: The sample page

Here's how I created the sample page (or as close to it as I could) with MyInternetBusinessPage. Figure 8-14 illustrates where you start; Figure 8-15 shows the finished product.

1 Start the program.

MyInternetBusinessPage (which I think I'll call MIBP from here on out) opens to a new, untitled document like the one in Figure 8-14 when you start the program.

2 Save the document.

Same-o, same-o. Choosing File⇨Save does the trick.

3 Enter the page's title.

Unlike all of the other programs I looked at for this unit, MIBP does not have a handy-dandy taskbar full of little buttons. Just about everything you do must be done from the pull-down menus. This may not be much of a bother for first-time users, but for experienced users who want to get where they're going as soon as possible, this can really slow you down.

Anyhow, to add a page title, click on the File menu and then select the Web Page Title option. Next, you have an opportunity to type in the title.

MyInternet-
BusinessPage is
good only if you're
super-inexperienced
on the Web and
you just want to
toss out a quick
and easy page

☑ Progress Check

If you can do the following, you've mastered this lesson:

❏ Go through the steps of creating a basic Web page in MyInternetBusinessPage.

4 **Change the background color to white.**

To do this, you click on the Color menu and then select the Background option. A window pops up where you choose from a number of different colors, including the desired white.

5 **Insert the header graphic.**

Again, it's back to another menu, this time the Insert menu. From there you select the Image option. This lets you browse through your system and select the desired image.

6 **Type the line of text.**

Thankfully, no menu option is required for this step.

7 **Insert the table.**

This is where MIBP really let me down. The program has no support in the program for tables, a Web page feature that's been around long enough to make this omission nearly inexcusable. Nevertheless, I had to push on, so I did the next best thing. I created a list of the items that I wanted to include in the table. This required a lot more "menuing" than I really care for.

First, I had to click on the Insert menu and then select New List. This created a bullet and positioned the cursor for me to type in the first list item. Now you'd think you'd be able to just tap the Return key and be all ready to type the next list item. Well, think again.

I next had to tell my secretary to hold all my calls. I was going to be awhile. For each subsequent list item, I had to click on the Insert menu again and this time select the List Item option. I can see the value of walking new users through a process one step at a time, but this seemed like overkill to me.

Because there is no table, these steps now skip to the image map steps, another area of disappointment.

8 **Insert the image map graphic.**

Take a look at Step 5.

9 **Create the image map.**

Not. By the time I got this far, it didn't come as much of a surprise that MIBP doesn't offer any kind of support for image maps, client-side or otherwise. Unlike HotDog Pro, where you can add any sort of HTML code you want — whether HotDog Pro supports it or not — you're stuck with what you've got with MIBP. Your only alternative is to save your MIBP document and then open it in a text editor, where you can add the extra HTML code for your image map. The only problem is that if you go back later and use MIBP to change something on your altered page, you may cause a nuclear meltdown.

Again, Figure 8-15 shows the finished product, with a list instead of a table and an image map that really isn't.

NetObjects Fusion

Fusion is currently the "hot ticket" for professional Web site design. At least that's the press that this particular product has been getting these days. Like FrontPage, Fusion is more oriented toward site management than creating individual Web pages.

Fusion: What's hot and what's not

Fusion offers very powerful site management tools, allowing you to keep track of links and other important site elements with minimum effort. Of course, the flip side to that is that all this extra power may seem a little intimidating to many first-time users.

If your goal is to crank out some Web pages with as few steps as possible, you may be happier with one of the other programs mentioned in this unit. On the other hand, if you're dealing with a very complicated site and you want to avoid some of the extra layers of effort that FrontPage seems to add, Fusion is its strongest competitor right now.

Fusion: The sample page

Here are the steps to create the Fusion version of our sample page: Figure 8-16 shows where I started (sort of); Figure 8-17 shows the finished product.

1 Ladies and gentlemen, start the program.

Because of the site-management focus of Fusion, this step is easier said than done. When you start the program, you have the opportunity to create a new Web site. This entails specifying a location on your hard drive for the new site and then giving the site a name. Fusion then creates a new folder using the name you gave in the location you told it.

After that, the program creates a document named index.htm. You have the option to base this document on a template, or you can tell Fusion to create a blank document. I opted for the blank document.

Fusion then displays a window that represents your site (much like FrontPage does) with your new home page sitting right in the middle. To actually start editing the page, you just double-click on it.

Much to my surprise, when I opened my blank document, it wasn't blank at all. It had a large graphic across the top that said HOME and another graphical button linking to index.htm on the left side. This was especially confusing since I was working with index.htm in the first place.

Along the bottom of the page, there was another text link called Home, which again linked to index.htm. Finally, there was a little NetObjects logo at the bottom of the screen that linked to the NetObjects Web site. That's so presumptuous. That's like my putting *http://www. komando.com* every place I can.

Notes:

Figure 8-16: This is supposed to be a blank page.

Figure 8-17: This is Fusion's rendition of the sample page.

Notes:

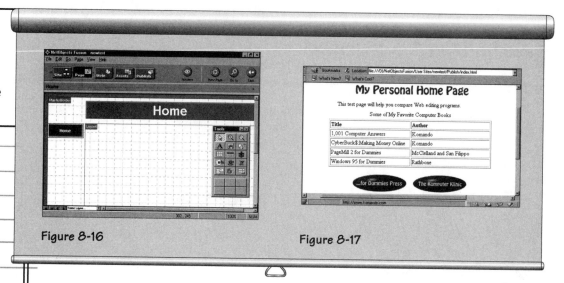

Figure 8-16   Figure 8-17

I didn't want any of this stuff on my page, so I had to waste time deleting it all. Figure 8-16 shows what the page looked like before I started deleting anything.

Because the document was already saved as index.htm, I was able to skip the save step.

2 Enter the page's title.

Fusion has a Properties palette that is very similar to PageMill's Inspector palette. From this little floating window, you have access to all sorts of options and functions. If you click on the Page tab, you can type the document title into the Name field. This threw me a little at first, because I expected such a field to be named Title instead of Name. Oh, well. On this same tab, you can also specify the background color, which I set to white.

3 Insert the header graphic.

Fusion has something of a taskbar, but there's not that much to it. Instead, most of the key functions are available from a floating Tools palette. To add a graphic, you click on the Picture button in the Tools palette.

However, all this does is turn the mouse pointer into a crossbar. You use this crossbar to specify a location on the page for your graphic by clicking and dragging. After you mark off the location of the graphic, a more or less standard Open dialog box appears in which to indicate the graphic you want to occupy that space.

If you've ever had an opportunity to use Quark Xpress (a major desktop publishing program), you already have a feel for how Fusion works. I've never cared much for Quark's "mark the location and then choose the graphic" approach, and it seems even more troublesome in a Web authoring program. However, if you're a die-hard Quark user, you'll probably love this program.

4 Type the line of text.

Text works the same way as graphics in Fusion. You select the Text tool from the Tools palette just as you would in a desktop publishing program. Then you use the crossbar to click and drag your way to a text box. Only after all that are you ready to actually start typing in your text.

5 Insert the table.

To insert a table, you click on the Table tool in the Tools palette and again use the crossbar to define the table area. When you do so, a Table window pops up that allows you to specify the size of the table, as well as some other table characteristics. When you click on OK, your new table appears.

6 Type the table caption.

For a high-end program like Fusion, I was very surprised that it doesn't offer any automatic captioning for tables. To create the table caption, I had to go through all the trouble of creating a new text box and then typing in the text for the caption. As minor as this may seem, for a program that promotes itself as a professional development tool, this really does seem inexcusable. Hey, I call 'em as I see 'em.

7 Enter the table data.

Amazing as it may seem, entering table data is pretty straightforward; it works like most of the other programs. Tab and type.

8 Insert the image map graphic.

Jump back to Step 3 for this cumbersome procedure.

9 Create the image map.

To create the image map, you must first select the image using the Tool palette's Selection tool, and then click on the Picture tool. When you do, a set of image-map editing tools magically (well, not magically; it actually involves a lot of 1's and 0's) appears in the tool palette. You then use these tools to mark off the various hotspots on the graphic.

Each time you mark off a hotspot, a Links window pops up on the screen. Here you click on the External tag (since the links on my sample page are to external URLs) and then type in the URL.

Fusion does offer one extremely handy feature in this area. Each time you type in a URL in the Links window, Fusion automatically adds that URL to a permanent list of links. The next time you need to link to that URL, you can just select it from the list in the Links window instead of having to retype it.

Again, Figure 8-17 shows what the sample page looks like done in Fusion.

☑ **Progress Check**

If you can do the following, you've mastered this lesson:

❑ Go through the steps of creating a basic Web page in Fusion.

Netscape Composer
Lesson 8-9

on the test

Netscape products. Are they free or not? That's a question that confuses many people. Technically, they're not. If you want the final, commercial version of any of Netscape's products, you have to pay for it. The thing is, Netscape always has a beta version available for free from its Web site. So for the most part, you can get the latest version of most Netscape products for free. That means you may be able to get Netscape's Composer for free — sort of.

Figure 8-18: Welcome to Netscape's Composer.

Figure 8-19: Don't bother clicking on the image map in Composer.

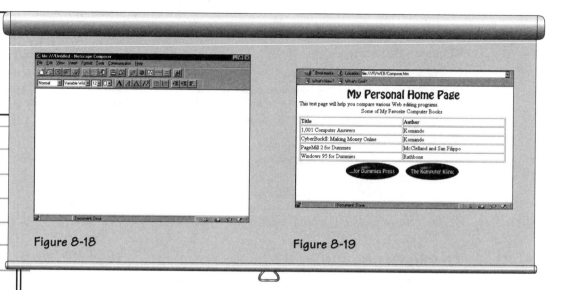

Figure 8-18   Figure 8-19

Notes:

Composer: What's hot and what's not

When the Web was young, one-fiftieth of a century ago, it was enough to put out a great Web browser. That's what Netscape did with its Navigator, and the company captured over 70 percent of the browser market in the process. Then along came Microsoft, giving away Internet Explorer for free with no strings attached, a browser that is (arguably) just as good as Navigator.

Competition heated up and suddenly a good browser wasn't enough. Both Netscape and Microsoft decided that the key to success was to build a whole suite of Internet tools around its Web browser. Netscape's answer is Communicator, which includes, among other components, a Web authoring tool called Composer.

I suppose the best thing about Composer is the price (free, if you download a beta version of Communicator). The problem is that since Composer is an add-on product and designing Web authoring tools is not Netscape's primary business, this program is not quite as robust as some of the others we covered in this unit. The biggest drawback of all, as you'll read shortly, is that Composer doesn't offer you any assistance in creating image maps.

Composer: (n) 1. Someone who, like Beethoven, creates great music 2. Netscape's Web page creation product

Composer: The sample page

Here's what it takes to create the sample page in Netscape's Composer. Figure 8-18 shows a new Composer document; Figure 8-19 shows our finished product.

1 Start the program.

When I first installed the Communicator suite, I was afraid that I'd have to start some main Communicator program to get at Composer, but such is not the case. You can start all of the Communicator components individually.

2 Save the document.

When you save your document, Composer automatically forces you to type in a document title, so you don't have to do that as an extra step.

3 Change the background color to white.

To change the background color, you click on the Format menu and then select the Page Colors and Properties option. Here you can change the background color, as well as many other page characteristics, including the document title.

4 Insert the header graphic.

To insert a graphic image in Composer, you click on the Insert Image button in the taskbar. This displays an Image Properties window. At this point, you click on the Browse button to go out looking for the desired image.

5 Type in the line of text.

6 Insert the table.

Clicking on the Insert Table button in the taskbar pops up a Table Properties window where you specify the size of the table and the positioning of the caption, among other things.

7 Type the table caption.

Based on what you entered in the Table Properties window, Composer provides a place for the caption.

8 Enter the table data.

This is the usual type and tab routine to which you've become so accustomed.

9 Insert the image map graphic.

Works just like Step 4.

10 Create the image map.

Oops! Looks like the programmers at Netscape forgot something. I can see a text-based program like HotDog Pro not supporting a popular technology like image maps. I can even see a low-end beginners program like My Internet Business Page not supporting image maps. But, come on. Netscape is supposed to represent the state of the art on the World Wide Web. Hey, it would be state of the art if this was 1992, but, as I'm sure some hillbilly once said some time or another, it just ain't right.

Again, Figure 8-19 shows what the sample (with its non-functional image map) looks like created in Netscape's Composer.

☑ Progress Check

If you can do the following, you've mastered this lesson:

❑ Go through the steps of creating a basic Web page in Composer.

Microsoft FrontPad   Lesson 8-10

As I mentioned in the previous lesson, Netscape is not the only company that's decided that the future lies in creating Internet suites. Microsoft has gotten in on the act with its Internet Explorer 4.0, which has not yet been released publicly as I write this. As does Netscape Communicator, IE4 (as it's often called) includes a Web authoring component, called FrontPad. I looked at a beta of FrontPad to create this lesson's Web page so some steps and features may differ in the final product.

FrontPad: What's hot and what's not

I dislike few things about FrontPad, but at the very top of the list is the program's name. I suppose that because WordPad is like a "lite" version of Microsoft Word, and this Web authoring tool is (I suppose) like a lite version of FrontPage, the folks at Microsoft figured FrontPad was the perfect name. Oh, well. I suppose that's a minor concern compared to some of the technical areas where FrontPad is lacking.

When I say that FrontPad is a lite version of FrontPage, I should really say that it's an extra light version. The program fails to provide some pretty basic features, as you'll discover on the pages that follow. Although there is a workaround to these problems, it hardly seems worth all the extra effort.

On the other hand, the price is right. Like all other Internet Explorer components, FrontPad is free for the downloading. (However, as of this writing, you have to download about 14MB of Internet Explorer to have FrontPad included — a real drag with even the fastest standard modem connection.) Basically, you click, download, and go to bed.

FrontPad: The sample page

FrontPad is a lot like a scaled-down version of FrontPage

This is what FrontPad required for our sample page. The before and after shots are Figure 8-20 and Figure 8-21.

1 **Start the program.**

Unlike its big brother FrontPage, FrontPad opens to an empty, untitled document something like the one shown in Figure 8-20 when you start the program.

2 **Save the document.**

FrontPad is a little peculiar in this area. When you first save the document, a Save As window pops up that apparently assumes you're saving the document on the computer that will ultimately act as the Web server for that document. To that end, this dialog box asks you for a document title and the URL of the saved document. To save the document as a plain, old HTML file, you have to click on the As File button in this dialog box. Then and only then do you get a more typical Save As dialog box that allows you to save the document as a file somewhere on your system.

3 **Enter the page's title.**

All this required was a click on the File menu and the selection of the Page Properties option, at which point I had opportunity to type the title.

4 **Change the background color to white.**

Just like FrontPage, new FrontPad documents default to a white background. However, if you want to change the background color to something else, you can click on the File menu and then select Page Properties.

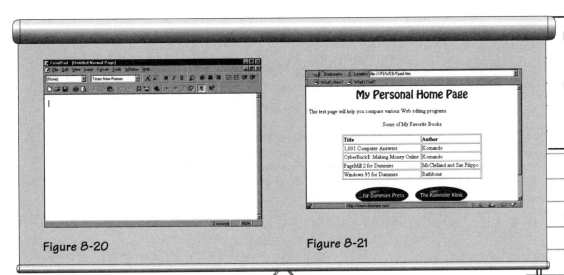

Figure 8-20

Figure 8-21

Figure 8-20: Starting FrontPad brings you right to a new document.

Figure 8-21: It took some extra effort, but FrontPad was able to create this page.

Notes:

5 Insert the header graphic.

To accomplish this, you click on the Insert Image button in the taskbar, which displays an Image window. This window asks you for a file name. If you don't know the exact file name and location, you click on the Browse button to poke around through your system and find the desired graphic.

6 Type in the line of text.

7 Insert the table.

Did you notice that I didn't say a single word in that last step? I was astounded to discover that you can't create tables in the FrontPad beta. God only knows what the Microsoft programmers were thinking when they got to this part of the program. This oversight earns FrontPad a Komando "No Brains" award.

If you think that oversight is strange, here's something even more strange. If you open an existing HTML document with FrontPad that already includes a table, FrontPad displays the document correctly! What do you think of that? I'll tell you what you think. You think one FrontPad doesn't know what the other FrontPad is doing.

Okay, so FrontPad can display tables; it just can't create them. By clicking on the View menu and selecting HTML, you can edit the HTML code directly. So that's exactly what I did. I went into the HTML code and manually typed in all the code for our little table. (If you need a refresher on tables and HTML code, check out Unit 6.) When I closed the HTML editing window, there the table was in all its glory. What a major hassle.

8 Insert the image map graphic.

It shouldn't come as any surprise that this works just like Step 4.

9 Create the image map.

Oh, no! Not again. Just as with tables, you can't create image maps in FrontPad. However, also like the table fiasco, FrontPad can handle the image map code (also discussed in Unit 6) if you enter it manually in the HTML editing window. Well, I wasn't about to try to figure out the coordinates for myself. Instead, I went into my sample PageMill (big hint here) document and copied

☑ Progress Check

If you can do the following, you've mastered this lesson:

❑ Go through the steps of creating a basic Web page in FrontPad.

all the map code from there. Back in FrontPad, I pasted the code into the HTML editing window in just the right location. Once I exited the HTML editing window, FrontPad knew exactly how to handle the image map.

Keep in mind that as I was writing this, only the beta version of Internet Explorer 4.0 was available. That being the case, I suppose there's some chance that the final version will address some of these shortcomings. Maybe they'll read this book. On the other hand, since providing a Web authoring tool isn't a primary goal of IE4, and since I'm sure Microsoft would much rather have you buy FrontPage than grab FrontPad for free, I'm not holding my breath waiting for this all to be fixed.

Despite all the extra effort I had to put into it, I was able to create a sample page with all the desired components. Again, Figure 8-21 shows the results.

Lesson 8-11

Getting by with a Little Help from Your Word Processor

By the time you make it through this lesson, one thing will be perfectly clear. You don't want to rely on your word processor as your primary Web development tool, no matter how awesome the packaging and manual say the program is at creating Web pages from word processing documents.

on the test

That's not to say that this functionality in word processors is not without value. If you already have word processing documents that you need to convert to Web pages, converting them to HTML in your word processing program is an easy and sensible way to get started. When you make that conversion, you can then open the resulting documents with one of the other programs covered in this unit and fine-tune your documents.

Nevertheless, I took a crack at creating our sample page in both Microsoft Word and WordPerfect just to see what kind of results I got. The rest of this lesson is a recap of the results. I'm not going to go through all the steps like I did with the previous programs. Instead, I'll just touch on a few noteworthy points.

WordPerfect version 7

The basic creation of a document in WordPerfect is pretty straightforward. Word processors have had table creation capabilities for quite some time, and have had the ability to import graphics for even longer. As you may expect, however, there's no way to create hypertext links in WordPerfect, via hyperlinks or otherwise.

One little quirk showed up when I inserted the two graphic files. Both files popped in as teeny-tiny versions, just a fraction of the original size. Fixing this took a couple of steps.

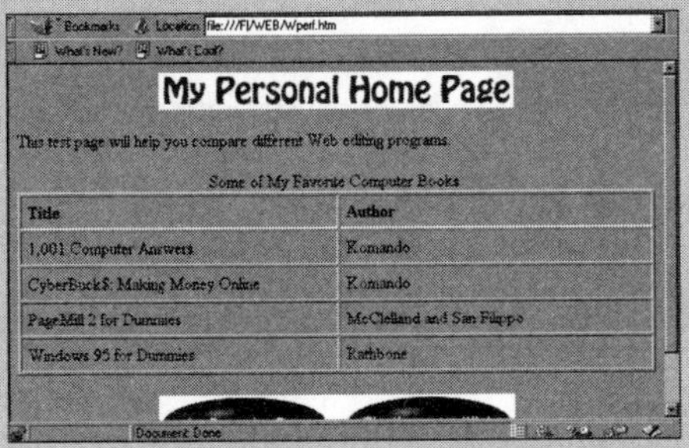

Figure 8-22

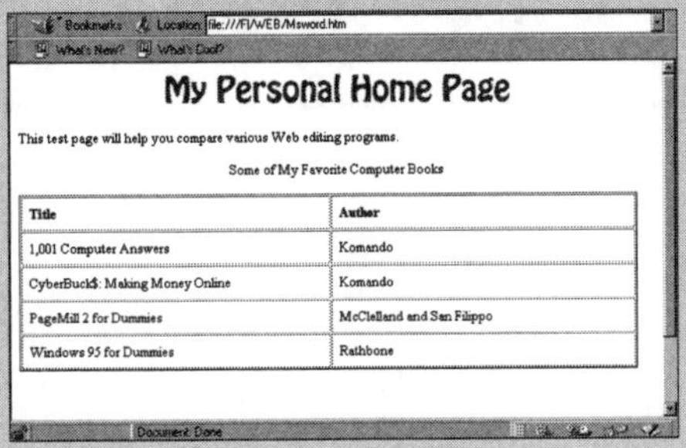

Figure 8-23

Figure 8-22: A page created in WordPerfect isn't always much to look at.

Figure 8-23: Word did better than WordPerfect in terms of appearance.

A little Edit button appears, attached to each image. Double-clicking on that button pops up a window wherein you can specify a number of image options. Clicking on the Size button pops up another window with even more options. For whatever reason, clicking on the Maintain Proportions check box in this window fixed the problem and the images returned to their normal sizes.

Figure 8-22 shows the unretouched results of the sample page as created in WordPerfect.

Microsoft Word 97

Creating the sample page in Word was not substantially different from creating it in WordPerfect (although, as you can see from Figure 8-23, the results were a little more attractive). As with WordPerfect, you can't do anything with image maps or background colors. However, there are a couple of minor differences worth noting.

For starters, when you tell Word that your new document is going to be a Web page, Word offers to go out on the Internet and check with Microsoft to see if there have been any updates to the Web authoring portion of Word. I thought that was a nice touch.

Unlike the tables in all of the other programs we've looked at in this unit, Word tables start out by default with no borders. To add borders, you have to click on the Table menu, select the Table Borders option, and then click on the Grid option in the resulting Window.

Once last thing that bugged me about Word: For the life of me, I couldn't get the table to center on the page. That drove me nuts. I mean, I'm already nuts, but it didn't help.

Anyhow, Figure 8-23 shows the results.

☑ Progress Check

If you can do the following, you've mastered this lesson:

❑ Understand the downside of creating a Web page in a word processing program.

❑ Explain the differences and difficulties of creating Web pages in both Word and WordPerfect.

Unit 8 Quiz

Notes:

Select the best answer to each question. I'll try to keep this simple, because I don't honestly expect you to remember every single feature of every single program we covered.

1. **WYSIWYG stands for . . .**

   A. What You See Is What You Generate

   B. What You See Is What You Get

   C. What You Sample Is What You Get

   D. Where You See Is Where You Go

2. **You pronounce WYSIWYG like . . .**

   A. Woosy-woog

   B. Why-see-wig

   C. Whatsa-wig

   D. Wizzy-wig

3. **A good Web authoring program should be able to . . .**

   A. Create tables

   B. Automatically create table captions

   C. Create client-side image maps

   D. All of the above

4. **Word processors are especially good for . . .**

   A. Creating new Web pages

   B. Converting existing word processing documents to Web pages

   C. Writing letters to your Mom

   D. Creating hyperlinks

5. **Netscape Communicator components are free . . .**

   A. Always

   B. Never

   C. When you download beta versions

   D. When you illegally steal them

6. **Microsoft Internet Explorer components are free . . .**

   A. Always

   B. Never

   C. When you download beta versions

   D. When you illegally steal them

7. **HotDog Pro . . .**

   A. Is a WYSIWYG program

   B. Has powerful image map features

   C. Lets you see the HTML code as it's created

   D. All of the above

8. **Site management tools let you . . .**

   A. Control many aspects of an entire Web site

   B. Allow you to check links automatically

   C. Make it easier to manage complicated sites

   D. All of the above

Unit 8 Exercise

No, I mean really exercise. You've been reading too long.

By now, I think there's a pretty good chance that you're considering at least one of these programs. Maybe you've ruled out a couple already. But so many of them seem so similar, it's hard to choose the one that's right for you. Well, I'm going to make it a little easier for you.

Table 8-1 shows a list of all the products and features we covered in this unit. What I'd like you to do is study this table and then decide which program you think will best meet your needs. Then, if it's in your budget, go out and buy that program. No matter which one you choose I can all but guarantee that it will make your Web authoring time much more productive.

The column marked *Extra Tools* indicates programs that come with extra stuff "above and beyond the call of duty" that makes creating Web pages even easier.

Table 8-1			Web Page Editors			
Product	*WYSIWYG*	*Tables*	*Captions*	*Image Maps*	*Site Management*	*Extra tools*
PageMill	Y	Y	Y	Y	N	Y
Home Page	Y	Y	N	Y	N	N
FrontPage	Y	Y	Y	Y	Y	Y
Web.Graphics Suite	Y	Y	N	Y	N	Y
HotDog Pro	N	Y	Y	P	N	N
MyInternet-BusinessPage	Y	N	N	N	N	N
Fusion	Y	Y	N	Y	Y	N
Composer	Y	Y	Y	N	N	N
FrontPad	Y	P	P	P	N	N

Key: Y = full support, P = partial support, N = no support

Web Publishing
with Online Services

Prerequisites
▶ Know the basic steps of creating a Web page (Parts I, II, and III)
▶ Want your online home to be a part of the big online high-rise with lots of tenants on the Web (independent study)

Objectives for This Unit

Publish your very own Web pages through:

✓ America Online

✓ CompuServe

✓ Prodigy

✓ The Microsoft Network

✓ The Kim Komando Komputer Klinic

Not too many years ago, each commercial online service (such as America Online or CompuServe) — was its own little digital island. If you joined one of these services, you had access to only the content provided by those services and, perhaps more important, you had e-mail access to only other people who were also members of the same service.

Then along came the Internet. The Internet was a tremendous boon for the online services because, by adding Internet e-mail gateways, these online services were able to connect their members to members on other services, as well as to those people who just had straight e-mail access.

For better or worse, the public's interest in the Internet didn't stop at e-mail. (Better for you, worse for them.) Soon, members of these online services began clamoring for more Internet services. First there was Gopher and FTP access. Then along came the biggie — access to the World Wide Web directly through a commercial online service.

before you create
a Web page with
an online service,
you need to have
an account with
that service

on the test

But even that wasn't big enough. Members weren't satisfied to just view Web content; they wanted to create it, too. That brings us to today, when every major online service on the planet offers personal Web publishing as part of its standard membership package. This way, the services can give members their own little piece of online real estate, well, as long as the member's account status is paid up.

In this unit, you get to figure out how to use those online services to publish your Web page. For those online services that offer extra tools to make Web publishing even easier, I describe those tools in detail, too. No, don't thank me.

Lesson 9-1

Web Publishing with America Online

America Online is the biggest commercial online service in the entire United States that's branching out globally, and with good reason, too. In addition to being the home of my original Kim Komando Komputer Klinic (keyword: **KOMANDO** or **COMMANDO** *for you people who can't spell*), it boasts what I believe to be the easiest-to-use interface of the Big Four service providers. While the others primarily have gone to a Web browser-based interface, AOL has stuck with its own software for accessing its own content, while simultaneously offering complete access to the Internet over the same connection.

on the test

AOL offers an online Web publishing tool called Personal Publisher that enables you to create a simple Web page while you're connected to AOL. I describe how to use Personal Publisher first; then I tell you about the other Web publishing options that AOL has to offer.

Easy Web publishing with Personal Publisher

Personal Publisher is an online Web publishing tool that helps you create a simple Web page by having you answer just a few questions and select a few options. Here are the steps to create a simple business page using Personal Publisher. I assume here that you've already established an AOL account.

1 **Connect to America Online.**

Go ahead and check your e-mail and take care of whatever other online business you need to take care of. You may want to:

> Delete all the junk e-mail piling up in your mail box
>
> Go into the teen chat rooms and lecture them about good behavior
>
> Mute that "You've got mail!" guy

2 **Click on the Go To menu and select the Keyword option.**

When you do this, a dialog box pops up where you can type your keyword.

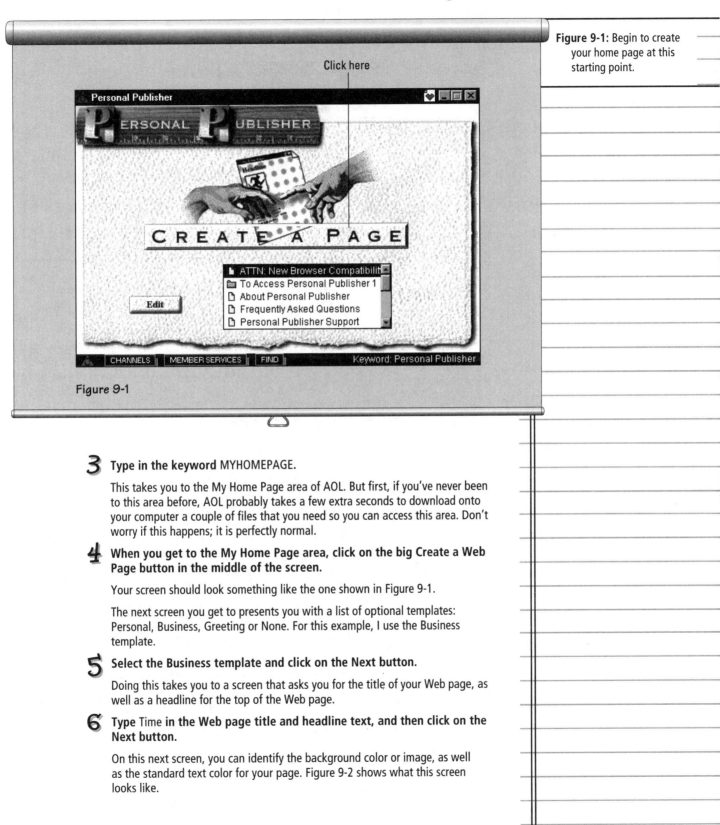

Click here

Figure 9-1

Figure 9-1: Begin to create your home page at this starting point.

3 **Type in the keyword** MYHOMEPAGE.

This takes you to the My Home Page area of AOL. But first, if you've never been to this area before, AOL probably takes a few extra seconds to download onto your computer a couple of files that you need so you can access this area. Don't worry if this happens; it is perfectly normal.

4 **When you get to the My Home Page area, click on the big Create a Web Page button in the middle of the screen.**

Your screen should look something like the one shown in Figure 9-1.

The next screen you get to presents you with a list of optional templates: Personal, Business, Greeting or None. For this example, I use the Business template.

5 **Select the Business template and click on the Next button.**

Doing this takes you to a screen that asks you for the title of your Web page, as well as a headline for the top of the Web page.

6 **Type** Time **in the Web page title and headline text, and then click on the Next button.**

On this next screen, you can identify the background color or image, as well as the standard text color for your page. Figure 9-2 shows what this screen looks like.

Figure 9-2: Choose your
colors on this screen.

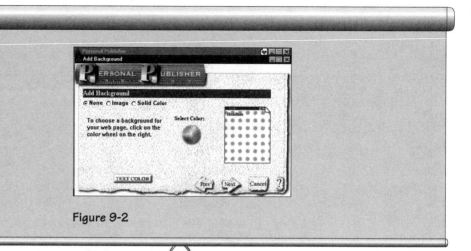

Figure 9-2

Notes:

7 **Make your color and/or image selections and click on the Next button.**

Now you have the opportunity to add a graphic to your Web page. The interesting thing here is that you have the option to add a graphic from a group of images that AOL offers you, or you can click on the Browse My Files button (shown in Figure 9-3) and select a file from your own hard drive. If you go this route, Personal Publisher automatically uploads that graphic when it gets ready to create your Web page. Personal Publisher uploads the file from any folder, but image files still need to be in the GIF or JPEG formats.

8 **Specify an image to add to your Web page, then click on the Next button.**

The next screen lets you enter some miscellaneous information about you and your business.

9 **Enter the requested information and click on the Next button.**

This next and final creation screen allows you to enter the main body text for your Web page.

10 **Enter whatever text you want to use for the body of your new Web page, then click on the View (not the Next) button.**

Personal Publisher now displays an approximation of what your page will look like on the World Wide Web. I say approximation because, as you already know, no Web page looks exactly the same through any two different Web browsers.

The screen offers an Edit button that lets you go back and change anything you don't particularly like. (Don't you wish the rest of life was like that?) If you're like me, you probably won't get it just right the first time — or the second time or the third time either. Just keep editing until you like what you see. That's what my editor does. And a very fine job too!

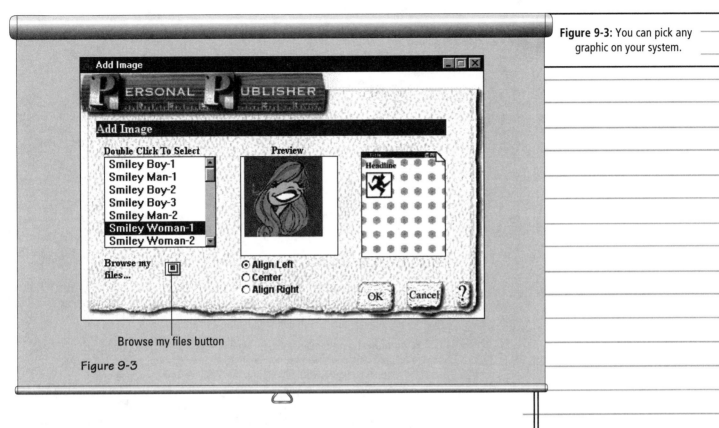

Figure 9-3: You can pick any graphic on your system.

Figure 9-3

11 When you are satisfied with how your Web page looks, click on the Publish button.

Personal Publisher automatically creates your Web page on the AOL Web server. If you used any graphics from your own system, Personal Publisher now uploads them to the AOL Web server. Personal Publisher automatically names your page index.html.

In a matter of seconds, your Web page will be out on the World Wide Web for the entire planet to see. So be careful what you say about your boss. Naturally, you'll want to check it out, too, so there's just one more step . . .

12 Launch your Web browser and visit your new home page.

Oops! Not quite sure what your new Web address is? That's easy enough. Your Web address is:

```
http://members.aol.com/yourscreenname
```

. . . where *yourscreenname* is really your America Online screen name, minus any spaces you may normally include.

Other AOL Web publishing options

If you've created your own Web pages and simply want to post them on the World Wide Web through your AOL account, you have a couple of options. The simplest way (and cheapest, since it's included in your regular AOL membership) is to go to keyword: **MYPLACE**. This takes you to the My Place area of AOL, which is just an upload area through which you can transfer files from your computer to the directory on the AOL Web server that holds your Web pages. Basically, you're doing the work that Personal Publisher may otherwise do for you. That means that your Web address is still the same.

In the My Place area, you can see what files are already in your directory. For example, if you have already created a Web page using Personal Publisher, you see that file and any other related files (like graphics files) listed there. From the My Place area, you can upload files to your directory, or you can download the files in your AOL directory to your computer in case you want to store them or edit them. This area also offers buttons for creating new subdirectories within your AOL directory, and for deleting files and subdirectories.

If you want to do some heavy-duty business Web publishing, America Online also offers a separate business Web publishing service called PrimeHost (keyword: **PRIMEHOST**). PrimeHost isn't free like the basic Web site that I just showed you how to do. Here's a rundown of the three service packages you can get through PrimeHost (as of this writing).

- **Domain:** This is the least expensive PrimeHost package. Domain includes Web hosting with your own domain name (for example, www.yourcompany.com). This package gives you a maximum of 50MB of storage space on a PrimeHost Web server, and limits you to 1,500MB of traffic per month. Let me explain how traffic is measured. On your Web page, you will have files that take up space that is measured in megabytes. Each time a person visits your site, the contents of the page are automatically downloaded so that they can view them. When this happens, the Internet server keeps a log and running total of the megabytes that are exchanged between the user and the server. The setup for this package costs $199, and the monthly fee is $99.

- **Commercial:** In addition to domain name hosting, Commercial offers a variety of extra Web publishing tools, including support for CGI scripts, which, as you know from Unit 6, are necessary if you want to use any online forms. ("Online forms" sounds like something the DMV cooked up.) The Commercial package offers you up to 100MB of storage space on the Web server, and limits you to 3,000MB of traffic per month. This package costs $249 to set up, with a monthly fee of $199.

- **Dedicated:** In addition to all the benefits of the other two packages, this one offers you a dedicated Web server just to host your site. Among other things, this means that you can use multiple domain names for your site or sites if you so desire. With Dedicated, you get 4,000MB of storage space, plus a monthly traffic allowance of 15,000MB. Of course, all this doesn't come cheap. The setup for the dedicated package is $499 and the monthly charge — I hope you're sitting down — is $1,799. That's no chump change. If you spend that, you'd better be dedicated.

in addition to its basic service, AOL offers some services that are geared for businesses with more elaborate needs

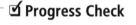

☑ Progress Check

If you can do the following, you've mastered this lesson:

❑ Go through the steps of publishing a basic Web page on AOL. (Of course, you need an account for that)

❑ Explain briefly the other AOL Web publishing options.

Recess

Take a break and ponder what life was like way back when online services were king:

- Bill Clinton was a president without too many scandals
- If you had a 14.4 modem, you were the envy of your friends
- 16MB of memory was more than enough
- Java was only coffee
- Bill Gates hadn't heard of the Internet (Uh, don't tell Bill I said that.)

Web Publishing with CompuServe

Lesson 9-2

on the test

Like America Online, CompuServe offers its own Web creation software to help make your job a little easier. The main difference is that unlike AOL Personal Publisher, CompuServe Home Page Wizard is a downloadable program that runs on your PC. After you download the software, you don't have to connect to CompuServe until you're ready to upload your new creation to CompuServe. This way, your phone line remains open for important calls. Phone calls like:

- Your kids wondering why you haven't picked them up from school. Reason: You wanted to change "one little thing" to your page before you left.
- Your spouse's lawyer with divorce papers. Reason: "You love that damn computer more than me."
- Janet Reno and the Bureau of Alcohol, Tobacco and Firearms (ATF). Reason: They think you are hiding out in your "compound," because you haven't left your house (or your desk) in a month as you work on your Web page.

heads up

Also like America Online, CompuServe doesn't require you to create your Web pages with their Home Page Wizard. You can create them any way you want and then upload them to CompuServe using another program called the Publishing Wizard. One catch: Unfortunately, the Publishing Wizard comes in the same file as the Home Page Wizard, so you have to download both of them together, even if you don't plan to use the Home Page Wizard. Oh — one more thing — these programs work only on Windows. If you're a Mac user, you're out of luck on this one.

Notes:

Figure 9-4: Click here to download your free software.

Figure 9-4

Download button

the Web page
publishing program
from CompuServe
doesn't work on
Mac machines

Don't think that you cannot use your own images on your home page. If you want to put photos on your Web page, you need to use the JPEG file format for them. (I seem to have read that somewhere before. Oh yeah, this book.) One thing to remember, is as I said before, the Home Page Wizard and the Publishing Wizard come together as a package deal; there's just one file to download, so you end up getting (and using up the download time for) the Home Page Wizard even if you don't ever plan to use it. However, note that both of these programs are only for Microsoft Windows users.

heads up

When I walk you through these steps, I assume that you're using the Home Page Wizard. If you've created a page of your own that you just want to post using the Publishing Wizard, that's cool: Just do Step 6 and then skip to Step 11. Therefore, in this lesson, I give you only one set of steps, which include instructions for using the Home Page Wizard. If you don't plan to use the Home Page Wizard, you can skip to Step 11 after you finish Step 6.

Once again, these procedures (and I) assume that you've already established an account with CompuServe and are using the latest CompuServe software (version 3.02 at this writing).

1 **Connect to CompuServe in the normal manner.**

2 **Click on the Go button.**

After you do this, a dialog box pops up. This pops up a little box for you to type a Go word into.

3 **Type in HPWIZ and click on the Go button at the bottom of this little box.**

If you visit CompuServe's help files to figure out how to publish your Web page, you discover that they call for you to go to **OURWORLD** instead of **HPWIZ**. If you do that, you have to click through a bunch of image-laden screens before

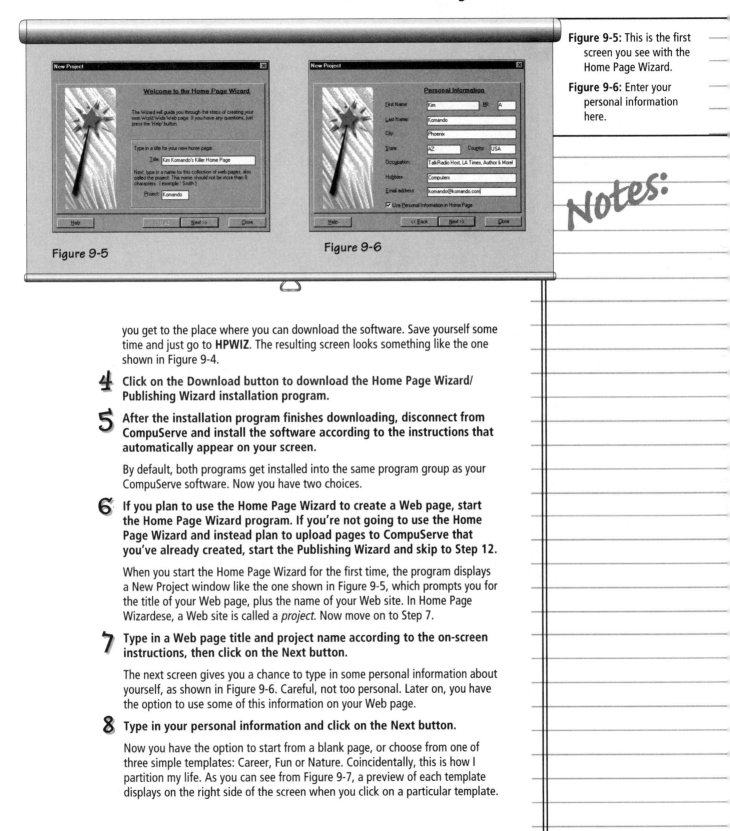

Figure 9-5

Figure 9-6

Figure 9-5: This is the first screen you see with the Home Page Wizard.

Figure 9-6: Enter your personal information here.

Notes:

you get to the place where you can download the software. Save yourself some time and just go to **HPWIZ**. The resulting screen looks something like the one shown in Figure 9-4.

4 **Click on the Download button to download the Home Page Wizard/ Publishing Wizard installation program.**

5 **After the installation program finishes downloading, disconnect from CompuServe and install the software according to the instructions that automatically appear on your screen.**

By default, both programs get installed into the same program group as your CompuServe software. Now you have two choices.

6 **If you plan to use the Home Page Wizard to create a Web page, start the Home Page Wizard program. If you're not going to use the Home Page Wizard and instead plan to upload pages to CompuServe that you've already created, start the Publishing Wizard and skip to Step 12.**

When you start the Home Page Wizard for the first time, the program displays a New Project window like the one shown in Figure 9-5, which prompts you for the title of your Web page, plus the name of your Web site. In Home Page Wizardese, a Web site is called a *project*. Now move on to Step 7.

7 **Type in a Web page title and project name according to the on-screen instructions, then click on the Next button.**

The next screen gives you a chance to type in some personal information about yourself, as shown in Figure 9-6. Careful, not too personal. Later on, you have the option to use some of this information on your Web page.

8 **Type in your personal information and click on the Next button.**

Now you have the option to start from a blank page, or choose from one of three simple templates: Career, Fun or Nature. Coincidentally, this is how I partition my life. As you can see from Figure 9-7, a preview of each template displays on the right side of the screen when you click on a particular template.

Figure 9-7: Select a
template — or not.

Notes:

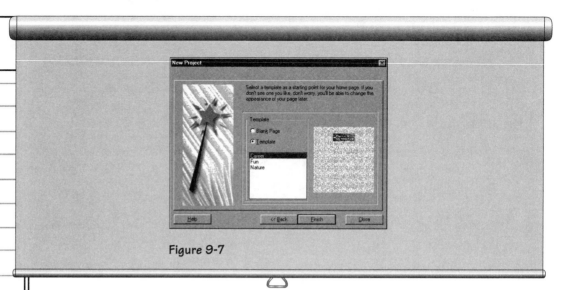

Figure 9-7

9   Choose whichever option you want and click on the Finish button.

Before you get going, the Home Page Wizard displays a Tip of the Day. These
tips help you with both the program and Web page creation, but if you don't
want to see the tips, uncheck the Show Tips on Startup box. Either way, you
need to click on the Close button to get past this tip box.

Next, you're finally ready to edit your Web page using the Home Page Wizard.
The Home Page Wizard provides push button tools for adding text, graphics,
links, and other HTML elements. I'm not going to provide detailed instructions
on using this feature; that's not really the point of this book. Fiddle around with
the various tools to get your page looking just the way you want. If you have
any problems, the Help file is comprehensive and should assist you. When you
are done creating the perfect digital masterpiece, go ahead and continue on to
Step 10.

10   Click on the File menu and select Publish Pages.

This starts up the Publishing Wizard.

**11   When you see the opening screen to the Publishing Wizard, click on the
Next button.**

The next screen offers you two options: Upload Files or Delete All Files. If you
select Upload Files, the Publishing Wizard gathers all the files you need for your
Web site and allows you to upload them to the CompuServe Web server. If you
select Delete All Files, the Publishing Wizard deletes all files that you currently
have stored on the CompuServe Web server. This doesn't affect any files you've
saved on your own computer. For our purposes, I assume you want to upload
your Web page.

**12   Accept the default selection of Upload Files and click on the Next
button.**

The next window lets you modify the personal information you've already
entered. To be honest, I'm not really sure why. This only helps people who
second-guess themselves.

13 **Change any information if you want to, or just click the Next button.**

This next screen also allows you to modify your personal information, again for no apparent reason. The only thing that's changed since then is that I'm a little older and a little more frustrated.

14 **Change any information if you want to, or just click the Next button.**

The next screen prompts you for your CompuServe user name and password.

15 **Type in your account information, but before you click on the Next button, reestablish your modem connection to CompuServe.**

You have to do this through the regular CompuServe software, because the Publishing Wizard does not prompt you to make the connection; it simply assumes that you are connected and delivers an error message if you're not. When you establish the connection, go back to the Publishing Wizard and click on the Next button. This displays a relatively useless screen that simply tells you to click on the Next button again. Don't you just *love* useless screens? It's like the developers put them in just to make sure that you are still awake.

16 **Click on the Next button again.**

The Publishing Wizard now uploads your files to the CompuServe Web server. If you were working in the Home Page Wizard, the Publishing Wizard should know where all your Web page files are on your hard drive. If you're just posting your own file using the Publishing Wizard, the program gives you the opportunity to tell you where the files are that you want to upload. When the upload is complete, the program displays a window the shows the Web address for your home page. Your Web address is . . .

```
http://ourworld.compuserve.com/homepages/mailalias
```

. . . where *mailalias* is the mail alias you specified for your CompuServe account. For more information about mail aliases, check with CompuServe member services.

17 **Click on the Finish button.**

That's it; you're done. Your Web page is now available to anyone who has access to the World Wide Web. You can now exit the Home Page Wizard and also disconnect from the CompuServe service.

☑ **Progress Check**

If you can do the following, you've mastered this lesson:

❑ Download CompuServe's Web page creation software.

❑ Walk through the steps of creating a Web page with that software.

❑ Post your creation.

Web Publishing with Prodigy

Lesson 9-3

Prodigy is an online service in transition. The company still offers its traditional service, now called Prodigy Classic (just like Coca-Cola became Coca-Cola Classic), which uses special software to connect to the service. (Not Coca-Cola . . . Prodigy.) However, the more recent addition to the product offering is Prodigy Internet, which is entirely Web-based. Since the whole idea is to publish on the Web, I'm going to cover Prodigy Internet in this lesson. If you have plain ol' Prodigy and you want to publish a Web page, you probably want to check with the company to see if you can get the Prodigy Internet software. The pricing plans for the two different services are about the same.

Figure 9-8: If you use the WS_FTP program to post your Web page on Prodigy's Web Server, all you have to do is add your user name and password.

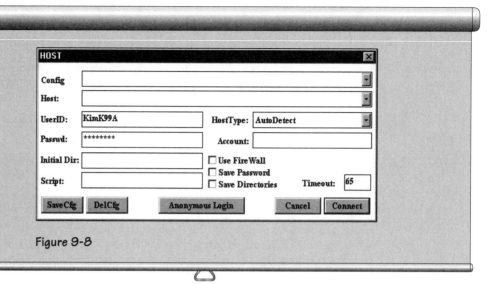

Figure 9-8

As I said, Prodigy Internet is entirely Web-based. That means that when you connect to the service, you do so using your Web browser. Prodigy Internet software comes with Microsoft Internet Explorer, but you can elect to use Netscape Navigator.

Prodigy Internet doesn't offer any custom software for creating or uploading your Web pages to the Prodigy Web server. However, there is a Web publishing support area that offers loads of tips and tricks, as well as links to a wide variety of shareware and freeware that can help you create those pages. Getting to this area by navigating through the system takes a little while, so I'll give you a shortcut. Simply go to this Web address:

```
http://science.prodigy.net/internet
```

on the CD

After you create your Web pages, you upload them to the Prodigy Web server using a standard FTP program. Now, I know you don't really know a lot about FTP yet, so let me give the briefest of explanations. FTP stands for File Transfer Protocol, and it's basically the way you transfer your Web page files from your computer to the Internet. If you want to learn more about FTP, just skip over to Unit 11. At any rate, to post your Web page through Prodigy Internet, you can use WS_FTP for Windows or Anarchie for Macintosh. I've included both of these programs on the CD.

heads up

The advantage to using the WS_FTP program is that it comes with all the Prodigy server information already included. That saves you a few steps. All you have to do is type in your Prodigy user name and password and the program knows right where to look. Figure 9-8 shows the initial Session Profile window for WS_FTP.

Assuming that you've installed WS_FTP and are using it to upload your files, here are the steps to get your pages on the Prodigy Web server.

 Establish your connection to the Prodigy Internet in the normal manner.

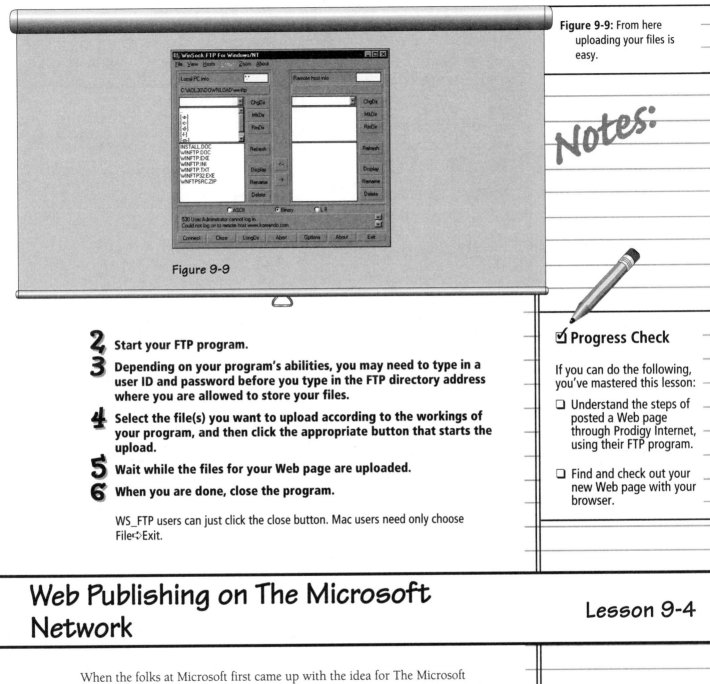

Figure 9-9

Figure 9-9: From here uploading your files is easy.

Notes:

2 Start your FTP program.

3 Depending on your program's abilities, you may need to type in a user ID and password before you type in the FTP directory address where you are allowed to store your files.

4 Select the file(s) you want to upload according to the workings of your program, and then click the appropriate button that starts the upload.

5 Wait while the files for your Web page are uploaded.

6 When you are done, close the program.

WS_FTP users can just click the close button. Mac users need only choose File➪Exit.

☑ **Progress Check**

If you can do the following, you've mastered this lesson:

❑ Understand the steps of posted a Web page through Prodigy Internet, using their FTP program.

❑ Find and check out your new Web page with your browser.

Web Publishing on The Microsoft Network

Lesson 9-4

When the folks at Microsoft first came up with the idea for The Microsoft Network (MSN), the Internet was already a hot item. The original plan was to make MSN another online service, competing with the likes of AOL and CompuServe.

Then the Internet got to be even more popular. So by the time MSN and Windows 95 were ready to roll, Microsoft decided to follow the lead of the other big commercial online services and transformed itself into an online service that offered Internet access.

Figure 9-10: Welcome to online Web creation.

Figure 9-11: You're about to start building.

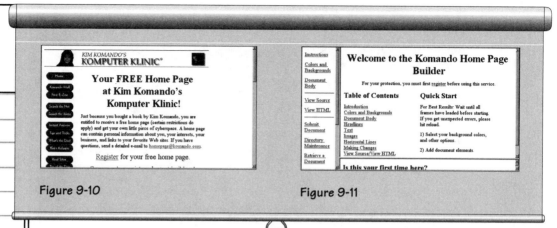

Figure 9-10   Figure 9-11

on the test

☑ Progress Check

If you can do the following, you've mastered this lesson:

❏ Consider sending Microsoft an e-mail to ask them what's taking them so long to offer a personal home page service.

Just one problem: The world doesn't really need another online service. Just as Apple Computer found out when it introduced its now-defunct eWorld online service, the world just wasn't ready for yet another online service. So Microsoft began pushing MSN as more of an Internet Service Provider instead of an online service. What does that make MSN today? Your guess is as good as mine.

Regardless of what the Microsoft Network is, however, there is one thing that MSN isn't — at least at this writing — and that's a place where you can go to publish Web pages. Weird for an Internet Service Provider, huh? Here's a quote taken directly from an MSN online FAQ.

> Q. *Can I Have a Home Page on MSN?*
>
> A. *MSN is currently working diligently to develop Internet services that meet your needs and interests. At this time we are still in the process of developing the best personal home page service for our members. In the coming months you will hear more about our plans for offering home pages on MSN. We look forward to your participation in testing this feature at that time. Thank you for your ongoing support and we will announce all relevant information as we roll out the feature.*

There's a special toll-free number for a translation of the above. For the time being, that pretty much says it all.

Lesson 9-5   One More Online Tool — from Me

The World Wide Web is really redefining what constitutes an online service. Take my Komputer Klinic Web site (http://www.komando.com), for example. I suppose that technically, you couldn't call it an online service, because I don't offer online access accounts to the general public. However, the Komputer Klinic is obviously online and, if you've ever dropped by, you know it offers plenty of services.

One great service that I created for my readers (and fans, of course) is a special Web development tool that lets you create your own Web page just by making

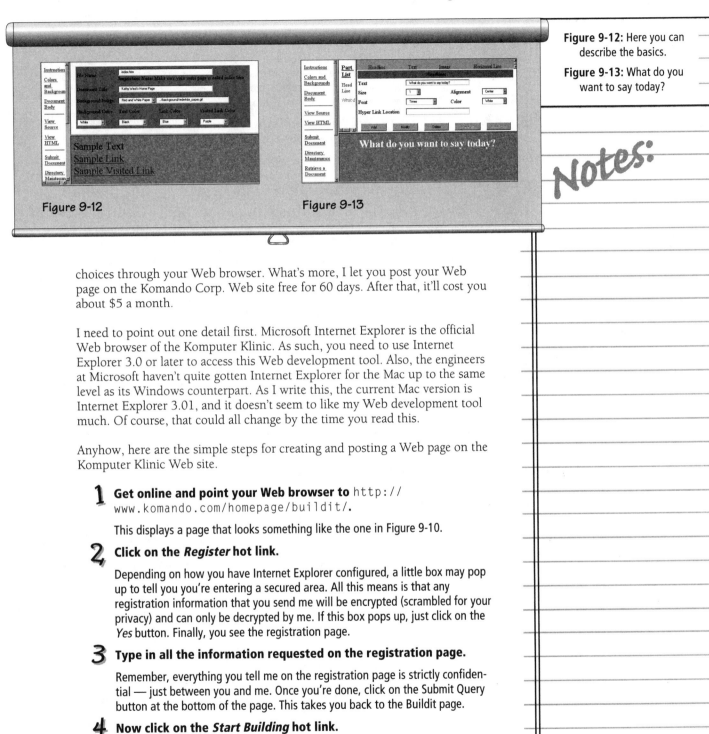

Figure 9-12: Here you can describe the basics.

Figure 9-13: What do you want to say today?

Figure 9-12   Figure 9-13

Notes:

choices through your Web browser. What's more, I let you post your Web page on the Komando Corp. Web site free for 60 days. After that, it'll cost you about $5 a month.

I need to point out one detail first. Microsoft Internet Explorer is the official Web browser of the Komputer Klinic. As such, you need to use Internet Explorer 3.0 or later to access this Web development tool. Also, the engineers at Microsoft haven't quite gotten Internet Explorer for the Mac up to the same level as its Windows counterpart. As I write this, the current Mac version is Internet Explorer 3.01, and it doesn't seem to like my Web development tool much. Of course, that could all change by the time you read this.

Anyhow, here are the simple steps for creating and posting a Web page on the Komputer Klinic Web site.

1 Get online and point your Web browser to http://www.komando.com/homepage/buildit/.

This displays a page that looks something like the one in Figure 9-10.

2 Click on the *Register* hot link.

Depending on how you have Internet Explorer configured, a little box may pop up to tell you you're entering a secured area. All this means is that any registration information that you send me will be encrypted (scrambled for your privacy) and can only be decrypted by me. If this box pops up, just click on the *Yes* button. Finally, you see the registration page.

3 Type in all the information requested on the registration page.

Remember, everything you tell me on the registration page is strictly confidential — just between you and me. Once you're done, click on the Submit Query button at the bottom of the page. This takes you back to the Buildit page.

4 Now click on the *Start Building* hot link.

This takes you to the Komando Home Page Builder, as shown in Figure 9-11.

5 Click on the Colors and Backgrounds link in the left frame.

Once you click on this link in the left frame, the upper-right frame changes so you can enter some basic information about your site. Take a look at Figure 9-12 to see what I mean.

Progress Check

If you can do the following, you've mastered this lesson:

❏ Join me on the Internet and publish a fabulous Web page using the tools at my site.

This form provides pop-down menus for selecting colors of various Web page components, as well as background images that I've created just for you. As you choose different color combinations, the frame at the bottom of the window shows you an example of what to expect.

6 **After you finish making your color selections, click on the Document Body link in the left frame.**

This brings up a different form in the upper-right window, a form that lets you tell my Home Page Builder exactly what you want your Web page to say. You can see what I mean in Figure 9-13.

The View Source and View HTML links in the left frame let you switch back and forth between viewing your document as plain HTML (View Source) and as a regular Web page (View HTML) in the lower-right frame. When you're done...

7 **Click on the Submit Document button in the left frame.**

In the lower-right frame, a form appears for you to enter your Komando user name and password — the ones you chose during the registration process. (Please don't tell me you forgot them already!)

8 **Type in your user name and password, and then click on the Submit button.**

Once you submit your page, you'll see the complete URL of your site in that same lower-right frame. If you want to submit more pages, feel free. I've even got tools to create internal links if you want to do that. Don't forget to jot down your Web page address so you can hand it out to all your friends!

Unit 9 Quiz

Select the best answer for each of the following questions.

1. **The first Internet service to be offered by most commercial online services was . . .**

   A. E-mail

   B. Web browsing

   C. Web publishing

   D. FTP

2. **As it was introduced, the most popular Internet feature soon became . . .**

   A. FTP

   B. Gopher

   C. WAIS

   D. Web browsing

3. **Most major online services now offer their members . . .**

   A. Internet e-mail

   B. Web browsing

   C. Web publishing

   D. All of the above

4. **The most notable exception to question Number 3 is . . .**

   A. America Online

   B. CompuServe

   C. Microsoft Network

   D. Prodigy

5. **America Online offers a Web creation tool that lets you create Web documents . . .**

   A. Online in your pajamas

   B. Offline while you are talking on the telephone

   C. Both A and B

   D. Neither A nor B

6. **You can download CompuServe's Publishing Wizard . . .**

   A. All by itself

   B. Packaged with the Home Page Wizard

   C. Both A and B

   D. Neither A nor B

7. **Web files are sent to the Prodigy Web server by . . .**

   A. A special publishing wizard

   B. E-mail

   C. A standard FTP program

   D. Telepathy

Notes:

Unit 9 Exercise

heads up

If you saw something you liked in this unit in terms of an online service, the good news is that every single one of the services offers a free trial period. That way, you can try one or more of them out to see if they really meet your needs. I should warn you, however, that even though your first month or so is free, all of the commercial online services collect your credit card number up front just in case you do something that's not covered by the free trial.

You can find floppies and CDs for many of these services shrink-wrapped with various computer magazines down at the local drugstore. Also, many new computers often come bundled with access software for one or more of them. However, if you're not a magazine reader and you didn't just buy a new computer, you can reach your favorite online service at one of the following numbers (even the call is free):

- America Online: (800) 433-7300
- CompuServe: (800) 848-8990
- Prodigy: (800) 213-0992
- Microsoft Network: (800) 386-5550

Part IV Review

Unit 8 Summary

▶ **Web Page Creation Programs:** You can do every ounce of HTML coding yourself, but lots of different programs can do the bulk of the work for you. In most of these programs, you can just tell it how you want your page to look, and the program adds the HTML code. That way, you never have to see a single HTML tag. These programs are WYSIWYG (*What You See Is What You Get*) programs. In other programs, you actually see and work with the HTML code.

▶ **Different Programs:** This unit goes through the steps of creating a basic Web page using nine different programs. Of the nine, seven of the programs you would buy in the store. They include Adobe PageMill, Claris HomePage, Corel Web.Graphics Suite, Microsoft FrontPage, MySoftware My Internet Business Page, NetObjects Fusion, and Sausage Software HotDog Pro. The two remaining programs are free tools that come with Netscape Navigator and Microsoft Internet Explorer browsers. In addition, I show you how you can use some of the common word processing programs to help create your Web page.

Unit 9 Summary

▶ **Creating Web pages on online services:** Online services offer tools to their members so it's easier to create and publish Web pages. In this unit, you learn how to use those tools in America Online, CompuServe, and Prodigy Internet. When I wrote this book, Microsoft Network couldn't publish Web pages.

Part IV Test

The questions on this test cover all the material presented in Part IV (Units 8 and 9).

True False

T   F   1. WYSIWYG is pronounced wizzy-wig.

T   F   2. In a WYSIWYG program you never have to see the HTML code.

T   F   3. Adobe PageMill is the most recent Web-page-creation product to come to the market.

T   F   4. Site management has to do with ISP construction projects.

T   F   5. Corel Web.Graphics Suite comes with 15 different programs.

T   F   6. Client-side image maps are harder to create than server-side image maps.

T   F   7. Netscape Composer is always free.

T   F   8. Microsoft FrontPad is always free.

T   F   9. Some word processors can help with some very basic Web page creation.

T   F   10. The Web page creation tool that comes with America Online is called Personal Publisher.

T   F   11. America Online has some additional Web publishing plans if you want more than a basic Web page with basic service.

T   F   12. Prodigy Classic has the best Web publishing tools of all the Prodigy services.

Multiple Choice

For each of the following questions, circle the correct answer or answers. Some questions may have more than one right answer, so read all the answers carefully.

13. Adobe PageMill incorporates

A. File-translation tools

B. Site-management tools

C. A vacation to Hawaii

D. A taskbar

14. A taskbar is

A. A place where getting a drink is a real chore

B. A row of function buttons at the top of the screen of a program

C. Sometimes called a toolbar

D. None of the above

15. Which of the following programs include site management tools?

A. PageMill

B. FrontPage

C. Fusion

D. FrontPad

16. CompuServe's Web page creation tools include

A. Home Page Wizard

B. Publishing Wizard

C. An FTP Program

D. All of the above

17. **Microsoft Network**

    A. Includes all the bells and whistles

    B. Is missing Online Service basics like Web publishing capabilities

    C. Is the best way to publish on the Web

    D. Offers lots of hand-holding for Web page creation

Matching

18. **Match each product to the company that offers it:**

A. My Internet Business Page	1. Netscape
B. Publishing Wizard	2. MySoftware
C. Composer	3. Claris
D. HomePage	4. CompuServe

19. **Match the acronym with the phrase it stands for:**

A. WYSIWYG	1. Why Do I Have To Do This Test
B. WYSIABOCTYHWR	2. What You See Is What You Get
C. WDIHTDTT	3. Because I Want To Check Your Alphabet Skills
D. BIWTCYAS	4. What You See Is a Bunch of Code That You Hope Works Right

Part IV Lab Assignment

This Lab Assignment gives you a choice of two assignments, based on whether you'll be using a Web page editing program. By now, if you're going to buy a Web page editing program that helps you with Web page design, you should already have done your shopping. But before you design your own Web page, here's what I want you to do for a little practice:

Step 1: Use the program to go through the Unit 8 steps

Go through all the steps that I've outlined in Unit 8. In other words, design a table, add a head, do all that stuff.

Step 2: Sit back and contemplate your work

Don't post the page you create. I just want you to go through the steps so you can get used to the tool you're using.

If you don't think you'll be using a Web page editing program but you've got an account with an online service, you should familiarize yourself with those tools. Do this exercise:

Step 1: Open your standard Lab Assignment Web page

Open the same Web page design that you've been using in the past Lab Assignments.

Step 2: Use the online tools to design that same exact page

Again, you may not want to post this page. Just do it for practice.

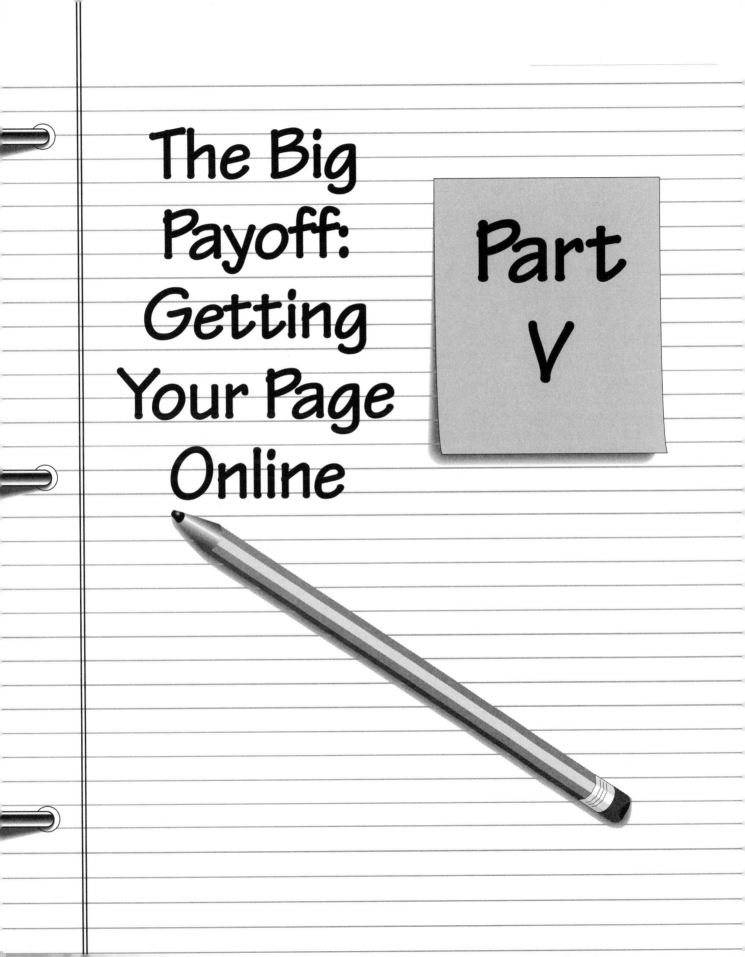

The Big Payoff: Getting Your Page Online

Part V

In this part . . .

In Part IV, you learned everything you need to know about putting your Web page online with one of the big commercial online services. Using a major service provider is a perfectly acceptable way to go, especially if you're uploading a personal Web page. However, if you're putting up a business Web page, exploring the possibility of hooking up with an Internet Service Provider (ISP) for your Web hosting is probably a good idea. Even if you're not putting up a business page, your ISP can offer some extra flexibility and benefits that the online services can't. Before you make a decision one way or another, work through Unit 10 to see what's involved with taking the ISP route to the Information Superhighway. In this unit, I also tell you a little of what it takes to set up your own server, although I don't recommend that for most of you.

If you don't use a commercial online service, you have another problem: getting all of the files for your fantastic work of cyberart from your computer to somewhere the rest of the world can get to them. How? You need to put your files on the Web server of your ISP or online service. For most people, this procedure means using *File Transfer Protocol* (FTP), which is the Internet protocol for moving whole files around on the Internet. This procedure isn't extremely difficult, but you do need to follow all the steps to the letter if you want the whole thing to work right. FTP is covered in Unit 11. Oh, but you know that. You're a smart cookie. After all, you bought this book and now you want to buy copies to give to all your friends and family as gifts. Right?

Getting Space on a Web Server

Objectives for This Unit

✓ Understanding what a Web server does

✓ Learning what a domain name is and how to register your own

✓ Evaluating different ISPs and what they have to offer

✓ Using other services offered by your ISP

✓ Preparing for the launch of your Web site

✓ Setting up your own Web server

Prerequisites

▶ You should have some Internet Web publishing skills and lingo down. How much? If you understand this sentence, you've got it: "The HTML in my Web page produced some 404 errors until I created a new index.htm file."

By now, your Web page should be just about finished — if not in final HTML code, then in basic design. In other words, you should have a pretty good idea of what your Web site consists of. (Remember, though, as I said in earlier units, your Web page is never finished.) Now you need to find a safe, happy home for your page. Perhaps you've already posted your page on a commercial online service. Keep in mind, oh wondrous student, that the beauty of the Web is that nothing is permanent unless you want it to be. If you try out one online service and don't find it to your liking, you can switch easily to another online service, or to an ISP. On the Web, you have complete freedom (unlike some of those fast-food restaurants that want you to think you can have it your way, and then someone behind the counter tells you otherwise). Like, who's the customer here?

Lesson 10-1   # Exactly What Is a Server, Anyway?

on the test

I use the term *Web server* many times throughout this book, and, just from the context, you probably already have a basic idea of what a Web server is. In short, a Web server is a computer (your computer, your ISP's computer, your online service's computer) that houses your Web site and makes your site available to any computer on the World Wide Web.

on the test

To accomplish this amazing feat, the Web server must run special Web server software. This software acts as the agent between your Web page and the rest of the world. When a user types your Web address in the Web browser, that request routes through this software, which in turn decides which Web page of yours the person wants to look at. The server software then finds that Web page and *serves* it to the person who requested it. The concept is amazing when you picture that someone in Japan can type in a few characters and that a Web server in Boise, Idaho, knows that the request is for a Web page on its server within a few seconds. This request may route through many Internet *hubs* (major junction points on the Internet), and yet it all happens so quickly. (Although it doesn't feel so quick when an image on a page freezes at 35 percent of 125K.)

All of this information travels back and forth through various types of phone lines, and many factors can affect the speed at which the information moves. Of course, the speed of the computer being used for a Web server makes some difference, but that's minimal. Any computer you're likely to find being used as a Web server is probably fast enough for the job. Other, more significant factors can affect performance.

Phone line fun

on the test

You may be amazed at how many different types of phone lines are available, each with its own maximum speeds. First, if you connect to the Internet through a standard modem, you connect over a regular voice-grade phone line that carries a speed of 33.6 Kbps. Keep in mind that 33.6 Kbps is your *maximum* speed on the Info Superhighway. If there is any *noise* on the line (what you would call a "bad connection" on a voice call), your 33.6 Kbps modem makes its connection at a lower speed to make up for the extra trouble of handling the line noise.

Notice that I said 33.6 Kbps is the maximum speed of a voice line, even though 56 Kbps modems are beginning to appear on the market. These 56 Kbps modems actually use some technical trickery to move data *to you* that fast. When you send out any data, you're still limited to the true 33.6 Kbps line speed. Again, that 56 Kbps coming in to you is only under optimum line conditions.

The next step up from regular phone lines is Integrated Services Digital Network, or *ISDN*. With an ISDN phone line, you can achieve a maximum rate of 128 Kbps, twice that of those new 56 Kbps modems. The down side is that an ISDN line is more expensive to install and run than a regular phone line. In addition to hefty up-front charges (installation, special equipment), you

be sure you know the terms here or you may sound like a dope when you talk to someone who knows anything about the Internet

current FCC regulations limit the download speed to 53 Kbps over regular phone lines

typically get billed by the minute when using an ISDN phone line. You can outlay a hefty chunk of change if you use ISDN to connect to the Internet (in which case, ISDN means, "I Should Disconnect Now").

Beyond ISDN, there are several different "industrial strength" phone lines, such as Frame Relay, T1 and T3. So far, I've talked about line speeds in terms of kilobits, or thousands of bits, per second. These high-speed, industrial strength lines are measured in terms of *megabits*, or millions of bits, per second. Suffice it to say that such lines are all very fast data lines — and they are also very expensive. I have a T1 line in my office that took the phone company three months to install. I wasn't very happy.

The point here is that any connection to your Web site is only as fast as the slowest line between your Web server and the person who wants to look at your page. For example, suppose your Web server connects to the Internet *backbone* (the series of hubs that form the basic skeleton of the Internet) via a T1 line. The backbone consists of extremely high-speed lines, as well. Then suppose that your visitor's ISP connects to the Internet via a T1 line, as well. Finally, your visitor dials into the ISP using a 28.8 Kbps modem. Obviously, no matter how fast the interim lines are, your pages can travel to that visitor's computer at only 28.8 Kbps, max. Figure 10-1 illustrates this point. On a side note: If you'd like to know more about the Internet's technical workings, there are numerous university sites on the Internet for your browsing pleasure.

Battling traffic jams

on the test

No matter how fast your connection to the Internet is, other things can slow you down. Conditions are seldom optimum, due in large part to the fact that you're not the only person on the Internet. As more people get online and attempt to make connections around the world, the more traffic that you'll have to bear. And the Information Super Highway is just like any other highway: Too much traffic can jam things up.

A good example of what can happen with too much traffic comes from the so-called cable modems that some cable television carriers around the country are beginning to offer. Using these special modems, cable companies can connect you to the Internet over the same lines used to connect your television to your local cable system. Under ideal conditions, a cable modem is many times faster than even the fastest phone lines. But cable modems are a shared medium. If you are the only person in town to subscribe to the modem service with your cable company, you probably have a mighty fast connection. However, as more of your neighbors begin subscribing to the service (and competing for the cable's bandwidth), the performance on your system will drop.

Don't get me wrong. I'm not slamming cable modems. I'm just using them as an example. Assuming your cable carrier is competent, you get performance far superior to a standard modem, even if everybody on your block signs up for a cable modem. So if you are first on your block with a cable connection, and your neighbors ask you if you're happy with the service, tell them, "No, it's very slow." That's just a joke. You know the spirit of the Internet is sharing. Speaking of sharing, Figure 10-2 shows a hot site where you can get the latest scoop on cable modems (http://www.cablemodems.com).

even if you have a very fast connection to the Internet, high traffic and phone-line conditions can slow you down

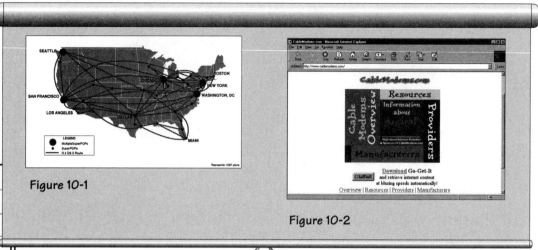

Figure 10-1: The Information Superhighway can be a long and winding road. UUNet is a company that makes it possible.

Figure 10-2: For the latest developments in cable modems, look on the Internet.

Figure 10-1

Figure 10-2

For the record, a regular modem isn't a shared service. If you have a 33.6Kbps modem, your connection to the Internet is the same. Of course, what the traffic is like once you get out to the Web can vary.

You and your server

Maybe you're the computer guru in your neighborhood and you're thinking of setting up your own server. Or maybe you're considering setting up a Web server at your place of business so that the availability of your Web site doesn't hinge on the success or failure of any ISP. The good news is that you can do that. The bad news is that you probably don't want to. Here's why.

For starters, you need a computer dedicated to the task. Just about any Pentium or Macintosh PowerPC system can serve as a foundation for a reasonable Web server. But you may want more than just a reasonable server. Although a server can be just a middle-of-the-road Pentium with 32MB of RAM, having one that's beefed up with plenty of RAM (at least 64MB) and hard drive space (2GB or more) is best. The server that runs my Web page is a 166MHz Pentium with 64MB of RAM, a 2GB hard drive, a 2GB tape backup drive, a 3Com Ether Link III 3C509B-COMBO network card, a Cisco 2501 router, ADC Kentrox D-Serve T1, a 10BaseT Ethernet Hub (which varies, depending on the number of users in the office), and a 3Com Office Connect Hub/TPC8.

You also need the server software. While there are some reasonably priced packages out there, you'd *better* be the neighborhood computer guru because you also need the expertise to install, run, and maintain this software. Of course, you're not going to plug into the Internet through your modem port. You need some special network equipment between you and the Internet. The software I have on my server includes Windows NT 4.0, Microsoft Internet Information Server 3.0, PCanywhere32 V7.5, and Post Office Email Server.

☑ Progress Check

If you can do the following, you've mastered this lesson:

❑ You know basically how a Web server works.

❑ You know the two things that can have a negative impact on access speed.

❑ You understand that setting up your own server is a monumental task and is probably the right move for only a very small number of people.

If you want to make sure your Web site is always available, it wouldn't hurt to have two of these systems, so the second can take over if and when the first one fails. Notice I say, "when." It's like that old joke about the British car, the Jaguar: You have to buy two — one to drive while the other is in the shop.

Then there's the issue of the phone lines, which you already know something about. Obviously, you can't connect your server to the Web with a 33.6 Kbps modem. How about an ISDN line? An ISDN line connection is technically possible, but if your site gets any action at all, ISDN is way too slow. ISDN would then mean, "It Slows Down to Nothing." Nope. If you want a respectable connection to the Internet, you have to spring for at least a T1 line.

How much can a T1 line cost? Well, I'll skip the installation costs (which are pretty stiff) and cut right to the monthly charges. For a T1 line, the fee is easily $1,000 or more per month. And exactly what do you connect that T1 line to? The answer is an Internet Service Provider, the very people you thought you could avoid by setting up your own server. Sorry.

Maybe your company already has a high-speed Internet connection. What then? Well, you don't have to worry about the connection part, but the other issues are still there. Is your company willing to invest the time and money in equipment and staff required to keep a Web server running smoothly? Why go to all that trouble when you're likely to just duplicate the efforts of the ISP that you're going to connect to anyway? The ISP has the trained staff and (hopefully) the state-of-the-art equipment. Let the ISP staff do what they do best, and you do what you do best — which is creating and maintaining a useful and engaging Web site.

> you can set up your own server, but it may be too much of a hassle to bother with (and you may need a second mortgage to pay for it)

What's in a Domain Name?   Lesson 10-2

If you're going to put up a business site — and perhaps even if you're not — you should consider getting your own *domain name*. Sounds important. It should. It is. Your domain name is your company's Internet name. For example, my company's domain name is komando.com. You can get to my company's Web page by typing in www.komando.com using your favorite Web browser, and you can send me e-mail by typing komando@komando.com using your favorite e-mail program. As you can see, the common denominator here is komando.com.

So what?

Maybe you're wondering why you need your own domain name. To be frank, it's a combination of vanity and common sense. From the vanity standpoint, having your own domain name gives you a little stature on the Internet. (Maybe very little, but every little bit helps.) Your domain name says to the

Notes:

registering your
own domain name
makes it easier
for people to find
you on the
Internet
(especially
important if you
put up a business
site)

world, "Hey, I'm my own entity out here on the Internet and beholden to none." Even if that declaration is not true and you're connected via an ISP who *services* the domain name for you, the *perception* remains.

But a domain name also serves a very practical purpose. Suppose for a moment that I never told you my company's domain name, but you knew there was something on my site that you'd find very valuable. (Of course, I'd like to believe that every smidgen of information on my Web site is very valuable.)

If you had to guess at my Web address, what would you guess? The first thing that comes to mind is www.smartbeautiful.com, right? After that, you'd probably guess www.komando.com. If my company's Web address happened to be www.MyISP.com/~komando, for example, it would be a lot harder for people to find my site. I've found many, many company Web sites simply by typing the company name in the standard Web address format (for example, www.adobe.com, www.microsoft.com, and www.motorola.com).

In the next section, you figure out how to discover whether somebody else is already using your desired domain name.

Just in the InterNIC of time

A Web address is like a phone number. If everyone in town could select his or her own phone number, there would undoubtedly be some duplicates and your local phone system would get really fouled up. So it stands to reason that no two entities (companies, individuals, organizations, and so on) can use the same domain name. The responsibility to make sure this doesn't happen by approving and keeping track of all domain names in use rests with an organization called InterNIC — at least, until InterNIC's contract runs out in 1998.

When you want to *register* your domain name with InterNIC, you send them an e-mail message formatted in a very specific way that includes all of the information that InterNIC needs to complete your request. The formatting, which I cover shortly, is very important because a real person doesn't process your request (as opposed to a fake person, like actors, lawyers, insurance salespeople, and politicians. Was I too harsh? Sorry).

Instead, the computer at InterNIC reads through your e-mail, pulls out the information it needs and then processes your request automatically. Without the proper formatting in your e-mail message, the computer cannot find the information it's looking for. Those pesky computers.

The initial cost to register a domain name is currently $100, which covers you for two years. After that, you receive an annual bill (by e-mail) from InterNIC for $50. Obviously, you can't send a check for $100 by e-mail, so you must return your payment by regular surface mail. Remember that. If you fail to pay your bill, InterNIC simply "turns off" your domain name, and you vanish from cyberspace without a trace.

Naturally, you don't want to waste time registering a domain name that somebody has already taken. If you do, InterNIC rejects your application, and you have to start all over again.

extra credit

Tips for choosing a domain name

Selecting the right domain name can be a little tricky. On one hand, you want to keep things brief so there aren't too many characters to type. On the other hand, you don't want to be too cryptic, either. You want your domain name to be at least somewhat obvious.

If you're considering a domain name for your personal Web page, you may want to think about using your whole name. For example, you can use *johndoe.com*, or maybe *john-doe.com*. Obviously, you can't have the same domain name as someone else. However, because individuals don't commonly register their own domain names, you may find your name unused (as described in the next section), even if you have a fairly common name. But hurry. Every `www.tom`, `www.dick`, and `www.harry` is reading this book too.

For a company domain name, you can apply these same basic guidelines. If the company name consists of one or two words, use them as the domain name. If the company name is longer, consider using initials. The only problem is that if your company name consists of pretty common words, a company with a similar name has probably already registered the same domain name. InterNIC doles out domain names on a strictly first come, first serve basis. Al's Tow and Transmission certainly couldn't get `www.att.com`.

What about the `.com` part? Choosing the extension that's appropriate is up to you.

In the United States, the four common domain name extensions are:

▶ `.com` (for commercial organizations)

▶ `.net` (an alternate often used by telecommunication companies and other networking businesses)

▶ `.org` (used by non-commercial organizations)

▶ `.gov` (reserved for use by government agencies)

But in May 1997, a group of Internet heavyweights (the International Ad Hoc Committee, or IAHC, which you can reach at `http://www.iahc.com`) met in Geneva and agreed on a list of seven new domain extensions:

▶ `.firm` (for businesses)

▶ `.store` (for companies selling products)

▶ `.web` (for sites emphasizing the World Wide Web)

▶ `.arts` (for cultural sites)

▶ `.info` (for information services)

▶ `.nom` (for individuals)

▶ `.rec` (for recreational services)

The new naming system will take time to become stable. But don't wait. Register your domain name today!

If you want to check on a domain name ahead of time, follow these steps:

1 **Point your Web browser to** `http://rs.internic.net/cgi-bin/whois`.

2 **In the box at the top of the page where it says,** *Type in your target string (i.e., "example.com") or "help,"* **type the name of the domain you'd like to register.**

3 **Press the Enter key on your keyboard.**

Up pops the results of your search on a new Web page. Figure 10-3 shows what this Web page looks like.

Notes:

If your domain name is already taken, detailed information about the current owner of the domain name appears on your screen. If the name is not in use, you find that out, too. See Figure 10-4 for an example.

But don't forget; even though you can't have the exact same domain name as someone else, you can have a similar one. For example, if your company is ABC Business Services and you discover that `abc.com` is already registered (in this case by ABC Television), try abcbiz.com or something similar.

By visiting InterNIC's Web site at `http://www.internic.net`, you can get everything you need to register your own domain name. On the main page, look for the link to Registration Services. The process involves filling in all sorts of information in a preformatted document that InterNIC calls a *template*. Figure 10-5 shows you the steps outlined at the InterNIC site that you need to take to register a domain. But because the steps happen on the Internet, it's real easy.

Assuming you fill out the template with all the correct information in all the correct places, InterNIC's computer processes your application automatically. You don't even need to know who is going to service your domain name (which ISP you're going to use) to get it registered and make sure that nobody else sneaks in ahead of you. However, if you do register your domain name before you know who your ISP is, you need to send in a new completed template later to tell InterNIC exactly who is servicing your domain name.

heads up

I recommend that you take the time to carefully go through the instructions and other information on the InterNIC Web site. As you do, you may get the feeling that registering your domain name is a complicated process — and it is, to some extent. Some ISPs may help you out and register your domain name for you. Should you let them? There are pros and cons.

On the pro side, it's *professional* to have your ISP help you. You can (presumably) be assured that the template is filled out correctly. Your ISP may just ask you for the information, or they may have you fill out the template yourself. Either way, the ISP is likely to check out the template before forwarding it on to InterNIC. This check-up assures you a greater probability of success on the first go-around.

On the other hand, some greedy ISPs have been known to charge exorbitant fees for this service. An ISP usually includes the registration fee in the cost (currently $100) and then adds a little for their effort. So exactly how much "extra" is appropriate to fill out and e-mail a form that shouldn't take more than 10 minutes to complete? In the long run, you need to be the judge, but in my opinion, anything more than $25 to $35, and you're being *conned*.

heads up

An ISP normally includes the registration fee in the cost and forwards the appropriate funds to InterNIC after the ISP receives your payment. However, after the two years covered by that first payment, the annual bill goes directly to you, not your ISP. Don't expect the ISP to handle this for you; they won't even know the bill has come. When you get your annual billing from InterNIC, you need to pay it yourself.

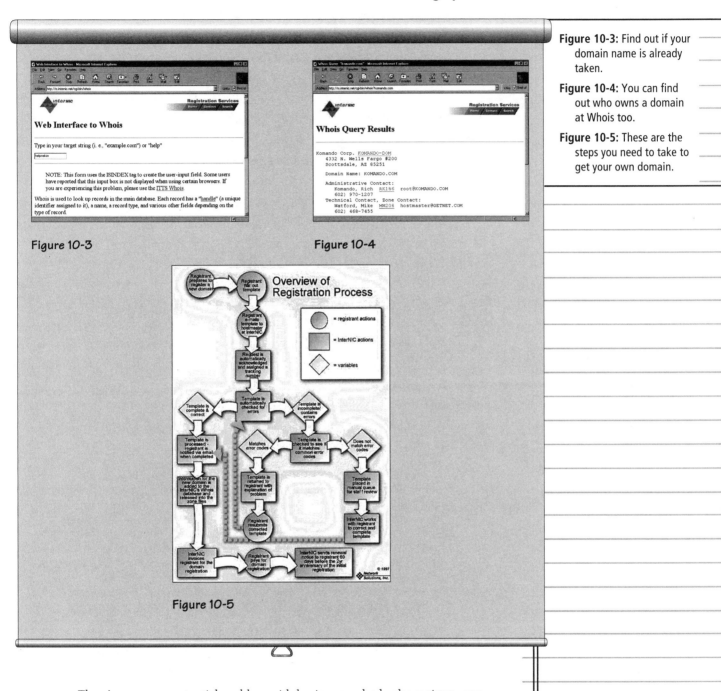

Figure 10-3: Find out if your domain name is already taken.

Figure 10-4: You can find out who owns a domain at Whois too.

Figure 10-5: These are the steps you need to take to get your own domain.

Figure 10-3

Figure 10-4

Figure 10-5

There's one more potential problem with having somebody else register your domain name. After a person registers a domain name, only the registered owner can make any changes to that domain name. See the potential problem?

heads up

A good ISP makes sure that you are the registered owner of your domain name. However, some less-than-honest ISPs have registered themselves as the owners of their customer's domain name. So what happens when you finally realize that this ISP isn't worth your trouble and decide to switch your domain

Notes:

if your ISP registers
your domain name
for you, be sure
the ISP designates
you as the
registered owner
of your domain
name

you can also use
your domain name
in your e-mail
address, assuming
your ISP is on the
ball ... check with
your ISP to find
out exactly how
this works

name over to a more reputable ISP? Oh, no! Suddenly you find that you can't change your domain name over to a new ISP, because as far as InterNIC is concerned, you don't own that domain name. This means that your current ISP can basically extort some sort of conversion fee from you to turn over to you the domain name that's rightfully yours anyway.

If this situation happens, don't think about going to InterNIC with your complaints. This organization intentionally stays neutral over domain name disputes. You have to work out the matter with the ISP or, failing all else, you may have to get an attorney involved. Since online law is a relatively new field, I can only suggest that if you have to find a lawyer, find one with some experience regarding online issues.

Using your domain name

on the test

Registering a domain name doesn't do you a bit of good if you can't use it. After you register your domain name, you have to make sure that, in addition to the other items I cover in the next section, your ISP can provide *virtual domain hosting*. This magic makes folks who visit your Web page think you have your own server but you really don't.

In the old days of the Web, every domain name had to have its own dedicated server. Today, though, most ISPs can host lots of domain names. This means that when people type in `www.YourDomainName.com`, they can get to your Web page even though your Web site resides on the ISPs server along with hundreds of others.

When you sign up with your ISP, you select a user name. For instance, say your user name is `kim` and your ISP's domain name is `isp.com`. This makes your real e-mail address `kim@isp.com`. However, if your domain name is `MyDomainName.com`, then e-mail would also get to you if it was addressed to `kim@MyDomainName.com`. Using one method, your ISP may ensure that any mail that's addressed to `kim@MyDomainName.com` really goes to `kim@isp.com`, and mail to any other user name `@MyDomainName.com` goes to whoever has that user name with that ISP. If someone addresses e-mail to `bob@MyDomainName.com`, then `bob@isp.com` (assuming there is such a person) gets that e-mail, even if he has nothing to do with your company.

The other option for your ISP is to have any e-mail that uses your domain name go directly to you, regardless of the specified user name. For example, e-mail can be addressed to `mary@MyDomainName.com`, `fred@MyDomainName.com`, or `rocko@MyDomainName.com` and it would all come directly to you. If you rely on this method to let several people in your company use a single e-mail account, you must sort the incoming e-mail. I touch on this a little more in the next section.

Recess

And now, boys and girls, it's time for Kim Komando's 10th inning stretch! Stand up and sing along!

> *Take me out to the Do-main.*
> *Take me out to the com.*
> *Buy me some e-mail and I-S-P.*
> *I don't care*
> *How much it costs me!*
>
> *For it's root, root, root for the home page.*
> *If it's not up it's a shame.*
> *You get just one chance,*
> *So hurry-to-register*
> *Your own name!*

Crowd cheers. Now sit down and take the progress check.

☑ **Progress Check**

If you can do the following, you've mastered this lesson:

❏ Identify what a domain name is and how to use it.

❏ Understand and explain how and why domain names are registered with InterNIC.

❏ Resolve not to get ripped off if you decide to have somebody else register your domain name.

What to Look for in an ISP

Lesson 10-3

ISPs come in two basic flavors: big, national companies such as Microsoft Network and PSI, or smaller, local companies like the ones you're likely to find listed in your local Yellow Pages. In addition to all the other considerations in the rest of this lesson, there are some things that set the big guys apart from the little guys, and these may or may not be important to you.

on the test

The two main benefits of going with one of the big guys are ease of use and national coverage. When I say ease of use, I mean that most of the big companies have developed automated installation programs that take a lot of the guesswork out of setting up the software you need to connect to the Internet. For example, many companies offer customized versions of either Netscape Navigator or Microsoft Internet Explorer that can help guide you through the use of that particular ISP. In contrast, many of the smaller ISPs simply provide you with a written set of instructions for installing the various shareware components you need to get online.

When you choose a national ISP, you can also rest assured that you can get online just about no matter where you go in the country — unless your local provider is in Los Angeles, where natural (and unnatural) disasters seem to occur weekly. The reason for such easy access is that the big guys set up local call-in numbers across the country. If you live in Los Angeles, you can't call into the Microsoft Network on the same number when you travel to Orlando, but you can find a local MSN number for Orlando.

on the test

One of the advantages to a local ISP — at least a good local ISP — is better customer service. The local ISP is a member of the community and generally has a more vested interest in keeping other community members satisfied with its service. If you have a problem, you may be able to go in and discuss it face-to-face with a customer service representative, something that generally is not possible with one of the big guys.

A local ISP may often, but not always, offer you a more reliable and flexible service. Because the local company has to deal with only one small geographic region, you never have to worry about going offline because of some natural disaster on the other side of the country. A good local company is also more likely to control its growth in new users, an area where America Online had some problems toward the end of 1996. When AOL got a big boom of new users, there were so many folks trying to get online, you couldn't even get connected.

Finally, because the big service providers are more interested in mass-marketing a consumer product, they're much less likely to provide other services you may want. Such services can include your own FTP site or the ability to set up extra e-mail accounts, and logging on!

The Web hasn't been around that long, so you're not going to find any ISP that's been hosting Web sites for more than a couple of years. However, experience still makes a difference. A lot of fly-by-night ISPs (FBNISPs) are springing up these days, so even two years of experience in hosting Web sites is a positive indicator for a local ISP. One thing you won't find is Ted's ISP: In Business for Over a 50th of a Century. And if you do, run. They are lying.

heads up

Almost as important as what to look for in an ISP is what to *look out* for. I tell you about a little of both in this section. Whether you decide to go with a national or local provider, make sure you read this section carefully.

Serving up your Web site

As you discover later in this lesson, there are plenty of things to consider when choosing an ISP, many of which depend on your particular situation. But there's one thing that's extremely important, no matter what your situation, and that's how well a given ISP can serve up your pages to everyone else out there on the World Wide Web.

I often hear comments like, "Find out how many T1 lines they have," or, "See what their user-to-dial-in-modem ratio is." The implication here is that the more T1 lines, the better it is. Why? Well, because your pages get served up faster, and the lower this ratio, the less likely you are to encounter the dreaded busy signal when *you* try to dial into the Internet right when you're expecting that critical e-mail. All of this is absolutely true, except for a couple of things. Do you know how many T1 lines are considered "enough?" And do you happen to know what a good modem-to-user ratio is? I didn't think so.

All the facts, figures, and statistics in the world don't tell you as much as one (satisfied or dissatisfied) user. Your first course of action when evaluating any ISP should be to get input from some of its current customers. Most ISPs have some sort of customer directory — at least for their business accounts — that includes clickable links to the customer Web sites.

you may get docked for an extra per-minute charge by an ISP if you use its supposedly toll-free number to sign on for service

First, try out a couple of these sites for yourself. See if performance is acceptable when you access their Web site just as someone else would access yours. If the ISP passes muster at this point, contact the ISP's customers directly by e-mail (using the e-mail link that's most likely included on their Web page). When people have very good or very bad experiences, they're usually willing to talk about them. All you have to do is ask.

on the test

After you're satisfied that you've found a reasonably good ISP, you need to start considering other practical matters:

▶ **What does the ISP charge to host your Web site?** Most ISPs charge a flat monthly rate. This rate includes storage of a certain number of megabytes of your files and also a certain amount of traffic on your site. Traffic is the amount of activity on your site, and is measured in terms of how many megabytes of data the server serves up from your site each month. This all means that there are two variables here that can cause your supposed flat rate to fluctuate: traffic and disk space.

For example, if you're allotted 5MB of disk space for your files (which should be enough for most beginning efforts), but you discover that for some reason your files take up 6MB, the ISP still lets you put your site online, but you get charged a little extra. The charge probably isn't much, based on the amount you go over, but if you have a very large site, this may be an issue to consider.

Traffic charges can vary from one month to the next. Suppose your Web site takes up 1MB and you're allowed 50MB worth of traffic each month. That means that the first 50 people who visit your site don't cost you anything extra. But when visitor number 51 accesses your Web site, you begin racking up extra charges based on the extra traffic. This can be a large or small concern, based on whether you expect lots of visitors.

▶ **Will the ISP give you easy access to your files via FTP?** FTP doesn't stand for Fix This Page. It's the computer acronym for File Transfer Protocol, and you'll learn a lot more about that in the next unit. For now, just know that FTP is a way of downloading (or transferring) files from a computer on the Internet to your computer and vice versa. (A *protocol*, by the way, is an agreed-upon set of standards for doing something.) FTP makes sure that the file you copy to your computer arrives in perfect condition. Of course, you can use FTP to upload (or send) a file to another computer. For you, the Web page creator guru, this means that you can log on and update your Web site instantly. If an ISP forces you to use some other, slower and less efficient method for updating and adding to your site — like forcing you to send your files on floppy disk — I suggest you just keep on lookin'. Other slow methods to update your files include relaying the updates to someone on the phone, using carrier pigeons, and letting visitors guess.

▶ **Finally, can your ISP provide you with numbers on how many people are accessing your Web site?** When your site is up and running, you'll want to know if anyone is actually using it. How else can you measure its success? Your ISP should be able to give you the numbers. Some ISPs e-mail reports on a daily basis. Others provide you with online software tools to gather and analyze the information.

Notes:

if you get a lot of traffic to your Web site, your ISP may charge you more

make sure your ISP
offers some means
for you to monitor
your site's activity

many ISPs won't let
you use your free
personal Web pages
for business
purposes

signing any kind of
long-term contract
with your ISP is not
a good idea

Pricing and terms

How much should you expect to pay for sticking your Web page on somebody else's server and letting that server do its thing? The answer depends on the type of Web page you put up.

If you upload a personal page, your ISP may include hosting services with the cost of your Internet connection. This type of free Web page usually has some limitations. Typically, you're pretty limited in how much disk space you can use up. And you're also limited in what you can use the page for. Many ISPs prohibit the use of free personal Web pages for business purposes. Your ISP figures if that you're going to profit from being on the Web, they should profit from your profit. Hey, it's capitalism — what can you do?

The standard monthly cost of a personal Internet account these days — with or without a personal Web page — is around $20 for unlimited access. At this price point, you can go online whenever you want and stay online for as long as you want. If you want to publish only a personal Web page, just make sure that you look for an ISP that does indeed offer free personal Web pages. Note, however, that if you have registered your own domain name, you probably can't use your domain name with one of these free accounts.

The business account, however, is an entirely different matter. You pay extra for a business account, but you get more, too. You get more disk space. You get to use your own domain name, if you have one. You may even get some professional Web development assistance from your ISP. Prices for business services may range from $50 to $100 per month or more. (However, if you go higher than $100 a month, you should take a very close look at what you're getting for your money.)

on the test

The one thing you should never, ever do is agree to a long-term contract — no matter how attractive the price is. Suppose a new ISP shows up in town and offers unlimited Internet access, including hosting your Web page, for $10 per month. One of two things may happen.

First, there's a good chance that this price is too low to allow for a reasonable profit for the ISP. That means that the ISP may function like a pyramid scheme, relying on new members to pay the way for old members. Eventually, the ISP maxes out, files bankruptcy, and then you are left without an ISP. Assuming you're the registered owner of your domain name, you can switch to another ISP easily enough, but it may take a couple of weeks based on InterNIC's backlog. If you weren't using your own domain name, your entire Web address changes to reflect your new provider.

But just suppose that $10 really is a reasonable price for both you and your ISP. (Maybe you're on the ground floor of the pyramid.) If you've followed computer technology at all, you know that the tendency is for prices to go down. So what happens if a year from now, your ISP lowers prices to $5 per month and you still have two years left on your three-year contract? You'll be paying double what everybody else is, that's what!

No matter how you look at it, I really believe that anything other than a month-to-month agreement is a cyberdisaster just waiting to happen. For a sampling of actual pricing plans from ISPs around the country, see Appendix A.

The extras

So you've found a reliable ISP that can host your Web site at a price you're willing to live with. Is that really enough? It depends on you and your particular situation. If you're satisfied with just putting up your Web page and letting the page take its course, that's fine. However, you may want to consider other related services.

You already learned about virtual domain hosting in the previous lesson. If you want to use your own domain name, it's essential. And using your own name is also something that you may have to pay extra for. Check with your ISP to be sure.

What about e-mail? Any ISP includes one e-mail account with your service, but what if you need more? If you need three separate e-mail accounts, do you have to pay three times as much money — even if only one person has access to the account at any given time? Check with your ISP.

Many ISPs allow you to set up extra e-mail accounts (called *POP, or Post Office Protocol, accounts*) that don't include any Internet access or other features. You must dial in to your ISP using your regular account, and then check the e-mail for all three accounts while you're logged on. Popular e-mail programs such as Qualcomm's Eudora and Claris Emailer make it easy to check multiple e-mail accounts during a single online session. If you have the latest version of Microsoft Office that includes Microsoft Outlook, you can also check multiple-mail accounts too. You still pay a monthly charge for extra POP accounts, but the fee is small compared to the cost of a "full access" account.

Extra e-mail accounts are handy even if you're the only person involved with your Web site. For example, say you want to use a second e-mail account to handle what's called an *auto-responder*. Anyone who wants general information about your company can send e-mail to a different e-mail address. Any time mail comes addressed to that account, the auto-responder replies with a pre-typed message containing whatever information you want. Both of the e-mail programs I mention in the preceding paragraph can handle this process.

You also need multiple e-mail addresses if you want to run any sort of Internet *mailing list* from your computer. A mailing list is an e-mail-based discussion group. Assuming that you have the correct software on your computer, people can send e-mail to a POP account handled by that software. In turn, that software automatically distributes a copy of the message to everyone else who has subscribed to the mailing list. To run this type of program, you need two extra POP accounts: one for people to send their messages to and one to handle administrative tasks, such as subscriptions and cancellations.

Notes:

most ISPs include "lite" versions of popular e-mail programs within their membership kits

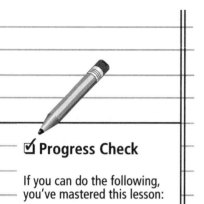

☑ Progress Check

If you can do the following, you've mastered this lesson:

❑ Explain the differences between local and national ISPs.

❑ Evaluate and compare different ISPs.

❑ List other services you may need from your ISP.

Do you plan to offer downloadable files? You need space on your ISP's FTP server to store those files. You can then create links on your Web page that automatically download the files to your visitor's computer system. Just as some ISPs offer free Web pages for personal accounts, some also have free FTP drop boxes where you can put downloadable files for personal accounts. As usual, though, if you have a business account, you're going to have to pay a few dollars extra each month for this service.

Last, do you plan to offer products for sale online? If so, you need to think about how you're going to get paid for these products. There are dozens of online payment options — ways to move funds from the buyer to the seller over the Internet — available today. Of course, like everything on the Web, some payment options are better than others are, but they all have their merits. The real problem is that none of these online payment options are compatible with each other. You pick one and miss out on anyone who prefers one of the others.

For the time being, there's not much you can do about the incompatibility. However, you can look for an ISP that offers some sort of online payment processing directly to its clients. This way, you avoid all the trouble of having to evaluate and experiment with different options on your own. Your ISP can take care of all that for you.

There's plenty to think about when you're choosing an ISP. Just remember that the ISP that's right for your neighbor is not necessarily the one that's right for you. Shop around and get just the right mix of features, pricing and reliability.

Unit 10 Quiz

Select the best answer(s) for each question.

1. **A Web server . . .**

   A. Lets you connect to the World Wide Web from your home

   B. Makes your Web pages available on the World Wide Web

   C. Lets you connect to the World Wide Web from your office

   D. Eliminates the need for FTP

2. **A hub on the Internet . . .**

   A. Acts as a major junction for the Internet

   B. Is the phone line that connects your home to the Internet

   C. Is the connection between the Web server and the FTP server

   D. Allows you to use an ISDN line

3. **The maximum true data speed over a standard voice telephone line is . . .**

   A. 28.8 Kbps   C. 56 Kbps

   B. 33.6 Kbps   D. 128 Kbps

4. **Your domain name can be just about . . .**

   A. Anything you want

   B. Anything you want, as long as it's not being used

   C. Anything you want, as long as you're willing to pay a higher fee

   D. Anything you want, as long as your ISP agrees

5. **The initial cost to InterNIC for your own domain name is . . .**

   A. $100   C. For two years only

   B. Often included in the   D. Whatever you feel like paying
      fee charged by your ISP

6. **If you're a business or individual, what should you use for a domain name extension?**

   A. `.com` or `.org`   C. `.net` or `.com`

   B. `.org` or `.gov`   D. `.net` or `.org`

7. **If you plan to use your domain name on your ISP's system . . .**

   A. You're out of luck

   B. You need a service called virtual domain hosting

   C. You need an ISDN line

   D. You need a national ISP

8. **When you use a national ISP, you get . . .**

   A. Nationwide access   C. Better service

   B. Greater ease of use   D. A free trip to the national headquarters

9. **When you use a local ISP, you get . . .**

   A. More personalized service

   B. Greater flexibility

   C. A pre-arranged meeting with the company president

   D. A care basket delivered to you at home

10. **Two things that can affect the cost of Web hosting are . . .**

    A. Distance to server and amount of line noise

    B. Modem speed and bandwidth

    C. Bert and Ernie

    D. Amount of disk space and amount of traffic

11. **When signing up with an ISP, you should . . .**

    A. Insist on a long-term contract

    B. Accept a long-term contract if the price is right

    C. Never sign a long-term contract

    D. Bring your own pen

12. **In addition to Web hosting, you may need . . .**

    A. Multiple e-mail accounts

    B. FTP server access

    C. Online payment services

    D. A couple of aspirin to deal with all these options

Unit 10 Exercise

1. Think carefully about what you plan to do with your Web site and then make a list of all the services you need from your ISP.

2. Go through your local Yellow Pages and make a list of potential ISPs.

3. Scan through some online-related magazines to get the names of some national ISPs.

4. Contact each ISP on your list to see if they have the services you need, and if so, what the cost is.

5. Do some price shopping online and offline.

Exposing Your Site to the World (And Having People Browse It)

Prerequisites
▶ A Web page (Parts II and III)
▶ Space on a Web server (Unit 10)

▶ WS_FTP
▶ Anarchie

on the CD

Objectives for this unit:

✓ Understanding FTP and how it works

✓ Using FTP to upload your site

✓ Making sure your upload was successful

✓ Updating your page

on the test

Exactly how you get your Web page and other documents to your Web server (called *uploading* your files) depends largely on how you create your Web page. For example, if you create your Web page through a commercial online service, your online service may provide special tools for getting your page online. If that's the case, all you need to do to post your Web creation is follow the instructions that the online service provides. Online services can offer even more complete help. For example, if you use Personal Publisher from America Online, that software takes care of everything for you. Personal Publisher puts your files where they need to be and you don't even have to read the first lesson in this unit. (However, I suggest you read this unit anyway. I have more to teach than just Web pages. Besides, you end up with a better understanding of what's going on. Even if you skip the first lesson, be sure you read through the other lessons — they are helpful even if you create your Web page through a commercial service.) And don't skip the unit exercise — it contains a very special Web page offer from me.

Another way to create a Web page is to use one of the programs you read about in Unit 8. All the programs make Web page creation easier, but some of them go an extra step by making it easy to upload your files without ever leaving that program. For example, using the Composer component of Netscape Communicator, you can specify your FTP parameters right in Composer and the program uploads the files for you without any need for a separate FTP program. This program is so smart, it won't upload any files it thinks are too boring. Just kidding. (Hey, you never know what's coming. Until recently, cloning meant only making a knock-off computer.)

on the test

Remember that FTP stands for File Transfer Protocol and is the method, or *protocol,* you use to move files back and forth across the Internet. Even if your Web creation software does include FTP, you need the information in Lesson 11-1 to know exactly what information to enter.

Now, that leaves all the rest of you. Those of you who do not fall into one of the above two categories create your Web pages with either some sort of text editor or with a Web page editor that doesn't have any built-in FTP capabilities. So you folks need to roll up your sleeves and get into the job of uploading your Web pages and all the other supporting files (graphics, and so on) to your ISP's Web server.

if you don't post your Web page through an online service, you may need to use an FTP program

Lesson 11-1 Putting FTP to Work

You need to use a separate FTP program when you post files to your ISP. The sole purpose of an FTP program is to move files back and forth across the Internet. That makes it a natural choice for moving your HTML files onto your ISP's Web server.

on the CD

Okay. So the first thing you need is an FTP program. When you signed up with your ISP, they should have given you some sort of start-up kit, which is typically just a floppy disk or two with a collection of freeware and/or shareware Internet programs. An FTP program should be among those programs. If you can't find the one supplied by your ISP (or if they're so stingy they didn't give you one), check the files that came on this book's CD for a shareware program called WS_FTP or Anarchie. These FTP programs are one of the more popular for Windows users, so I included them for you.

After you have a lock on the FTP program of your liking, you need to get some important information from your ISP. Actually, you probably have some of this information already. After you read through this checklist, though, you can give your ISP a call to make sure you get all the parts you don't have. Your ISP shouldn't have any problem providing you with what you need because every FTP program requires the same information to make a connection — including the FTP features built into programs such as Netscape Composer.

Here's what you need to make an Internet connection:

on the test

▸ **Server Name:** If your ISP is one of the biggies, they may actually have several servers to meet their subscribers' needs. The trick here is that every single server on the entire Internet has a unique name. That's why you need to have the exact name of the server on which your Web page will reside. This tidbit of information lets your FTP program know which server, out of the thousands out there, it needs to connect to. Talk about finding a needle in a haystack! The format for the server name can be as simple as `yourisp.com`.

heads up

The server name can also be a little longer, with one or more extra words at the beginning, each separated by a period (for example, `this.is.yourisp.com`). Whatever it is, make sure you use the server name exactly as it's provided by your ISP. Get one little dot where it shouldn't be, and you're toast.

on the test

▸ **User Name and Password:** When you signed up with your ISP, you selected a user name and password. Your user name is really the same as your online name — it's the name you use in your e-mail address. For example, if your e-mail address is `myname@myisp.com`, then your user name is `myname`.

Your password serves a pretty obvious purpose. It lets your ISP's server know that you're really who you say you are. A password is like the secret handshake of cyberspace. For this reason, it's super important that you keep your password an absolute secret. In fact, while I have the opportunity, ahem, allow me a minute or two to give you my complete password sermon.

My sermon starts with a little secret: I'm smart and computers aren't that smart. Really. They only do what you tell 'em. You know when your mom told you not to open the door to strangers and you could always tell who a stranger was because you could identify people from their voices or by the way they rang the doorbell? Well, computers aren't that sophisticated. All they know is your password. That's how they identify you. So if you tell them that your password is *balloons*, (gee, now I have to change mine) all they know is that the person with your user name should tell give them the word *balloons*. When the computer has that information, it lets you in, right?

heads up

But there's a glitch. Other people can figure out your user name and password. Here's the truth: As scary as it seems, figuring out people's user names and passwords is not that tough.

For example, *password* is about the dumbest word you can use for a password. Lots of people who are new to the online world think they're pretty darn clever by using such an obvious password. They're not. If you use one of these easy-to-guess passwords, you're just asking for trouble. Cybercriminals (often called *hackers*) know all the stupid little tricks people use when they're deciding on passwords.

heads up

Also, don't use regular words that you can find in any English-language dictionary. Programs exist that can run through the entire dictionary one word at a time trying to figure out your password. No, I'm not kidding you. This is serious stuff.

Notes:

*passwords are
important
protection, so
change yours often*

Notes:

on the test

One thing to keep in mind is that passwords are case-sensitive. That means that *arizona* is a completely different password from *ARIZONA* or even from *Arizona*. If you absolutely insist on using a regular word as your password, at least mix up the cases. For example, *expert* probably wouldn't be a very good password; It's too easy to guess. On the other hand, *ExpErT* may take some computer hacker a thousand years to figure out. Of course, he's no *ExpErT*.

If you live in a town that has a sports team — especially a winning sports team — don't change your password to the team name. Surveys have shown that it's not uncommon, for example, for people in Chicago to change their passwords to *Cubs* when the Cubs are doing well. Computer hackers are no idiots; they know these things and will take advantage of you if you fall into such a trap.

heads up

Finally, I strongly suggest you change your password on a regular basis. Even if you select *GilfRExzPQ* as your password and can memorize it so that you don't even have it written down anywhere, there's still always the chance that it can slip out somehow. For example, your FTP program probably allows you to save your password so you don't have to enter it again the next time you connect. It is possible for hackers to get access to that. You can probably go a lifetime with the same password, but when that long-shot incident comes along and you get burned because you didn't change your password, you'll wish you had listened to good, ol' Kim. And don't use *Kim*.

Aren't you relieved that I'm done with my sermon? On to the list of more stuff you need to post your Web page.

on the test

▶ **Directory:** Every FTP program out there allows you to enter the name of a particular directory or folder where you're going to post your Web pages. For most ISPs, you don't need to specify a directory, because the ISP's server can figure out the directory where your files go based on your user name and password. For example, say that you and I both have accounts with the same ISP. When I use my information to connect with my FTP program, I automatically log onto the directory that contains my files. However, when you connect with your FTP program using your user name and password, you automatically log onto the directory that contains your files.

heads up

(I hate to belabor a point, but this is another reason why your password is so important: If someone obtains your password, she can just go into your ISP directory and change your Web page at will.)

Keep in mind that there are no hard and fast rules for how an ISP must operate. Most ISPs don't require a directory name, but everyone is a little different. If your ISP tells you that you need to enter a particular directory name when you connect with your ISP program, then you need to enter a directory name — no ifs, ands, or buts about it. The only way to know for sure is to call your ISP and *ask*.

So now you should have the four things you needs to publish your page on the World Wide Web: the actual files that make up your Web page; an FTP program for copying your files from your computer to your ISP's Web server; the logon information you need to connect to your ISP's server; and a need for completion. Assuming you have all these items assembled and you're ready to go, just follow these simple steps to put your Web page online.

1 Launch your FTP program.

Your FTP program displays an initial screen.

On most Windows and Macintosh systems, launching your FTP program also acts as a trigger that tells you computer to automatically establish a connection to your ISP via your modem. If your computer makes the connection automatically, you can skip to Step 3. Otherwise, follow Step 2.

2 Establish a modem connection to your ISP.

The exact procedures to establish a modem connection vary from computer to computer and from ISP to ISP, as well. If you've been up on the Web millions of times before, this should be a breeze. Otherwise, follow the procedures provided by your ISP and from your modem manufacturer.

3 Enter the logon information (server name, user name, password) for your ISP's server.

Some FTP programs may prompt you for this information as soon as you start the program; with other FTP programs, you may need to select a menu option or click on a button to initiate an FTP connection.

You may see your FTP program flash some messages as it negotiates the connection to your ISP's server. When the program makes a connection, the FTP program displays a list of files currently found in your directory on the server. Believe it or not, making this connection is the toughest part. If you make it through this, you're home free. Otherwise, you can be pulling your hair out while you wait for a connection.

4 Let your FTP program know which files you want to upload.

Identifying the files to upload is another step that varies from program to program. For example, many current programs support "drag and drop." Using d&d, you simply drag the files you want to upload right onto the listing of files on the server and the FTP program automatically uploads those files for you.

With other programs, you may have to select a menu option to start an upload. You may be able to upload several files at one time, or you may have to do them individually.

extra credit

Two ways to FTP

FTP programs transfer files in one of two formats: text or binary. Text is just that — any file that consists only of text characters, including your HTML files. Binary files consist of, well . . . everything else. If a file isn't a text file, it's a binary file.

Most current FTP programs are pretty smart; they can figure out for themselves which type of file they're transferring. However, if your FTP program should happen to ask you how to transfer a particular file, don't question its intelligence, simply tell the program to transfer your HTML files as text and your graphics and other such files as binary.

upload your Web
files as raw
data — otherwise,
your ISP's server
can't understand
them

☑ Progress Check

If you can do the following, you've mastered this lesson:

❏ Gather the information you need to connect to your ISP's server.

❏ Go through the simple steps of posting your page online using an FTP program.

❏ Understand the difference between raw data and encoded data.

Some FTP programs give you the option to use different forms of *encoding* when you upload your files. Different types of encoding apply to different situations. For example, if you want to attach a graphic image to a posting to a *Usenet newsgroup*, you would need to *uuencode* the image. Without getting into a lot of detail, uuencoding is necessary in this situation because the Usenet was originally designed to handle only text messages, and uuencoding gets around this limitation. (Usenet is a portion of the Internet that houses over 20,000 discussion groups called *newsgroups*.)

heads up

So what's my point? Pushy, aren't you? Like I said, many FTP programs have options for different types of encoding. Remember that FTP programs transfer lots of different kinds of files over the Internet, not just files for Web pages. That's why these programs have a bunch of different encoding options. For your Web page to function properly, *you can't use any encoding on any of the files associated with it*. You just want to send the *raw data*: Don't change it with any encoding. If your Web browser is looking for a GIF image, it expects to find a GIF image, not a uuencoded GIF image.

When you upload your Web pages — the actual HTML files that define your Web site — you must upload them as *text only*. When you upload graphics or any multimedia files you may have, you have to be sure that they're not unencoded either.

Lesson 11-2

Making the Final Check

The instant your files hit your ISP's Web server, they're ready to be viewed by anyone on the entire World Wide Web. Here's the moment when you want to crack open that bottle of champagne to celebrate. But before you do, take a minute to check and make sure everything looks right. While you're still connected to your ISP after uploading your Web files, launch your Web browser and try your page out for yourself.

on the test

Right now, go ahead and launch your Web browser and enter in your Web address. Don't settle for just loading your home page. If your site includes other supplemental pages, check them too. Make sure that every single link on your site leads where it's supposed to lead, and make sure that every graphic loads fully with no problems. There's really no excuse for introducing an error-riddled Web site to the world — unless you're making a Web page called `http://www.chaos.com/riddled/mistakes/errors/didn't/even/check.html`.

So what can go wrong? Not much if you follow my instructions throughout this book and you check your work on your own computer using your Web browser. If you don't get the same results on your ISP that you got when you ran your site on your computer, it should be pretty easy to figure out the problem. There are a limited number of things that can be wrong. Let's explore some of the problems you may encounter.

When I enter my Web address, all I see is a list of files

Remember way back when I talked about naming your main page *index.htm* or *index.html*? If you didn't name it properly, your server is going to list all the files in your site, instead of jumping to your home page. This is a pretty easy problem to fix; just rename the file on your system and upload it again. Most FTP programs allow you to change file names in your directory on the server. It's important in this instance that you *don't* take that shortcut. The files on your ISP's server should be an exact duplicate of the files on your own computer. If you don't follow this simple rule, you're likely to run into some major problems when you try to update your site later.

The Web page loads, but the graphics don't load

If the graphics don't load and all you see is a broken-image icon for each graphic (as shown in Figure 11-1), this could be the result of one of two problems. First, did you remember to upload all your images as raw data without any sort of special encoding? If that's the problem, just upload the graphics again using the correct procedure.

Second, on your own computer, did you remember to keep all your graphics in the same folder as your other Web page documents? If you have your graphics in a different folder on your system, but uploaded all your files to the same directory on your ISP's server, the links aren't going to work right.

If that's the problem, you have a little work ahead of you.

1 Move all the graphics into the correct folder on your computer.

2 Edit each Web page and reestablish the links to all those graphics in their new locations.

3 After you're done, upload the HTML files again.

You don't have to upload all the graphics again as well since they're already in the right place on your ISP's server.

My skin's become pale, I recoil at sunlight, and I don't know what day it is

One of two things can cause these symptoms: Either you've been working on your Web page too long, or you're Dracula. If you're not Dracula, take a break and go outside. No, not www.outside.com. Go outdoors and recharge your batteries.

check, double check, and triple check to make sure your Web page is perfect

Figure 11-1: This is what a broken-image icon looks like. If you see this, you know you have some work to do on your graphics.

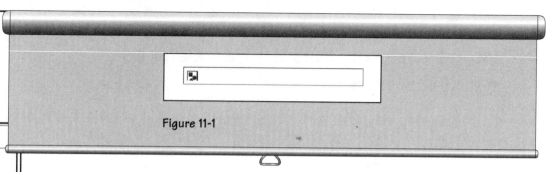

Figure 11-1

My Web browser can't locate the page that a link is supposed to lead to

Before you diagnose this problem, you need to determine whether the link is internal (a link to another page on your site) or external (a link to somebody else's site).

If the link is external, it could be that the site no longer exists. To check this, direct your Web browser to that site manually. If you are still able to get to the site that way, you know you've just miscoded some portion of the link in your Web page. Follow these simple steps:

1 Open the page with the broken link on your computer.

2 Fix the coding.

3 Upload the revised file to your ISP's server.

If you can't get to the site directly from your Web browser either, you know the site is probably gone for good — not all that uncommon in the ever-changing world of cyberspace. If that's the case, open your original file on your system and remove the reference to that link. Hopefully, it's just a stand-alone link. If the link is part of an image map, you have some extra work to do, either creating a new graphic for your image map or finding an alternative link to use in the old link's place. Remember, to be fair to your visitors, you don't want to leave a lot of loose ends. There are too many sites out there as it is that are under construction. Don't be one of them.

After you correct the file on your system, upload the file again and you're ready for action.

If all your internal links worked on your own computer, but are broken on your ISP's server, you've probably run into that old multiple folder problem I discussed earlier in relation to broken graphics. In short, you have your HTML files in different folders on your system, but you went ahead and put them all in the same directory on your ISP's server. Correcting the problem with links is just like correcting the problem with graphics. If you don't fix the errors, your Web page will look like Figure 11-2. The quick fix: Move all the files into the correct folders on your system, fix all the links to reflect the new location, and then upload the revised files to your ISP's server.

if you find that your links don't work, there are several possible solutions

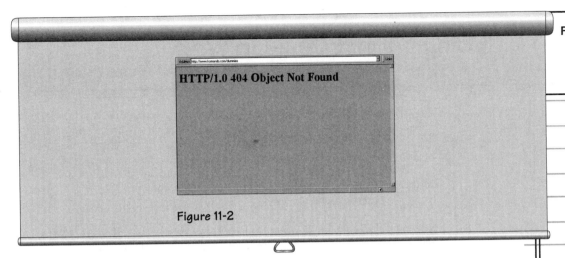

Figure 11-2

And the triple check

After you're absolutely, positively sure that your Web site is perfect, you're still not done! Remember my mentioning that any given Web page looks different when viewed through a different Web browser? Hopefully, you have some friends, acquaintances or business associates who use different browsers than you and are willing to give your site the old once-over. If so, have them check out your site and make sure you get their feedback on the look and flow of the site.

If you can, hang over a buddy's shoulder and watch him as he navigates your site: You may find extra places where it is helpful to add links, for example. This is really the best test of your site. If something doesn't work for him, you know it won't work for other visitors, either. After all, you know all the ins and outs of your site (you built it) so you may miss something that may be a problem for other folks.

Also, even if the site is functionally okay, you may discover that there is something offensive about your design. Maybe that fluorescent chartreuse background isn't quite as attractive as you thought. After all, beauty *is* in the eye of the beholder. If a large percentage of the people who behold your Web page think it's ugly, you've got some more work to do.

Recess

Here are five ways to ensure that your friends will love your site:

- Screen out the jealous ones
- Offer your pals a beer before they sit down
- Offer them "a page of their own" if they like it
- Threaten to write nasty things about them on your *Loser* page if they don't like it
- Tell them exactly where to click

☑ Progress Check

If you can do the following, you've mastered this lesson:

- ❑ Explain how to check through your Web page to make sure everything is working properly.

- ❑ Troubleshoot problems that may arise after you post your page.

- ❑ Recruit friends who can go through your page to do another check on your work.

Doing Your Follow-Up Work

After you have your Web site up and running, maybe you think your work is done. On the contrary, the fun has just begun. What makes the World Wide Web so different from books and magazines and other forms of print media is that you can create living, breathing documents — at least figuratively speaking. You can easily keep track of your site's most popular and least popular features, and make adjustments to your site on a moment's notice with virtually no extra expense to you.

Probably the first thing you want to do now is contact your ISP and see what they offer in terms of reporting. Some ISPs e-mail you a daily report that shows quite clearly how many people have accessed each component of your Web site. Each access is a *hit*. Other ISPs may compile this information in a separate directory and provide you with software tools to view and analyze the information. Otherwise, if you're feeling brave, you can add a visitor counter to your own page, as shown in Figure 11-3.

Adding a counter requires special programming outside of HTML. You can find counter programs on the Web that you can use, but be forewarned that you have to roll up your sleeves and do some programming. The one downside of a counter is that it may take a little while for it to load for visitors when they stop by. But adding a counter still may be worth the effort. It's a good way to keep track of how many people stop by to visit your page. Point your Web browser in these directions for some more information on Web page counters, sometimes referred to as "ego boosters" by Net veterans:

- Internet Counter: http://www.icount.com/
- JCount Animated Counters: http://www.jcount.com/
- Live Counter: http//www.chami.com/prog/lc/
- WebTracker: http://www.fxweb.holowww.com/tracker/

If you create your Web site to use, for example, as an online family photo album, maybe you don't really care how many hits you do or don't get. You put your page up for your own amusement, and that's fine.

However, if there are any business motives behind your move to the World Wide Web, you should have more than a passing interest in how popular your Web page is or isn't. After all, you wouldn't advertise your business in a magazine that nobody reads, would you?

The whole idea of putting up a Web page is to have people see it. If you keep track of how many people are viewing the different pages on your site, you have a measure of how well you've done and how successful your page is. You can also identify problem areas that need fixing. For example, if nobody goes to your links page, maybe this is an indicator that either the links don't work right, or maybe they're just not that interesting. Or you may only be getting guys named Link to hit it.

tracking the number of visitors who come to your site is often helpful

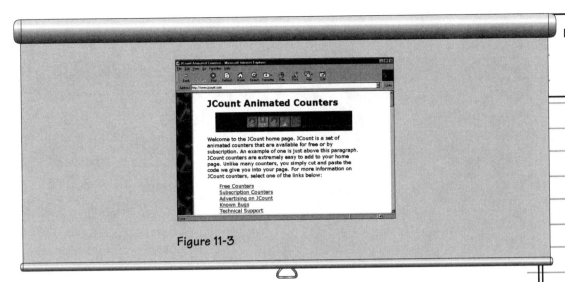

Figure 11-3

The whole idea is to have people see your page. But how can they see it if they can't find it? And how are people going find your page among the thousands and thousands out there? That's where *search engines* come into play.

A search engine is a Web site designed specifically to help people locate information on the World Wide Web. Typically, you go to one of these sites, enter one or more terms that describe the topic you're looking for, and then click on a Search button. The software on the search engine's server then searches through a database of Web sites that it has compiled by one method or another. The search engine than displays any matches, or *hits,* on your computer screen. You can then click on any listed Web address to go directly to that site.

Sounds great — if you could only get your site listed on these search engines. Well, you can. And it's probably easier than you think. Dozens of search engines are out there. The following ones are a few of my favorites, with some tips on how to get yourself added to each.

Yahoo! (ya' have to include the exclamation point) was the first big name in search engines and it's still the most well-known, if not the most popular. When you submit your Web address to Yahoo!, a live person eventually reviews your site to make sure it's appropriate to be added to the Yahoo! database. I still haven't quite figured out the Yahoo! definition of *appropriate,* because you can find a some pretty off-color material through Yahoo! I know. I've spent days discovering this stuff.

The address for Yahoo! is http://www.yahoo.com. When you get there, click on the main category that's appropriate for your site, as shown in Figure 11-4. Then continue to click on subcategories until you find the one that's just right for your site. Finally, click on the Add URL icon and follow the directions on the resulting page, shown in Figure 11-5.

be sure to register your new page with Yahoo!, one of the big names in search engines

Figure 11-4: This is the Yahoo! main screen.

Figure 11-5: This is the Yahoo! Add URL screen.

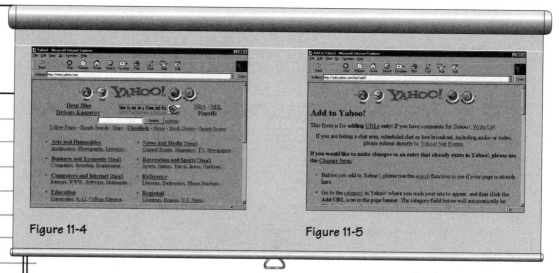

Figure 11-4   Figure 11-5

AltaVista is another extremely popular Web search engine, but it works a little differently than Yahoo!, at least in terms of how it collects Web addresses. Unlike the selective approach of Yahoo!, the goal of AltaVista is to catalog every single page on the World Wide Web. Instead of just relying on people like you to register their Web sites, AltaVista also sends out its own software *agents* (little automated programs) to scour the Web for new sites. This means that even if you don't register with AltaVista, your site may show up there someday. But someday could be a while from now. Best to speed up the process by registering.

The address for AltaVista is http://www.altavista.digital.com. When you go there, you find an Add URL button way at the bottom of the screen, as shown in Figure 11-6. Click there and just follow the instructions like you did with Yahoo!

Getting excited is a good thing. And Excite is another good search engine. What sets Excite apart from the others is that when this search engine displays a list of hits, there's also a button next to each hit that you can click on to display "similar sites." If you click on the button, Excite examines its database for related sites. You may discover a site that interests you, but that doesn't contain the exact search term you entered.

To register, go to http://www.excite.com. By now, you should be used to clicking on Add URL, as shown in Figure 11-7, and following the instructions. This one's no different.

on the test

Lycos is an older search engine, but it's still a goodie. I've discovered that I can often find sites through Lycos that don't pop up so easily on some of the other search engines. This is another reason why registering your site in lots of different places is a good idea: Different search engines work differently, so it's hard to say when your page will come up in a search. By registering with all the search engines, you cover all your bases.

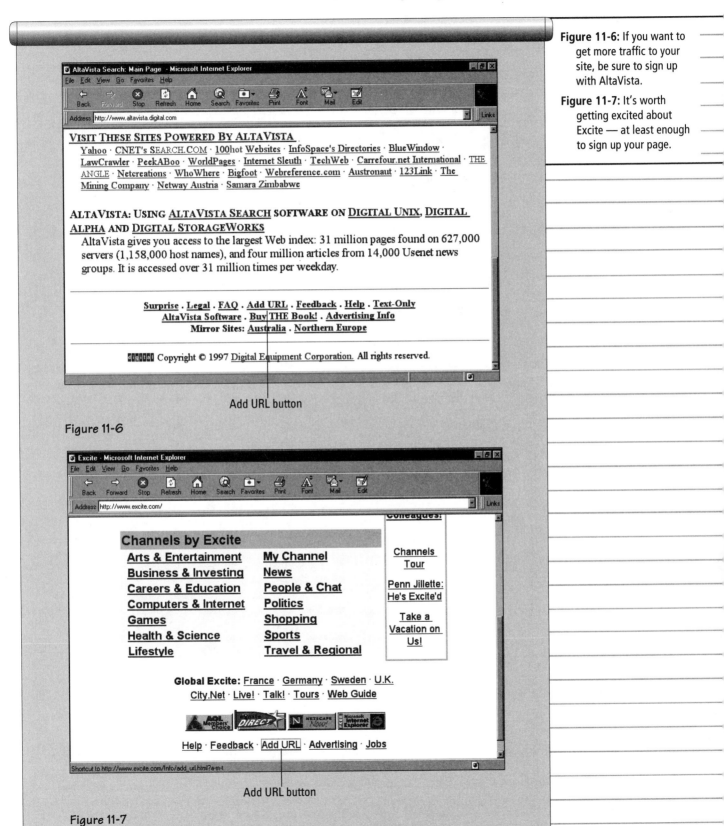

Add URL button

Figure 11-6

Add URL button

Figure 11-7

Figure 11-6: If you want to get more traffic to your site, be sure to sign up with AltaVista.

Figure 11-7: It's worth getting excited about Excite — at least enough to sign up your page.

Figure 11-8: Here's what
you see when you go to
the Lycos home page.

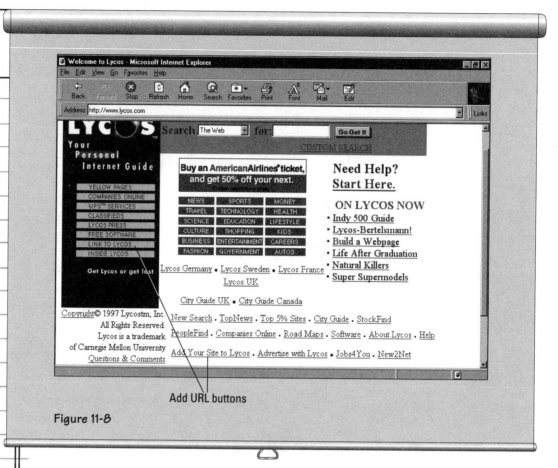

Add URL buttons

Figure 11-8

☑ Progress Check

If you can do the following,
you've mastered this lesson:

❏ Determine the type of
visitor-tracking you want
to do on your page.

❏ Add your page to some
or all of the listed search
engines.

❏ Plan for continual and
regular updates to your
Web site.

Ready for a big surprise? The Web address for Lycos is `http://www.lycos.com`. Here's another big surprise. Click on Add URL, as shown in Figure 11-8, and follow the directions.

The last search engine I'm going to mention — although there are admittedly many others — is WebCrawler. Because America Online owns and operates this search engine, AOL members are the ones who are most likely to stop by. And with AOL's membership going up almost by the millions annually, that's quite a few potential hits.

Point your Web browser to `http://www.webcrawler.com` and follow the usual routine, as shown in Figure 11-9.

People always ask me which one of these is my favorite search engine. That's easy. The one that brings them to my site.

Think you're done? Hate to disappoint you, but your trip down the Information Superhighway is a never-ending road. If your goal is to have as many people as possible see your site, particularly if you set up your site to promote your business, it's almost more important to get people to come back a second, third and fourth time than it is to get them to stop by the first time. The best way to *not* get people to come back to your site is to *not* update your site on a regular basis.

Add URL button

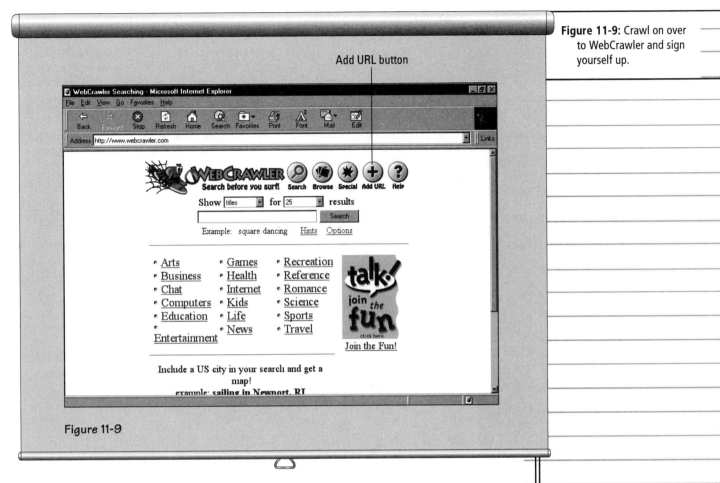

Figure 11-9

Figure 11-9: Crawl on over to WebCrawler and sign yourself up.

Maybe you look at your Web site like you look at a book. You publish some information and then let it run its course. Maybe in a few years, you come out with a revised edition that addresses some of the things that happened since the first go-around. This is the wrong way to look at your Web site. Because by then, you will be the only one *looking* at your Web site.

You need to think of your site more as a magazine, a place where people can come back weekly or monthly to get new and updated information. Keeping your site updated is so easy, there's really no excuse for not having completely up-to-date information.

Did you change the price on one of your products or services? The new price should be on your Web page the day it goes into effect. Do you have a new address, phone number or e-mail address? Old contact information on your Web page won't do you any good. Have you introduced a new service or side-lined into some related field? It takes you only a few minutes to let the whole world know.

on the test

I think you get the idea. Maintaining your site all goes back to that "living, breathing document" thing. To compete with the thousands of other Web sites out there, you must continuously keep your content fresh and engaging. If you don't, you're likely to discover that this whole effort was just a waste of time.

keep updating your site so your visitors get the most current information

The "how to" of updating your Web page is the easy part. Change the files you have on your computer and then just follow the same procedures you use for uploading your original files. Your FTP program copies the new files right over the old ones, and your revised site is available to the whole world the instant the upload is complete.

Unit 11 Quiz

Select the best answer(s) to each question.

1. **FTP stands for . . .**

   A. File Transfer Procedure

   B. File Transfer Protocol

   C. File Transit Protocol

   D. File Transit Procedure

2. **Putting your files on your ISP's server is commonly called . . .**

   A. Copying your files

   B. Moving your files

   C. Downloading your files

   D. Uploading your files

3. **The server name is . . .**

   A. The Internet name of the computer that holds your Web site

   B. The name of the company that owns your ISP

   C. Your user name

   D. The name of your waitress

4. **If your e-mail address is kim@komando.com, your user name is . . .**

   A. Kim

   B. Komando

   C. Komando.com

   D. One you can't have because that's me!

5. **You best choice for a password is . . .**

   A. A mix of upper- and lower-case letters

   B. A word not found in the dictionary

   C. A word that's not obvious

   D. The name of your pet Rover

6. **A directory is another word for a . . .**

   A. Listing of local ISPs

   B. Listing of files on your hard drive

   C. A folder on either your hard drive or your ISP's server

   D. None of the above

7. **HTML files should always be uploaded as . . .**

   A. Plain text

   B. Raw data

   C. Uuencoded documents

   D. Zipped files

8. **Graphics should always be uploaded as . . .**

   A. Plain text

   B. Raw data

   C. Uuencoded documents

   D. UNIX.tar file

9. **After you've uploaded all your files, you should . . .**

   A. Check every link

   B. Make sure every graphic loads properly

   C. Have your friends do the same

   D. Go out and party

10. **To ensure high visibility, you should register your site with . . .**

    A. The Better Business Bureau

    B. The National Web Page Developers' Society

    C. A search engine

    D. Several search engines

11. **You should update your Web site . . .**

    A. Weekly

    B. Monthly

    C. Annually

    D. As often as necessary to keep the content fresh and up-to-date

Unit 11 Exercise

In this unit, you learned that FTP (File Transfer Protocol) is a way of downloading (or transferring) files from a computer on the Internet to your computer. (A *protocol*, by the way, is an agreed-upon set of standards for doing something.) FTP makes sure that the file you copy to your computer arrives in perfect condition. Of course, you can use FTP to upload (or send) a file to another computer.

Because one purpose of the Internet is to share information, go ahead and share away. First, you need to create your home page by using a text editor or your favorite Web creating software program. Then, you can upload or FTP your Web page and post it for free for 90 days at the award-winning Kim Komando home page! Just drop by `http://www.komando.com/homepage/buildit/`.

If you have questions, send a detailed e-mail to `homepage@komando.com`.

10 reasons why you should FTP your home page at `Komando.com`:

1. If you want a location online, you need a good location.

2. It's cheap (although we prefer to say "inexpensive").

3. The site is accessible to people all over the world who browse the Internet.

4. You can update your page yourself.

5. You get to show the world your HTML skills.

6. You get your very own 2MB of space on the Internet for 90 days.

7. You tap into Kim Komando's audience and loyal followers.

8. You are not limited to the number of pages, only 2MB of space.

9. We have resources set up to help you out.

10. You got it free with this book. Period. End of story.

Part V Review

Unit 10 Summary

▶ **Getting Space on a Web Server:** In order to post your Web page, you need space on a server. A server is a computer that houses your Web site and also makes your site available to any other computer that hooks into the Web. Setting up your own server is difficult, so your best bet is to pay an *Internet service provider* (ISP) to rent space on its server. To connect to a server — and the Web beyond — you need a modem.

▶ **Choosing a Name:** Your name and address on the World Wide Web is very important. The best thing to do (if you can afford it) is to register your own domain name. Registration with InterNIC (the organization that keeps domain names straight) costs $100 for the first two years. If you decide to have an ISP help you register your domain name, make sure the domain name is registered in your name and not under the ISP's. Also, check with your ISP to be sure that it offers virtual domain hosting. Without it, the ISP can't host your site.

▶ **ISP Services:** You can choose a national or a local ISP. National companies have access numbers from anywhere in the country while local ISPs may provide better, more personalized service. ISP charges are generally based on two different factors: the size of your Web site and the amount of traffic that comes to visit it. Check with your ISP to see how easy it is to make changes to your page, to see if the ISP tells you how many visitors you get on your page, and to see how many email accounts come with your service.

Unit 11 Summary

▶ **Posting your Web site:** To post your site on the Web, you need a separate program called an FTP (*File Transfer Protocol*) program. When you use the FTP program to upload your documents for your site, be sure your password is tough to crack. If it's not, hackers can get into your files and change the look or text of your Web site.

▶ **Checking your site:** After you post your site, launch your browser and take a look. You need to check every link and make sure every graphic is where it should be. Be sure that you look at it in both Navigator and Internet Explorer browsers. Have some friends check the page and solicit their honest feedback.

▶ **Attracting visitors:** People won't come to your site if it's not up to date. Be sure you update yours regularly. Also, add your page to several different search engines so people can find your site more easily.

Part V Test

The questions on this test cover all the material presented in Part V (Units 10 and 11).

True False

T   F   1. A server is the waitress at the ISPs luncheon restaurant.

T   F   2. Federal Communications Commission regulations limit download speeds over regular phone lines to 53K.

T   F   3. ISDN stand for Integrated Services Digital Network.

T   F   4. A domain name is the name of the country where you live.

T   F   5. A domain name should relate to your name or the name of your company, and it should be easy to guess.

T   F   6. The InterNIC is the organization with which you register your domain name.

T   F   7. Some ISPs will register your domain name for you.

T   F   8. If you have the chance to sign a year contract for fixed-price ISP service, you always should.

T   F   9. You need an HTTP program to upload your Web page files to your ISP.

T   F   10. The best thing to use as your password is your first name.

T   F   11. If your Web browser can't locate the page that a link is supposed to lead to from your Web site, the page may not exist anymore.

T   F   12. The more hits you get, the worse you feel.

T   F   13. Signing up with lots of search engines can help you get more hits.

Multiple choice

For each of the following questions, circle the correct answer or answers. Some questions may have more than one right answer, so read all the answers carefully.

14. **FTP can transfer files in which format(s)?**

    A.   .avi

    B.   text

    C.   binary

    D.   secondary

15. **A good password**

    A.   Is a mixture of upper and lowercase letters

    B.   Is the same as your domain name

    C.   Is very hard to guess

    D.   Is something that your 3-year-old nephew can spell

16. **If the graphics don't load on your Web page, the problem may be**

    A.   Your browser is being lazy

    B.   You didn't keep all your graphics in the same folder as your other Web page documents

    C.   You forgot to upload the graphics

    D.   You encoded the graphics when you uploaded them

17. **A server should have**

    A.   At least 64MB of RAM

    B.   At least 2GB hard drive space

    C.   At least a Pentium chip

    D.   An operator to handle all the traffic

Part V Test

18. **ISP pricing**

    A. Probably includes a certain base size for your Web page

    B. Probably allows a certain amount of traffic to your page

    C. Probably will require a five-year contract

    D. Will change monthly

Matching

19. **Match the problem to the solution:**

    A. When I enter my Web address, I only see a list of files.

    B. The Web page loads, but the graphics don't.

    C. My browser can't locate the internal link I want to jump to.

    D. I don't know the answers to any of these questions.

    1. You didn't read the units carefully enough

    2. You didn't put the files in the same folder on your ISP directory

    3. You forgot to name your main page index.htm or index.html

    4. You forgot to upload the graphics

20. **Match the following terms to their definitions:**

    A. FTP

    B. Server

    C. Search Engine

    D. Internet Counter

    1. A tool that lets you find information on the Internet

    2. A computer that holds your Web page so people can view it from the Internet

    3. A tool that counts the number of people who have visited your site

    4. A program that allows you to upload your files to your server

Part V Lab Assignment

You've already posted your Web site, right? And you think it looks great, right? Well, here's what I want you to do:

Step 1: Look for mistakes on Web pages

Just get on the Web and start surfing around for mistakes. I'm not asking you to do this to be mean; I just want you to see how many careless mistakes people make on their Web sites.

Step 2: Check your site for mistakes

Now that you've found a couple of mistakes out there, double-check your own site and make sure you don't have any.

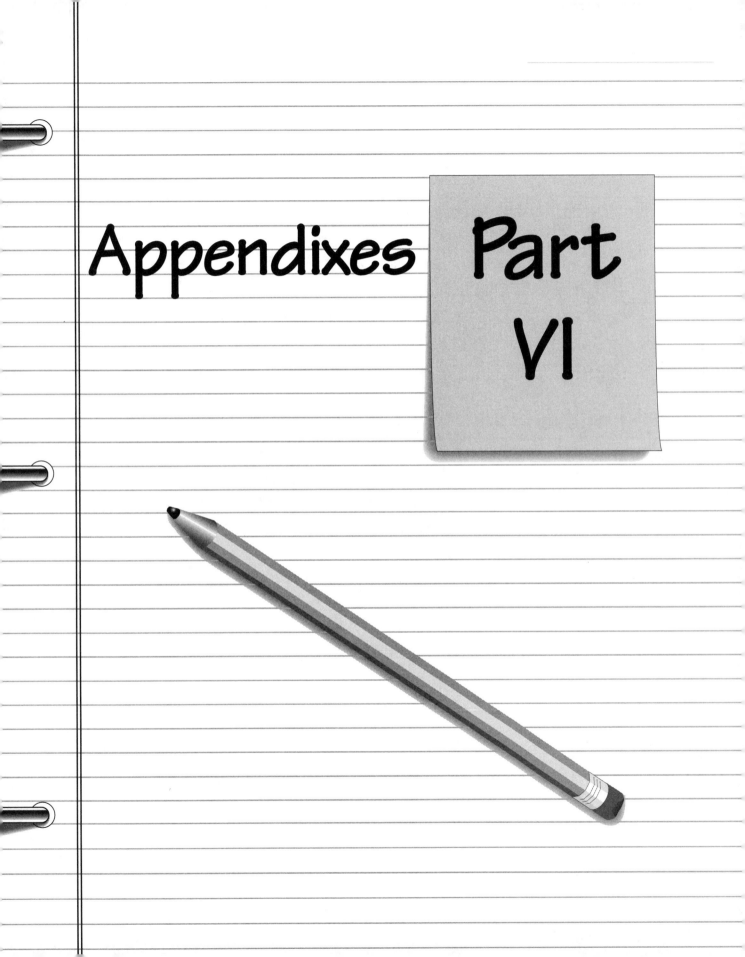

Appendixes

Part VI

In this part . . .

Ever hung up the telephone and suddenly remembered one more thing that you should have said? Sure you have. Well, the appendixes in this book give me that chance. And I don't even have to phone all of you.

Appendix A gives you some information on ISP costs. Not every ISP is listed — in fact, space limited the list to the biggest ISPs in America. But this should give you an idea of what you can expect to pay to share your cyberart masterpiece with the world.

Appendix B gives you the answers for all of the end-of-part quizzes in the book. You remember those quizzes, right? What — you didn't take the quizzes? Well, go back right now and do them. And when you get done, check out Appendix B for the correct answers and tips on where to look in case you get a wrong answer.

Finally, Appendix C tells you a little more about the files and programs that you can find on the CD that comes with this book. Installing these files is one of the first things you should do when you buy this book. So why did we put the "About the CD" appendix at the back of the book? Because that's where the CD is, that's why. Just one more question I've been able to answer for you — no extra charge.

A Sampling of ISP Prices

Exactly how much should you pay to get your wonderful work of art on the World Wide Web? Good question. The truth is that there are as many pricing plans out there as there are Internet service providers (ISPs). Every ISP works a little differently, and where you happen to live can make a difference, too. If Joe Blow owns the only ISP in town, he can charge you just about whatever he wants. On the other hand, if your town has 50 ISPs, pricing obviously will be much more competitive. Lucky for you, a few national ISPs exist, which should prevent good ol' Joe from taking advantage of you.

To help you in your never-ending quest for a good deal, I've compiled some pricing information for a few big, national ISPs. Use this as a guide when you go shopping around your town for an ISP.

Surprisingly, the Internet itself is a great place to find an ISP. In fact, Yahoo! has an entire section devoted to reviews of ISPs, as shown in Figure A-1. The URL to get there is a long one:

```
http://www.yahoo.com/Computers_and_Internet/Internet/
         Information_and_Documentation/Reviews/Internet
         Service Providers/
```

Or you can just search at Yahoo! using the phrase "ISP and reviews," and see what pops up in the search results page.

One of the categories mentioned in this appendix is *traffic charges*. Some ISPs charge you not only to keep your Web pages on their servers, but also according to how much other people access your Web site. Not every ISP does this, but the ISPs that do usually impose a maximum amount in megabytes that the general public can access from your site in a month. You see, each time a person visits your site, the graphics and images are transferred or downloaded from the ISP to the user's PC. And those graphics and images take up space that is measured in megabytes. ISPs keep track of how many megabytes are transferred. If your site exceeds the limit imposed by the ISP or the pricing plan you have selected with the ISP, you start incurring extra charges. This limit may make you think twice about visiting your own home page too often.

Also, a few words about set-up fees. Some of the ISPs in this appendix have set-up fees listed, while others don't. However, don't assume that just because a set-up fee isn't listed for an ISP that the ISP doesn't have one. This list was current as of the time of this writing, but rates and limitations change all the time. Call an ISP to verify this information before you enter into any agreement. When you do get the agreement, be sure you read the fine print. Also,

Figure A-1: Yahoo! lists the various reviews of ISPs available on the Internet.

Figure A-2: Be a smart consumer and check an ISP's reputation at the Better Business Bureau home page.

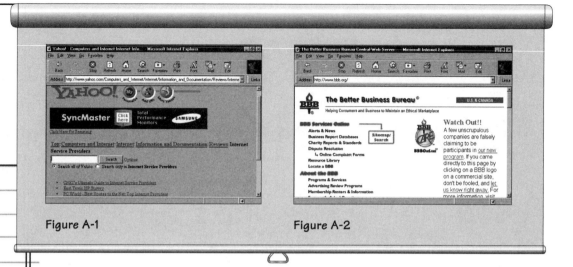

Figure A-1   Figure A-2

check for any complaints with the Better Business Bureau of the city where the ISP is doing business. You can find the Better Business Bureau on the Internet at `http://www.bbb.org` as shown in Figure A-2.

I already talked about the online services in Unit 9, but I wanted to throw AOL and CompuServe in here again just so you have something to compare the others to.

America Online

`http://www.aol.com`

Phone: 800 827-6364

Personal and business accounts:

- ♦ $19.95 per month unlimited access
- ♦ $17.95 per month paid one year in advance
- ♦ $14.95 per month paid two years in advance
- ♦ $4.95 per month for three hours, $2.50 for each additional hour
- ♦ 2MB of space per screen name for Web pages (with up to five screen names per account)
- ♦ No traffic charge

AT&T WorldNet Service

`http://www.att.com/worldnet/wis/`

Phone: 800 7HOSTIN (800 746-7846), business accounts; 800-967-5363 personal accounts.

Personal accounts:

- ◗ $19.95 per month unlimited access
- ◗ $4.95 per month for five hours (three hours if not an AT&T long-distance customer), $2.50 for each additional hour
- ◗ $1.95 per month for 2MB Web site
- ◗ $4.95 per month for 5 MB Web site

Business account:

- ◗ $2.95 per month
- ◗ Up to 100MB of storage
- ◗ 200MB traffic limit per month

CompuServe

http://www.compuserve.com

Phone: 800 848-8199

Personal and business accounts:

- ◗ $9.95 per month for five hours, $2.95 for each additional hour
- ◗ $24.95 per month for 20 hours, $1.95 for each additional hour
- ◗ 5MB of space for Web pages
- ◗ No traffic charge

Concentric

http://www.concentric.net

Phone: 800 939-4242

Personal accounts (may offer business accounts by the time you read this):

- ◗ $7.95 per month for five hours, $1.95 for each additional hour
- ◗ $19.95 per month unlimited access
- ◗ 5MB of space for Web pages
- ◗ No traffic charge

EarthLink

http://www.earthlink.com

Phone: 800 395-8425, personal accounts; 800 511-2044, business accounts

Personal accounts:

- ◗ $25 set-up fee
- ◗ $19.95 per month unlimited access
- ◗ 2MB of space for Web pages
- ◗ No traffic charge

Business accounts:

- ◗ $279 set-up fee
- ◗ $159 per month unlimited access
- ◗ 30MB of space for Web pages
- ◗ Maximum of 1.5GB (that's *gigabytes*) traffic per month

GTE Internet Solutions

`http://www.gte.net`

Phone: 888 GTE-SURF (888 483-7873)

Personal and business accounts:

- ◗ $19.95 per month unlimited access with your first 30 days free and no set-up fee
- ◗ $8.95 per month for 5 hours, $1.95 for each additional
- ◗ 5 MB of space for Web pages
- ◗ No traffic charge

Note: GTE Internet Solutions also offers various business services for Web development and hosting.

PSINet

`http://www.psi.net`

Phone: 800 395-1056

Business accounts (does not offer personal accounts):

- ◗ $145 per month for basic account that includes 256 IP addresses (this means that you could set up as many as 256 employees through this one account)
- ◗ $99 per month for basic Web hosting
- ◗ 10MB of space for Web pages
- ◗ No traffic charge

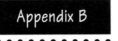

Appendix B

Answers

Part I Test Answers

Question	Answer	If You Missed It, Try This
1.	False	Review Lesson 1-1
2.	True	Review Lesson 1-1
3.	False	Review Lesson 1-1
4.	True	Review Lesson 1-1
5.	True	Review Lesson 1-2
6.	False	Review Lesson 1-3
7.	False	Review Lesson 2-5
8.	True	Review Lesson 2-4
9.	B, C, D	Review Lesson 1-1
10.	A, B	Review Lesson 1-2
11.	A, B, D	Review Lesson 1-3
12.	B, D	Review Lesson 2-1
13.	B, C	Review Lesson 2-2
14.	A	Review Lesson 2-4
15.	A-4, B-3, C-1, D-2	Common sense
16.	A-4, B-1, C-2, D-3	Review Lesson 2-4

Part II Test Answers

Question	Answer	If You Missed It, Try This
1.	True	Review Lesson 3-1
2.	False	Review Lesson 3-1

3.	False	Review Lesson 3-1
4.	True	Review Lesson 3-2
5.	True	Review Lesson 3-2
6.	True	Review Lesson 3-3
7.	True	Review Lesson 4-1
8.	False	Review Lesson 4-2
9.	True	Review Lesson 4-2
10.	False	Review Lesson 4-4
11.	C	Review Lesson 3-1
12.	A	Review Lesson 3-2
13.	C, D	Review Lesson 3-2
14.	B	Review Lesson 4-1
15.	A, C	Review Lesson 4-2
16.	A, C	Review Lesson 4-4
17.	A-2, B-4, C-1, D-3	Review Unit 4
18.	A-4, B-1, C-3, D-2	Review Unit 4
19.	A-3, B-2, C-4, D-1	Review Lesson 3-2

Part III Test Answers

Question	Answer	If You Missed It, Try This
1.	False	Review Lesson 5-1
2.	True	Review Lesson 5-1
3.	False	Review Lesson 5-2
4.	False	Review Lesson 5-3
5.	False	Review Lesson 5-5
6.	True	Review Lesson 5-6
7.	True	Review Lesson 6-1
8.	False	Review Lesson 6-2
9.	False	Review Lesson 6-3
10.	False	Review Lesson 6-4
11.	True	Review Lesson 6-5
12.	False	Review Lesson 7-1
13.	False	Review Lesson 7-2

14.	True	Review Lesson 7-3
15.	B, C, D	Review Lesson 7-3
16.	C, D	Review Lesson 7-1
17.	A, B, C, D	Review Lesson 5-1
18.	A, B, D	Review Lesson 5-2
19.	A	Review Lesson 6-1
20.	A, C	Review Lesson 6-1
21.	A-3, B-1, C-4, D-2	Review Units 6 and 7
22.	A-3, B-2, C-4, D-1	Review Units 5 and 7
23.	A-3, B-1, C-2, D-4	Review Units 5 and 6

Part IV Test Answers

Question	Answer	If You Missed It, Try This
1.	True	Review Lesson 8-1
2.	True	Review Lesson 8-1
3.	False	Review Lesson 8-2
4.	False	Review Lesson 8-2
5.	False	Review Lesson 8-5
6.	False	Review Lesson 8-5
7.	False	Review Lesson 8-9
8.	True	Review Lesson 8-10
9.	True	Review Lesson 8-11
10.	True	Review Lesson 9-1
11.	True	Review Lesson 9-1
12.	False	Review Lesson 9-3
13.	A, D	Review Lesson 8-1
14.	B, C	Review Lesson 8-1
15.	B, C	Review Unit 8
16.	A, B	Review Lesson 9-2
17.	B	Review Lesson 9-4
18.	A-2, B-4, C-1, D-3	Review Units 8 and 9
19.	A-2, B-4, C-1, D-3	Review Lesson 8-1

Part V Test Answers

Question	Answer	If You Missed It, Try This
1.	False	Review Lesson 10-1
2.	True	Review Lesson 10-1
3.	True	Review Lesson 10-1
4.	False	Review Lesson 10-2
5.	True	Review Lesson 10-2
6.	True	Review Lesson 10-2
7.	True	Review Lesson 10-2
8.	False	Review Lesson 10-3
9.	False	Review Lesson 11-1
10.	False	Review Lesson 11-1
11.	True	Review Lesson 11-2
12.	False	Review Lesson 11-3
13.	True	Review Lesson 11-3
14.	B, C	Review Lesson 11-1
15.	A, C	Review Lesson 11-1
16.	B, C, D	Review Lesson 11-2
17.	A, B, C	Review Lesson 10-1
18.	A, B	Review Lesson 10-3
19.	A-3, B-4, C-2, D-1	Review Lesson 11-2
20.	A-4, B-2, C-1, D-3	Review Units 10 and 11

About the CD

The *Dummies 101: Creating Web Pages* companion CD contains cool extra programs in addition to the exercise files that you use while you're following along with the lessons in the book.

I guide you through using most of these extra programs in the appropriate lessons, but I've also thrown in some other programs that I don't have the space to cover in this book. It's all stuff that you'll find extremely useful in creating Web pages!

Before you can use any of the CD files, you need to install them on your computer. But don't worry: The installation process is easy and fairly quick.

heads up

After you install the *Dummies 101: Creating Web Pages* exercise files, please don't open them and look around just yet. One wrong click and you can mess up a file, which would prevent you from following along with the book lesson that uses the file (you'd have to go through the installation process again to get a fresh copy). Your best bet is to follow the installation instructions given in this appendix, jump right into Unit 1, and wait until I tell you to use a particular file before opening it up. Besides, the exercise files don't mean much except in the context of the lessons.

In fact, I suggest not playing around with *any* of the CD files and programs until you've been through the book. You open and use most of the files and programs in the course of the book, and the ones that you don't probably won't be of much use to you until you're more comfortable with creating Web pages, anyway.

System Requirements

Before using the CD, make sure that your computer matches up to the minimum requirements listed below. If your computer doesn't have many of these items, you may experience problems in using the CD:

♦ A PC with a 486 or faster processor, or a Mac OS computer with a 68040 or faster processor.

♦ *At least* 8MB of total RAM (16MB recommended)

Notes:

♦ Microsoft Windows 95, Mac OS 7.5, or Microsoft Windows 3.*x* (that is, 3.1 or 3.11)

♦ At least 8MB of free hard-disk space available if you want to install all the items from this CD (you need less space if you don't install every item)

♦ CD-ROM drive — double-speed (2x) or faster

♦ Monitor capable of displaying at least 256 colors or grayscale

If you need more information on computer basics, check out *PCs For Dummies,* 4th Edition, by Dan Gookin; *Macs For Dummies* by David Pogue; *Windows 95 For Dummies* by Andy Rathbone; *Mac OS 7.6 For Dummies* by Bob Levitus; or *Windows 3.11 For Dummies,* 3rd Edition, by Andy Rathbone (all published by IDG Books Worldwide, Inc.).

Putting the CD Files on Your Hard Drive

The exercise files are sample documents that you use while following along with the lessons in the book. You need to put these files on your hard drive. After you're done with the book, you can remove the files easily.

Some of the extra programs are integrated with the lessons in the book; these programs are just some cool stuff that you'll find useful creating Web pages.

If you're a Mac OS user, skip to the section, "Installing the exercise files on a Mac OS computer."

Installing the exercise files in Windows

1 Insert the Dummies 101 CD (label side up) into your computer's CD drive.

Be careful to touch only the edges of the CD. The CD drive is the one that pops out with a circular drawer.

If your computer has the Windows 95 AutoPlay feature, the installation program should begin automatically. If the program does not start after 30 seconds, go to Step 2. If it does, go to Step 4.

2 If the installation program doesn't start automatically, click on the Start button and click on Run in Windows 95; in Windows 3.1 Program Manager, click on File⇨Run.

3 In the dialog box that appears, type d:\seticon.exe **(if your CD drive is not drive D, substitute the appropriate letter for** d**) and click on OK.**

A message informs you that the program is about to install the icons.

4 Click on OK in the message window.

After a moment, a program group called Dummies 101 appears on the Start menu, with an icon. Then another message appears, asking whether you want to use the CD now.

5 Click on Yes to use the CD now, or click on No if you want to use the CD later.

If you click on No, you can continue with the installation later in Windows 95 by clicking on the Start button, on Programs, on Dummies 101, and finally on Dummies 101 - Creating Web Pages CD. You can continue with the installation later in Windows 3.1 by double-clicking the Dummies 101 program group, and then on Dummies 101 - Creating Web Pages CD. If you click on Yes, you now see the End-User License Agreement window.

6 Read the license agreement and click on Agree.

If you don't agree to the terms of the license agreement, you can't continue with the installation. After you click on Agree, the Dummies 101: Creating Web Pages For Windows installation window appears.

7 Click on Install Exercise Files.

Another message appears, asking whether you want to go ahead and copy the exercise files to your hard drive.

8 Click on OK to continue with the installation or click on Cancel to stop the installation.

If you click on Cancel, you can install the files later by following these steps again (see Step 5 for instructions on how to get back to the installation window).

You see a window asking where to install the exercise files on your computer. To make the installation and the exercises in this book as simple as possible, let the installer place the exercise files in the recommended location. If you really want to put the files somewhere else, you can change the location by following the on-screen instructions (make sure that you remember where you put them if you customize the location).

9 Click on OK to install the files in the folder shown.

The installation program copies the exercise files to your computer. You see a little window telling you that the installation is done and referring you to this book for instructions on using the files.

10 Click on OK to make the little window go away.

The installation window reappears.

11 Click on the Exit button in the lower-right corner of the window.

The program asks whether you really, really want to exit.

12 Click on Yes.

Unless you change the location, the exercise files are installed to C:\101CWP. You don't have to do anything with the files yet — I tell you when you need to open the first file (in Unit 3).

Notes:

Installing the exercise files on a Mac OS computer

Follow these steps to install the exercise files on a Mac OS computer:

1 Insert the Dummies 101 CD (label side up) into your computer's CD drive.

In a moment, a CD-ROM icon appears on your desktop named **101 - Creating Web Pages**.

2 Double-click on the CD-ROM icon.

Inside the CD window are text files named Read Me First and License Agreement, a folder containing the exercise files, and a folder containing the additional software on the CD.

3 To install the exercise files, drag the 101CWP exercise files folder on the CD to your computer's hard drive icon.

Note: The files are meant to accompany the book's lessons. If you open a file prematurely, you may accidentally make changes to the file, which may prevent you from following along with the steps in the lessons. So please don't try to open or view a file until you've reached the point in the lessons where I explain how to open the file.

Tip: If at some point you accidentally modify an exercise file and want to reinstall the original version, just follow the steps for installing exercise files for your computer. If you want to save your modified version of an exercise file, either move the file to another folder before reinstalling the original or install the new replacement files to a different folder.

Removing the exercise files

Once you're done with the lessons in the book, you might want to delete the exercise files.

To delete the exercise files under Windows 95:

1 Double-click on the My Computer icon.

2 Double-click on the Drive C icon.

3 Double-click on the My Documents folder.

4 Click once on the 101CWP folder.

I assume that you let the CD installer copy the files to the folder it recommended. If you decided to change the recommended location for the exercise files, you may need to open additional folders to find where you saved the exercise file folder.

5 Choose File⇨Delete.

Depending on your Windows 95 settings, you might see a message asking if you really want to delete these items. Click on the appropriate button to indicate Yes.

To delete the exercise files in Windows 3.1:

1 **Start the File Manager. Most of you will find the icon for this program in the Main program group.**

2 **Click on the drive C button on the toolbar.**

The window now shows the files and directories (folders) on drive C.

3 **Click on the 101CWP directory.**

4 **Choose File⇨Delete.**

Depending on your File Manager settings, Windows may show a message that asks if you really want to delete this directory. Click on the Yes to All button to make the directory disappear.

To delete the exercise files on a Mac OS computer, just drag the 101CWP folder containing the exercise files from your hard drive to the Trash icon. To permanently delete the files, click the Special menu and choose Empty Trash.

heads up

Caution: As soon as you delete the exercise files, the exercise files are as good as gone, and the only way to get them back is to reinstall the exercise files again. (This won't bring back your changes to the files; they disappeared with the modified file.) If you want to keep any of the installed files, move them to a different folder *before* you delete the exercise file's folder.

Removing CD icons from Windows

If you installed icons for running the interface to your Windows 95 Start menu or the Windows 3.1 Program Manager, removing the icons after you're done with the CD is pretty simple.

To remove the icons in Windows 95:

1 **Click on the Start button, and choose Settings⇨Taskbar.**

2 **Click on the Start Menu Programs tab at the top of the window.**

3 **Click on the Remove button.**

A window appears that shows all the items on your Start menu.

4 **In the window, click on the tiny plus sign next to the Dummies 101 folder.**

If this is the only Dummies 101 CD you've used, you'll find only the Dummies 101 - Creating Web Pages CD icon. If you've used other Dummies 101 CDs, you'll see a few more icons here for those CDs. Your goal here is to remove only the Dummies 101 - Creating Web Pages icon.

5 **Click once on the Dummies 101 - Creating Web Pages CD icon.**

6 **Click on the Remove button, and then click on the Close button.**

If the Dummies 101 program group doesn't have any other icons in it, you can delete that as well by repeating the steps and selecting the Dummies 101 folder for removal.

Notes:

To remove the icons under Windows 3.1:

1 **In Program Manager, double-click on the Dummies 101 program group.**

2 **In the Dummies 101 window, click once on the Dummies 101 - Creating Web Pages CD icon to select it.**

3 **Choose File➪Delete.**

Depending on your Windows settings, the icon is deleted from your Program Manager.

Installing the Windows programs from the CD

To install the extra software included on the CD, start up the CD if necessary. Click on the Choose Software button and click on the category that you want to install. Next, click on the appropriate button for more information about the program. To install the software, click on the Continue button and follow the on-screen instructions. See "Extra Stuff" in this appendix for more information about each option.

Removing Windows programs from your PC

You might decide to uninstall the programs available from the Choose Software section of the CD. Most software designed for Windows 95 has some sort of uninstall feature that you can use to remove the program. The key word is "most." Not all Windows programs make it easy to remove a program.

To remove a program, look in these locations for the selections you need.

▶ Click on the Start button, and choose Programs. Here you might find the name of the program or the name of the company that made it. Open that program group, and choose the icon named Uninstall or Remove.

▶ Click on the Start button, choose Setting➪Control Panel, and double-click on the icon Add/Remove Programs. Listed on the Install/Uninstall tab of the window are any programs that Windows 95 can remove for you.

If these two options don't work, you have two more options.

▶ Drop by your computer store and pick up a program designed to uninstall programs from your computer, like CleanSweep, Uninstaller, and RemoveIt. These programs are also great for cleaning up the old files that build up on your computer over time.

▶ Locate the folder in Windows that contains the software for the program and delete it, and then delete the program's icons from the Start menu.

Deleting the program's folder is usually OK to do for some programs, but sometimes your computer may still have other information about the program that can't be removed in this way. Also, there is a chance that you could delete files that are shared by other programs you still use. Never delete anything from the Windows folder unless you know *exactly* what you are doing. Be careful once you begin the uninstall process. You should be absolutely certain that you want to delete all the files before you choose the Automatic option.

Note: Windows 3.1 itself does not contain a way to uninstall software; the programs copied to Windows 3.1 must include their own uninstaller, or you must buy and install a program designed to remove installed programs.

Installing and removing Mac OS programs

To install all the software *except* AT&T WorldNet Service and Disinfectant, just drag the folder containing the program from the CD and drop it on your hard drive's icon.

To install Disinfectant, just drag its icon from the CD and drop it on your hard drive icon in the same way.

To install AT&T WorldNet Service, follow these steps.

1 On the CD, double-click on the AT&T WorldNet Service folder.

2 Decide which World Wide Web browser you would like to use.

AT&T WorldNet Service offers two kinds of setup software. One version installs Netscape Navigator, the most popular Web browser as of this writing. The second version of the setup software installs a version of Microsoft Internet Explorer for your particular kind of Mac. Both Web browsers have many similar features. If your Mac has less than 16MB of RAM, you may want to consider Internet Explorer because of its lower RAM requirements. Otherwise, flip a coin if the choice doesn't matter to you.

3 Double-click on either the Setup with Internet Explorer folder or the Setup with Netscape Navigator folder.

4 Double-click on the Install AT&T WorldNet Service icon to start installation.

Read the Important Information window carefully. It contains special instructions you need to know for your particular computer. You may want to print the contents of this window for easier reading.

5 Once you know what to do for your particular computer, click on the Continue button and then follow the on-screen instructions to start installation.

During the setup and registration process, you will be asked to enter a registration number. If your home uses AT&T as your long-distance carrier, enter the following number: L5SQIM631. If you use any other long-distance carrier, please use this code: L5SQIM632.

To remove a program, drag the program's folder from your hard drive to the Trash.

Extra Stuff

In addition to the exercise files, the CD contains programs that you use with a couple of lessons, and extra programs that are not integrated with lessons.

heads up

Remember that you must already have Microsoft Windows 95 or Windows 3.*x*, if you own a PC, or a Mac OS computer with System 7.5 or better installed on your computer in order to use the Dummies 101 CD. Microsoft Windows and the Mac OS are sold separately at computer stores and are not included on this CD. Please see "System Requirements" earlier in this appendix for more requirement information.

- **AT&T WorldNet Service, from AT&T.** In case you don't have an Internet connection, the CD includes sign-on software for AT&T WorldNet Service, an Internet service provider. This version of the sign-on software provides you with Microsoft Internet Explorer, a program that lets you browse a very popular part of the Internet called the World Wide Web.

  For more information and updates of AT&T WorldNet Service, visit the AT&T WorldNet web site: `http://www.att.com/worldnet`

  If you're an AT&T long-distance residential customer, please use this registration code when prompted by the account registration program: L5SQIM631

  If you use another long-distance phone company, please use this registration code when prompted: L5SQIM632

heads up

  If you already have an Internet service provider, please note that AT&T WorldNet Service software makes changes to your computer's current Internet configuration and may replace your current provider's settings.

- **Anarchie 2.0.** Anarchie 2.0, from Stairways Shareware, is a shareware Macintosh File Transfer Protocol (FTP) program that you can employ to copy files between your Mac and a computer on the Internet. This is useful for such technical activities as uploading your own Web pages.

- **BBEdit Lite 4.0.** BBEdit Lite 4.0, from Bare Bones Software, Inc., is a Macintosh freeware text editor with powerful features that make creating HTML scripts for your Web pages easy.

  The commercial version of this program, BBEdit 4.0, has stronger HTML editing features. We've included a demo version of BBEdit 4.0 on the CD. This demo is fully-featured but cannot save files.

- **GifWeb.** GifWeb, from Informatik, Inc., is a tool for Windows that creates transparent GIF images. Creating a transparent GIF "removes" the image's background so that only the significant part of the image appears on the page. That way, an image that originally had a white background will not clash with the background colors of a Web page when the image is loaded.

  More information about the program can be found at `www.informatik.com` on the World Wide Web.

Notes:

- **GraphicConverter.** GraphicConverter, by shareware author Thorsten Lemke, is a Macintosh program that you can use to view images in virtually any graphics format that you're likely to encounter on the Internet.

   In addition, GraphicConverter lets you convert images from one file format to another, which can be very useful in helping you create your own World Wide Web pages. Also, GraphicConverter can help you create transparent GIF images.

- **HotDog.** HotDog, from Sausage Software, is a powerful but easy-to-use Windows shareware program that lets you create your own Web pages without requiring you to be an HTML programming whiz.

- **ImageMapper 2.5.** ImageMapper 2.5, from Stuart Snaddon, is a Macintosh shareware program that makes it easier to create clickable image maps that you can use on your Web pages. ImageMapper supports many of the popular image mapping formats.

- **LiveImage.** LiveImage, from Mediatech Inc., is an image mapping tool for Windows 95 and Windows 4.0. Using this tool, you can map out clickable hot spots on images used on the Web pages you construct. This shareware program works for 14 days before it disables itself. Updates to the program can be found at `www.mediatec.com` on the World Wide Web.

   Note: If the installer for this program asks for a missing DLL file, quit installation and install the LiveImage DLL Pack on the CD. Try installing LiveImage again.

- **RGB Color Box.** This freeware HTML utility for Windows 95 can create <BODY> tags with color information for your HTML documents. BODY tags normally mark out only the actual contents of a Web page, but other information, such as the page's background color, can also be added with the BODY tags. This program makes setting these colors easier. Updates can be found at `home1.inet.tele.dk/theill/rcb.htm` on the World Wide Web.

- **WS_FTP LE.** WS_FTP LE (Limited Edition), from Ipswitch, Inc., is a free (for noncommercial use) Windows File Transfer Protocol (FTP) program that you can employ to copy files between your PC and a computer on the Internet. This is useful for such technical activities as uploading your own Web pages.

If You've Got Problems (Of the CD Kind)

I tried my best to compile programs that work on most computers with the minimum system requirements. Alas, your computer may differ, and some programs may not work properly for some reason.

The two likeliest problems are that you don't have enough memory (RAM) for the programs you want to use, or you have other programs running that are affecting the installation or running of the program. If you get error messages like `Not enough memory` or `Setup cannot continue`, try one or more of these methods and then try using the software again:

- Turn off any anti-virus software that you have on your computer. Installers sometimes mimic virus activity and may make your computer incorrectly believe that it is being infected by a virus.

- Close all running programs. The more programs you're running, the less memory is available to other programs. Installers also typically update files and programs. So if you keep other programs running, installation may not work properly.

- On a Mac OS computer, turn Virtual Memory on from the Memory control panel. This will make your computer act like there is more memory installed. However, this will make your computer run more slowly. If you use a PowerPC Mac OS computer, always leave Virtual Memory on — it makes your programs require *less* memory to operate.

- Have your local computer store add more RAM to your computer. Adding more memory can really help the speed of your computer and allow more programs to run at the same time.

If you still have trouble with installing the items from the CD, please call the IDG Books Worldwide Customer Service phone number: 800-762-2974 (outside the U.S.: 317-596-5261).

Index

▸ Numbers ▸

8-bit color, graphics, 78
24-bit color, graphics, 78
33.6K modems, 15–17
56K modems, online service
  support, 16

▸ A ▸

absolute links, 66
ACTION attribute, form tag, 102
address (<ADDRESS>) HTML tag, 56
addresses, Web anatomy, 3–4
Adobe PageMill program, 19,
  144–148
Afterburner program, 29
aiff (Audio Interchange File
  Format), 125
ALIGN attribute, table cells, 111
alink (active link), colors, 51
AltaVista search engine, 228–229
America Online, 16, 176–181, 242
Anarchie program, 218, 256
anchors, 67–68
angle bracket (< and >) characters,
  HTML tags, 40
animated GIF graphics, 87–88,
  127–128
animated GIF gallery, 132
animations
  GIF files, 87–88, 127
  Shockwave plug-in, 28–29
anonymous FTP site, file
  downloads, 98
answers, test, 245–248
arts extension, domain name, 205
ASCII text file format, 42–43
AT&T WorldNet Service,
  242–243, 256
attributes
  form tag, 102
  frames, 115–116

table formatting, 109–111
au file format, 125
auto-responder, e-mail, 213

▸ B ▸

backbone
  described, 201
  Internet, 2
backgrnd.htm file, 89–90
backgrounds
  colors, 89
  images, 88–90
  logos, 89
  sounds, 126–127
BBEdit Lite program, Mac, 41, 256
Better Business Bureau, ISP
  record, 242
binary files, FTP, 221
bitmapped images, described, 78
blink (<BLINK>) HTML tag, 57
blinking text, browser support, 57
block quote (<BLOCKQUOTE>)
  HTML tag, 58
BMP (Windows bitmap) filename
  extension, 78
body (<BODY>) HTML tag, 53–54
body text, 53–60
  blinking type, 57
  boldface, 56
  indents, 58
  italics, 56–57
  line breaks, 54–55
  lists, 58–60
  monospaced type, 57–58
  paragraph breaks, 55
bold (<B>) HTML tag, 56
boldface, body text, 56
BORDER attribute, table HTML
  tag, 109
borders, linked graphics, 85–88
bottom-aligned graphics, 83–84

breaks.htm file, 55
broken image icon, 223–224
bulleted (unnumbered) list (<UL>)
  HTML tag, 58–59
bulleted lists, 58–60
buttons, hypertext links, 85–87

▸ C ▸

cable modems, traffic jams, 201
captions, table, 107
case, in passwords, 220
CD icons, removing from Windows
  253–254
CD-ROM programs
  Anarchie, 218, 256
  AT&T WorldNet Service,
    242–243, 256
  BBEdit Lite program, Mac, 41, 256
  GifWeb program, Windows,
    87–88, 256
  GraphicConverter program, Mac,
    79–80, 87–88, 257
  HotDog 16 program, Windows,
    158, 257
  HotDog Pro program, DOS,
    158, 257
  HotDog programs, 41
  ImageMapper program, Mac,
    117, 257
  installation of exercise files
    250–252
  installing Windows programs
    from, 254
  LiveImage program, Windows, 117
  Paint Shop Pro, Windows, 79–80
  putting files on hard drive,
    250–257
  qt.mov, 128
  removing CD icons from Windows,
    253–254
  RGB Color Box program,
    Windows, 52, 257

CD-ROM (*continued*)
  sample graphics images, 81
  SLIDES folder, 130
  software requirements, 256
  system requirements, 249–250
  troubleshooting, 257–258
  WS_FTP, Windows 186–187,
    218, 257
CELLPADDING attribute, table
    HTML tag, 110
cells
  contents, 108
  formatting attributes, 111–113
CELLSPACING attribute, table
    HTML tag, 110
CGI (Common Gateway Interface)
    scripts, 27, 101–107
characters
  angle brackets < and >, 40
  forward slash (/), 40, 51
checkboxes, forms, 104
citation (<CIT>) HTML tag, 56
Claris Emailer program, 213
Claris Home Page program, 148–151
clickable buttons, graphic links, 25
client-side image maps, 86, 157
clip art, graphics source, 81
code (<CODE>) HTML tag, 58
color schemes, hexadecimal color
    codes, 52
colors
  8-bit, 78
  24-bit, 78
  alink (active link), 51
  backgrounds, 89
  graphic images, 78
  hexadecimal codes, 52
  links, 51
  photorealistic, 78
  testing prior to publishing, 52–53
  text, 51
  vlink (visited link), 51
  Web page design consideration, 30
COLS attribute, frame HTML tag,
    115
COLSPAN attribute, table cells, 112
columns, headers, 108

com extension, domain name, 205
commands
  conventions used in book, 10
  File⇨Open, 46
  File⇨Save, 53
  File⇨Save As, 43
  View⇨Document Source, Internet
    Explorer, 41
  View⇨Source, Netscape
    Navigator, 41
commercial Web pages, 6, 30
components, URL (Web) address,
    3–4
CompuServe, 181–185, 243
computers, 14–15, 200
Concentric, 243
connections
  cable modems, 201
  Frame Relay, 201
  ISDN (Integrated Services Digital
    Network), 200–201
  ISP (Internet Service Provider), 2
  modem requirements, 15–17
  modem speed ratings, 15–16
  personal Web server cost consider-
    ations, 203
  T1, 201
  T3, 201
  traffic jams, 201–202
  voice-grade telephone lines, 200
contents
  table cells, 108
  Web pages, 29–30
conventions, file naming, 43–45
conversions, graphics files, 79–80
copyrights, graphics, 81
Corel Web.Graphics Suite, 143,
    154–157
counters, Web pages, 226

D

digital camera images, 79
Director program, 122–123
directory (<DIR>) HTML tag, 59
directory, Web pages, 220

documents
  frame pointer, 114
  htm/html filename extension, 44
  HTML creation, 41
domain names, 203–209
  cost considerations, 204
  determining availability, 205–206
  extensions, 205
  InterNIC registration, 204–208
  ISP registration support, 206
  owner concerns, 207–208
  selection tips, 205
  template registration, 206
  virtual domain hosting, 208
  Web address component, 4
download times, text versus
    graphics, 23
download.htm file, 68
downloadable files, 68

E

e-mail
  addresses, 30
  auto-responder, 213
  automatic, 94–96
  mailing list accounts, 213
  mailto links, 94–96
  protocol, described, 94
  readers, 213
EarthLink, 243–244
editing programs, 142–174
  Adobe PageMill, 144–148
  Claris Home Page, 148–151
  Corel Web.Graphics Suite, 154–157
  HotDog Pro, 158–160
  Microsoft FrontPad, 167–170
  Microsoft FrontPage, 151–154
  Microsoft Word 97, 171
  MyInternetBusinessPage, 160–162
  NetObjects Fusion, 163–165
  Netscape Composer, 165–167
  system requirements, 143
  word processors, 170–171
  WordPerfect version 7, 170–171
email.htm file, 96
Emailer program, 213

(<EMBED>) tag, 127
emphasis (<EM>) HTML tag, 56
encoding files, 222
Eudora program, 213
Excite search engine, 228–229
extensions, domain names, 205
external links, 26, 66

›F‹

FCC, download speed regulations, 16
feedback
    forms, 105
    mailto link, 30
fields, table, 108
file formats
    graphics, 77–79
    multimedia, 128
    sounds, 125
    Web page supported types, 42–43
filename extensions, supported
        types, 43–45, 78
files
    binary, 221
    case-sensitive naming
        conventions, 44
    downloadable, 68
    FTP, 68
    FTP downloads, 96–98
    graphic conversions, 79–80
    HTML, 4
    map, 157
    naming conventions, 43–45
    saving as plain text, 42–43
    text, 221
    text only, 222
firm extension, domain name, 205
flattenmoov program, Mac, 129
focus, Web pages, 5
folders
    SLIDES, 130
    Web page file storage, 45
fonts, 57–58
form (<FORM>) HTML tag, 102
form.htm file, CD-ROM, 106
forms, 101–107
    CGI (Common Gateway Interface),
        101–107

checkboxes, 104
    creating, 102–106
    described, 27
    feedback, 105
    form (<FORM>) HTML tag
        attributes, 102
    free-form text area, 105
    radio buttons, 105
    resetting, 105
    scrolling lists, 104
    submit buttons, 105
    Web page element, 26–28
forward slash (/) character, 40, 51
Frame Relay phone line, 201
frames, 18, 26–28, 113–116
frameset, described, 113
free-form text area, forms, 105
freelance artists, graphics, 81–82
freeware, 28
FTP (File Transfer Protocol), 2, 218
    anonymous FTP site, 98
    binary files, 221
    described, 94, 186
    file downloads, 96–98
    files, 68
    ISP support, 211
    non-anonymous FTP site, 98
    text files, 221
FTP dropbox, 68
FTP programs, move files across
        Internet, 218–222
FTP servers
    downloadable files, 68
    FTP file download links, 96–98
FTP sites, flattenmoov program, 129
ftp.htm file, 97–98

›G‹

GIF (Graphic Interchange Format)
    animations, 87–88
    file format, 78
    filename extension, 44
    transparencies, 87–88
GifWeb program, Windows,
        87–88, 256
Gopher protocol, 94, 98–99
Gopher, Internet text-based data, 2

gopher.htm file, 99
gov extension, domain name, 205
graphic artist, Web page develop-
        ment support, 7
GraphicConverter program, Mac,
        79–80, 87–88, 257
graphics, 77–92
    animated GIF, 127–128
    backgrounds, 88–90
    CD-ROM samples, 81
    clip art, 81
    conversions, 79–80
    copyright considerations, 81
    design considerations, 90
    download time considerations,
        23, 78
    file formats, 77–79
    file size considerations, 78
    freelance artists, 81–82
    gif (Graphics Interchange Format)
        filename extension, 44
    horizontal lines, 25, 62–63
    hyperlinks, 25
    image maps, 25, 86–87, 117
    Internet presentations, 3
    jpg (Joint Photographic Experts
        Group) filename extension, 44
    linked border, 85–86
    links, 85–87
    locating, 81–82
    royalty-free clip art, 81
    scanned images, 80
    sources, 79–82
    throbbers, 132
    versus text, 23
    Web page element, 21, 23–25
GTE Internet Solutions, 244

›H‹

hackers, 219
hard drives
    CD-ROM files, 250–257
    Web page folder, 45
head (<HEAD>) HTML tag, 51
headers, table column/row, 108
heading (<H1> through <H6>)
        HTML tags, 61

headings, 60–63
headings.htm file, 61
HEIGHT attribute, table cells, 112
hexadecimal codes, colors, 52
hobby-related Web pages, 5
home pages, index.htm/html filename, 45
horizontal lines, 62–63
horizontal rule (<HR>) HTML tag, 62
horizontal rules, 25
horzrule.htm file, 63
hot spots, image maps, 86, 117
HotDog 16 program, Windows, 158, 257
HotDog Pro program, 158–160, 257
HotDog programs, Windows, 41
htm/html filename extension, 44
HTML (HyperText Markup Language), 3, 14, 39–70
    borrowing source code, 42
    described, 19
    horizontal lines, 62–63
    tags, 40–41
    viewing source code, 41–42
HTML codes
    creating, 41
    horizontal rules, 25
HTML ColourTool program, Mac, 52
HTML documents
    alink (active link) colors, 51
    anchor links, 67–68
    blinking text, 57
    body text, 53–60
    boldface text, 56
    creating, 41
    described, 4
    forms, 101–107
    frames, 113–116
    frameset, 113
    FTP dropbox link, 68
    headings, 60–63
    hexadecimal color codes, 52
    horizontal lines, 62–63
    htm/html filename extension, 44
    indents, 58
    italicized text, 56–57
    line breaks, 54–55
    link colors, 51

links, 63–68
lists, 58–60
monospaced type, 57–58
paragraph breaks, 55
saving as plain text files, 42–43
tables, 107–113
testing in browser prior to publishing, 45–46
text colors, 51
titles, 50–51
vlink (visited link) colors, 51
HTML file, Web address component, 4
HTML tags. See individual tags
HTML/Java programmers, Web page development support, 7
http (HyperText Transfer Protocol), Web address component, 4
hubs, Internet, 200
hybrid CD, described, 149
hypertext links, 2, 85–87

icons
    broken image, 223–224
    removing CD from Windows, 253–254
    used in book, 10
image maps, 86–87, 117
    client-side, 86
    client-side versus server-side, 157
    defined, 25
    graphic links, 25
    hot spots, 86, 117
    map file, 157
    server-side, 86
image.htm file, 82–83
image2.htm file, 86–87
ImageMapper program, Mac, 117, 257
Image Surfer, 132
images
    alignment options, 83–84
    backgrounds, 88–90
    bitmapped, 78
    CD-ROM samples, 81
    copyright considerations, 81
    design considerations, 90

digital camera, 79
GIF versus JPEG, 78
image maps, 86–87, 117
inline, 83–84
Photo CD, 79
raster, 78
scanned, 80
sources, 79–82
vector-based, 78
Web page insertion, 82–84
indents, 58
index.htm file, 65
index.htm/html filename, primary Web page, 45
info extension, domain name, 205
info.htm file, 64
information, text-based, 98–99
inline images, 83–84
installation
    exercise files, 250–252
    Windows programs from CD, 254
internal links, described, 26, 64
Internet connection requirements, 219–220
Internet Explorer, 14
    blinking text non-support, 57
    Komputer Klinic support, 189
    viewing Web page source code, 41–42
    viewing Web pages, 17–19
Internet
    backbone, 2, 201
    connection types, 200–201
    described, 1–2
    development history, 1–2
    e-mail protocol, 94
    FTP (File Transfer Protocol), 2
    Gopher service, 2
    graphic presentations, 3
    HTML (Hypertext Markup Language), 3
    hubs, 200
    hypertext links, 2–3
    ISP (Internet Service Provider), 2
    versus LAN (local area network), 1
    netiquette, 30
    online services access, 175
    porno site scams, 31

protocols, 94–101
services, 94–101
traffic jams, 201–202
InterNIC, domain name registration,
    204–208
ISDN (Integrated Services Digital
    Network), 15, 200–201, 203
ISP (Internet Service Providers), 2,
    241–244
  56K connect speed support, 16
  CGI script source, 101
  America Online, 242
  AT&T WorldNet Service,
    1242–243, 256
  CompuServe, 243
  Concentric, 243
  contract length limitations, 212
  domain name registration
    support, 206
  e-mail accounts, 213
  EarthLink, 243–244
  file download links, 214
  FTP protocol support, 211
  GTE Internet Solutions, 244
  hit statistics, 211
  host fees, 211
  local versus national, 209–210
  locating, 209–214
  online payment processing, 214
  POP (Post Office Protocol)
    accounts, 213
  pricing and terms, 212–213,
    241–244
  PSINet, 244
  T1 connection lines, 210
  traffic charges, 211
  virtual domain hosting, 208
  Web page size limitations, 211
  Web server, 15
italic (<I>) HTML tag, 56–57

♦ J ♦

Java, described, 6
JPEG (Joint Photographic Experts
    Group) file format, 78
jpg (Joint Photographic Experts
    Group) filename extension, 44

♦ K ♦

K56flex technology, Rockwell, 16
keyboard (<KBD>) HTML tag, 58
Kodak, Photo CD images, 79
Komputer Klinic, 188–190

♦ L ♦

LAN (local area network), versus
    Internet, 1
left-aligned graphics, 83–84
lettercase, in passwords, 220
levels, headings, 60–63
line break (<BR>) HTML tag, 40,
    54–55
line breaks, 54–55
lines, horizontal, 62–63
linked graphics, 85–87
links, 63–68
  absolute, 66
  anchors, 67–68
  anonymous FTP site, 98
  colors, 51
  described, 26
  downloadable files, 68
  external, 26, 66
  frame, 116
  FTP dropbox, 68
  FTP files, 96–98
  Gopher sites, 98–99
  graphical, 25, 85–87
  hypertext, 2–3
  image maps, 25, 86–87, 117
  internal, 26, 64–65
  mailto, 30, 94–96
  missing, 66–67
  newsgroups, 100–101
  non-anonymous FTP site, 98
  plug-ins, 124
  relative, 64–65
  sounds, 125–126
  testing in browser prior to publish-
    ing, 45–46
  text-based, 30
  Web page element, 21
lists, 58–60, 104
lists.htm file, 60

LiveImage program, Windows, 117,
    257
local ISP, 209–210
logos, backgrounds, 89
lowercase, passwords, 220
Lucent Technologies, Rockwell
    K56flex technology, 16
Lycos search engine, 228, 230

♦ M ♦

Mac OS
  installing exercise files, 252
  programs, installing and removing,
    255
Macintosh
  html filename extension, 44
  QuickTime movies, 129
  system requirements, 14–15
  Web page editing program
    requirements, 143
Macromedia
  Afterburner program, 29
  Director program, 28–29, 122
  Shockwave plug-in, 28–29,
    122–124
mailing lists, multiple e-mail
    accounts, 213
mailto links
  automatic e-mail, 94–96
  Web page feedback, 30
map files, server-side image map, 157
MARGINHEIGHT attribute, frame
    HTML tag, 116
MARGINWIDTH attribute, frame
    HTML tag, 116
MasterSoft, Word for Word
    program, 146
megabits, described, 201
menu (<MENU>) HTML tag, 59
messages, HTTP/1.0 404 Object Not
    Found, 66
METHOD attribute, form tag, 102
Microsoft FrontPad program,
    167–170
Microsoft FrontPage program,
    151–154
Microsoft Network, Web publishing
    non-support, 187–188

Microsoft Outlook program, 213
Microsoft Word 97 program, 17, 171
middle-aligned graphics, 83–84
modems
　connect speeds, 200–201
　FCC download speed
　　regulations, 16
　ISDN, 15
　online service 56K connect speed
　　support, 16
　speed ratings, 15–16
　Web publishing requirements,
　　15–17
monospaced type, 57–58
mov (QuickTime) filename exten-
　sion, 44
movies
　avi (Windows AVI) filename
　　extension, 44
　flattening, 129
　mov (QuickTime) filename
　　extension, 44
　QuickTime, 128–129
multimedia
　animated GIF, 127–128
　animations, 28–29
　cost considerations, 122–124
　described, 121
　download time considerations, 124
　file formats, 128
　file size considerations, 124
　freeware, 28
　online slide shows, 130–132
　plug-in requirements, 123–124
　pros/cons, 122–125
　public domain, 124
　QuickTime movies, 128–129
　Shockwave plug-in, 28–29
　sounds, 125–127
　system requirements, 122–124
　Web browser plug-ins, 28
　Web sources, 132
MyInternetBusinessPage program,
　160–162
MySoftware, MyInternetBusinessPage
　program, 160–162
My Shareware Page, 132

N

national ISP, 209–210
net extension, domain name, 205
netiquette, described, 30
NetObjects Fusion program,
　163–165
Netscape Composer program,
　165–167
Netscape Navigator, 3, 14
　blinking text support, 57
　viewing Web page source code,
　　41–42
　viewing Web pages, 17–19
networks, LAN (local area
　network), 1
newsgroups, 100–101, 222
newsgrp.htm file, 101
nom extension, domain name, 205
non-anonymous FTP site, 98
Notepad, text editor, 17
NOWRAP attribute, table cells, 111
numbered list (<OL>) HTML tag, 59

O

online forms, 101–107
online services
　See also ISP
　CompuServe, 181–185
　Internet access, 175
　Komputer Klinic, 188–190
　Microsoft Network, 187–188
　Prodigy, 185–187
　Web publishing, 175–192
online slide shows, 130–132
operating systems, Web servers, 15
org extension, domain name, 205

P

page2.htm file, 85–86
PageMill program, 19
pages, uploading, 217–232
Paint Shop Pro program, Windows,
　79–80
paragraph break (<B>)HTML tag, 55
paragraph breaks, 55

paragraphs, indented, 58
password, 219
personal Web pages, 5
personal Web servers, cost consider-
　ations, 202–203
phone lines, 200–201, 203
Photo CD images, 79
photorealistic color, described, 78
plain text (ASCII) file format, 42–43
plug-ins, 28–29
　See also programs
　described, 28, 123–124
　freeware, 28
　links, 124
　multimedia, 28
　QuickTime, 128–129
　Shockwave, 28–29, 122–124
　Web site visitor considerations,
　　28, 124
pointer document, frames, 114
POP (Post Office Protocol), 213
pornography, moral issues, 31
postal address, commercial Web
　page component, 30
posting Web pages, 217–232
preformatted (<PRE>)HTML tag, 58
prices, online service providers,
　242–244
primary Web page, index.htm/
　index.html filename, 45
Prodigy, 16, 185–187
programmers, Web page develop-
　ment support, 7
programming
　CGI (Common Gateway
　　Interface), 27
　HTML, 49–70
programming languages
　HTML, 14, 19
　Java, 6
programs
　See individual program names
　See plug-ins
　site management, 145
　Web page editing, 142–147
　WYSIWYG, 142
proofreading, prior to publishing, 30

proportional font, described, 57
protocol, 218
PSINet, 244
public domain, 124

▸Q▸

qt.mov file, 128
Qualcomm, Eudora program, 213
QuickTime movies, 128–129
  mov filename extension, 44

▸R▸

radio buttons, forms, 105
raster images, 78
raw data, upload Web pages, 221, 222
raw HTML code, viewing, 41–42
rec extension, domain name, 205
relative links, 64–65
requirements
  multimedia, 122–124
  Web page editing programs, 143
  Web servers, 200, 202–203
RGB Color Box program, Windows, 52, 257
right-aligned graphics, 83–84
RoadRunner cable modem services, 124–125
Rockwell K56flex technology, 16
rows, 108
ROWS attribute, frame HTML tag, 115
ROWSPAN attribute, table cells, 112
royalty-free clip art, 81
rules, horizontal, 25

▸S▸

sample (<SAMPLE>) HTML tag, 58
Sausage Software, HotDog Pro program, 158–160
scams, porno sites, 31
scanners, image source, 80
screens, Yahoo!, 228
scripts
  CGI (Common Gateway

Interface), 27
  described, 101
SCROLLING attribute, frame HTML tag, 115–116
scrolling lists, forms, 104
search engines, 81–82, 227–231
server name, 219
server-side image maps, 86, 157
servers
  FTP, 68, 96–98
  Web, 3, 15, 199–216
shareware
  ImageMapper program, Mac, 117
  LiveImage program, Windows, 117
Shockwave plug-in, 28–29, 122–124
shopping cart application, described, 6
SimpleText, text editor, Mac, 17
site management, described, 145
SiteMill program, 145
slide shows, 130–132
SLIDES folder, 130
software requirements, Web publishing, 14–15, 17–19
sound.wav file, 125
sounds, 44, 125–127
source code, viewing, 41–42
store extension, domain name, 205
strong (<STRONG>) HTML tag, 56
subdirectory, Web address component, 4
submit buttons, forms, 105
system requirements, 14–15
  CD-ROM, 249–250
  multimedia, 122–124
  Web page editing programs, 143
  Web servers, 200, 202–203

▸T▸

T1 phone lines, 201
T3 phone lines, 201
tables, 107–113
  described, 28
  Web page element, 26–28
tables.htm file, 112
tags, HTML, 40–41
taskbar, defined, 145

technical support, Web page development, 7
telephone lines, 201–203
telephone numbers
  America Online, 242
  AT&T WorldNet Service, 242
  commercial Web page component, 30
  CompuServe, 243
  Concentric, 243
  EarthLink, 243
  GTE Internet Solutions, 244
  PSINet, 244
teletype (<TT>) HTML tag, 58
Telnet protocol, described, 94
templates, InterNIC preformatted document, 206
test1.htm file, 114
test2.htm file, 114
text, 21–23, 51, 53–60
text area, forms, 105
text editors, 17
text files, FTP, 221
text only files, 222
text-based
  data, 2
  information, Gopher sites, 98–99
  browser graphics non-support, 30
text-only browsers, 30
text.htm file, 53
throbbers, described, 132
TIFF (Tagged Image File Format), 78
Time Warner, RoadRunner cable modem services, 124–125
title (<TITLE>) HTML tag, 50–51
titles
  HTML documents, 50–51
  table, 107
top-aligned graphics, 83–84
traffic jams, 201–202
transparent GIFs, 87–88
troubleshooting
  CD-ROM, 257–258
  Web pages, 222–225
Tucows, 132
txt (ASCII text) filename extension, 44
type.htm file, 58

• U •

under constructionitis, Web site turn-off, 31
UNIX, Web server operating system, 15
uploading, Web pages, 217–232
upper case, passwords, 220
URL (Uniform Resource Locator), 3–4
US Robotics, x2 technology, 16
Usenet, 222
Usenet newsgroup protocol, 94, 100–101
user name, 219
uuencode files, 222

• V •

VALIGN attribute, table cells, 112
variable (<VAR>) HTML tag, 56
vector-based images, described, 78
virtual domain hosting, ISP, 208
vlink (visited link), colors, 51
voice-grade telephone lines, 200

• W •

wav (WAVE)
   file format, 125
   filename extension, 44
Web address
   anatomy, 3–4
   URL components, 3–4
Web authoring, described, 154
Web browsers
   cannot locate page to link to, 224
   described, 3
   download sites, 18
   filename extensions, 43–45
   frames support, 18
   Microsoft Internet Explorer, 14, 17–19
   Netscape Communicator, 17–19
   Netscape Navigator, 3, 14, 17–19
   plug-ins, 28, 123–124
   supported sound file formats, 125
   testing Web pages prior to publishing, 45–46, 52–53

text-only, 30
viewing raw HTML code, 41–42
viewing Web pages, 17
web extension, domain name, 205
Web pages
   animated GIF, 127–128
   background sounds, 126–127
   broken image icon, 223–224
   browser cannot locate link, 224
   checking after uploading, 222
   color considerations, 30
   commercial, 6
   content essentials, 29–30
   counters, 226
   described, 2–3
   design elements, 21–32
   editing programs, 142–147
   file naming conventions, 43–45
   filename extensions, 43–45
   focus, 5
   form addition, 101–107
   forms, 26–28
   frames, 26–28
   frames addition, 113–116
   getting listed on search engine, 227
   graphic elements, 21, 23–25
   graphics don't load, 223
   graphics file format support, 78
   graphics sources, 79–82
   hard drive folder storage, 45
   hobby-related, 5
   image insertion, 82–84
   index.htm/html filename, 45
   line breaks, 40
   link elements, 22, 26
   links don't work, 224
   mailto link feedback, 30
   online slide shows, 130–132
   only seeing a list of files, 223
   overwork by author, 223
   personal, 5
   posting, 217–232
   proofreading, 45–46
   QuickTime movies, 128–129
   saving as plain text, 42–43
   shopping cart application, 6
   supported file formats, 42–43
   table addition, 107–113

tables, 26–28
technical support, 7
testing prior to publishing, 45–46
text element, 21–23
text-based links, 30
tracking number of visitors, 226
under constructionitis, 31
updating, 231
uploading, 217–232
USA Today approach, 23
uses for, 4–6
view with a different browser, 225
viewing, 14
viewing source code, 41–42
Web publishing
   America Online, 176–181
   CompuServe, 181–185
   Komputer Klinic, 188–190
   Microsoft Network non-support, 187–188
   modem requirements, 15–17
   online services, 175–192
   Prodigy, 185–187
   software requirements, 17–19
   system requirements, 14–15
Web servers, 199–216
   connect speeds, 200–201
   cost considerations, 202–203
   described, 3, 15, 200
   domain name, 203–209
   Internet backbone, 201
   Internet hubs, 200
   phone line types, 200–201
   server-side image maps, 86
   software requirements, 200, 202–203
   system requirements, 200, 202–203
   traffic jams, 201–202
Web sites
   AltaVista, 228
   America Online, 242
   Animated GIF Gallery, 132
   AT&T WorldNet Service, 242
   Better Business Bureau, 242
   cable modems, 201–202
   Clip Art Searcher, 81–82
   CompuServe, 243
   Concentric, 243

EarthLink, 243
Excite, 228
For Dummies, 142
GTE Internet Solutions, 244
IAHC (International Ad Hoc
  Committee), 205
Image Surfer, 132
InterNIC, 206
Komputer Klinic, 3–4, 18, 142,
  188–190
Lycos, 230
MacUser Software Central, 52
My Shareware Page, 132
porno site scams, 31
Prodigy Web publishing support
  area, 186
PSINet, 244
QuickTime plug-in, 128
reviews of ISPs, 241
Tucows, 132
WebCrawler, 230
Yahoo!, 27
WebCrawler search engine, 230–231
WIDTH attribute, 109–110, 112
Windows NT, Web server operating
  system, 15
Windows PC
  htm filename extension, 44
  system requirements, 14–15
  Web page editing program
    requirements, 143
Windows programs
  installing from CD, 254
  removing from PC, 254–255
Windows, installing exercise files,
  250–251
Word for Word program, 146
word processors, 17, 42–43
Wordpad, text editor, 17
WordPerfect version 7 program, 17,
  170–171
WS_FTP program, 186–187,
  218, 257
WWW (World Wide Web), 2–3
WYSIWYG (what you see is what
  you get), 19, 142

X

x2 technology, US Robotics, 16

Y

Yahoo!, 227–228
  listing your Web pages, 227
  review of ISPs, 242
  Web designer keyword search, 82

AT&T WorldNet℠ Service

A World of Possibilities...

Thank you for selecting AT&T WorldNet Service — it's the Internet as only AT&T can bring it to you. With AT&T WorldNet Service, a world of infinite possibilities is now within your reach. Research virtually any subject. Stay abreast of current events. Participate in online newsgroups. Purchase merchandise from leading retailers. Send and receive electronic mail.

AT&T WorldNet Service is rapidly becoming the preferred way of accessing the Internet. It was recently awarded one of the most highly coveted awards in the computer industry, *PC Computing*'s 1996 MVP Award for Best Internet Service Provider. Now, more than ever, it's the best way to stay in touch with the people, ideas, and information that are important to you.

You need a computer with a mouse, a modem, a phone line, and the enclosed software. That's all. We've taken care of the rest.

If You Can Point and Click, You're There

With AT&T WorldNet Service, finding the information you want on the Internet is easier than you ever imagined it could be. You can surf the Net within minutes. And find almost anything you want to know — from the weather in Paris, Texas — to the cost of a ticket to Paris, France. You're just a point and click away. It's that easy.

AT&T WorldNet Service features specially customized industry-leading browsers integrated with advanced Internet directories and search engines. The result is an Internet service that sets a new standard for ease of use — virtually everywhere you want to go is a point and click away, making it a snap to navigate the Internet.

When you go online with AT&T WorldNet Service, you'll benefit from being connected to the Internet by the world leader in networking. We offer you fast access of up to 28.8 Kbps in more than 215 cities throughout the U.S. that will make going online as easy as picking up your phone.

Online Help and Advice
24 Hours a Day, 7 Days a Week

Before you begin exploring the Internet, you may want to take a moment to check two useful sources of information.

If you're new to the Internet, from the AT&T WorldNet Service home page at www.worldnet.att.net, click on the Net Tutorial hyperlink for a quick explanation of unfamiliar terms and useful advice about exploring the Internet.

Another useful source of information is the HELP icon. The area contains pertinent, time saving information-intensive reference tips, and topics such as Accounts & Billing, Trouble Reporting, Downloads & Upgrades, Security Tips, Network Hot Spots, Newsgroups, Special Announcements, etc.

Whether online or off-line, 24 hours a day, seven days a week, we will provide World Class technical expertise and fast, reliable responses to your questions. To reach AT&T WorldNet Customer Care, call **1-800-400-1447**.

Nothing is more important to us than making sure that your Internet experience is a truly enriching and satisfying one.

Safeguard Your Online Purchases

AT&T WorldNet Service is committed to making the Internet a safe and convenient way to transact business. By registering and continuing to charge your AT&T WorldNet Service to your AT&T Universal Card, you'll enjoy peace of mind whenever you shop the Internet. Should your account number be compromised on the Net, you won't be liable for any online transactions charged to your AT&T Universal Card by a person who is not an authorized user.*

*Today, cardmembers may be liable for the first $50 of charges made by a person who is not an authorized user, which will not be imposed under this program as long as the cardmember notifies AT&T Universal Card of the loss within 24 hours and otherwise complies with the Cardmember Agreement. Refer to Cardmember Agreement for definition of authorized user.

Minimum System Requirements

IBM-Compatible Personal Computer Users:
- IBM-compatible personal computer with 486SX or higher processor
- 8MB of RAM (or more for better performance)
- 15–36MB of available hard disk space to install software, depending on platform
  (14–21MB to use service after installation, depending on platform)
- Graphics system capable of displaying 256 colors
- 14,400 bps modem connected to an outside phone line and not a LAN or ISDN line
- Microsoft Windows 3.1x or Windows 95

Macintosh Users:
- Macintosh 68030 or higher (including 68LC0X0 models and all Power Macintosh models)
- System 7.5.3 Revision 2 or higher for PCI Power Macintosh models: System 7.1 or higher for all 680X0 and non-PCI Power Macintosh models
- Mac TCP 2.0.6 or Open Transport 1.1 or higher
- 8MB of RAM (minimum) with Virtual Memory turned on or RAM Doubler; 16MB recommended for Power Macintosh users
- 12MB of available hard disk space (15MB recommended)
- 14,400 bps modem connected to an outside phone line and not a LAN or ISDN line
- Color or 256 gray-scale monitor
- Apple Guide 1.2 or higher (if you want to view online help)
  If you are uncertain of the configuration of your Macintosh computer, consult your Macintosh User's guide or call Apple at 1-800-767-2775.

Installation Tips and Instructions

- If you have other Web browsers or online software, please consider uninstalling them according to the vendor's instructions.
- If you are installing AT&T WorldNet Service on a computer with Local Area Networking, please contact your LAN administrator for setup instructions.
- At the end of installation, you may be asked to restart your computer. Don't attempt the registration process until you have done so.

IBM-compatible PC users:
- Insert the CD-ROM into the CD-ROM drive on your computer.
- Select *File/Run* (for Windows 3.1x) or *Start/Run* (for Windows 95 if setup did not start automatically).
- Type *D:\setup.exe* (or change the "D" if your CD-ROM is another drive).
- Click *OK*.
- Follow the onscreen instructions to install and register.

Macintosh users:
- Disable all extensions except Apple CD-ROM and Foreign Files Access extensions.
- Restart Computer.
- Insert the CD-ROM into the CD-ROM drive on your computer.
- Double-click the *Install AT&T WorldNet Service* icon.
- Follow the onscreen instructions to install. (Upon restarting your Macintosh, AT&T WorldNet Service Account Setup automatically starts.)
- Follow the onscreen instructions to register.

Registering with AT&T WorldNet Service

After you have connected with AT&T WorldNet online registration service, you will be presented with a series of screens that confirm billing information and prompt you for additional account set-up data.

The following is a list of registration tips and comments that will help you during the registration process.

I. Use one of the following registration codes, which can also be found in Appendix C of *Dummies 101: Creating Web Pages*. Use L5SQIM631 if you are an AT&T long-distance residential customer or L5SQIM632 if you use another long-distance phone company.

II. During registration, you will need to supply your name, address, and valid credit card number, and choose an account information security word, e-mail name, and e-mail password. You will also be requested to select your preferred price plan at this time. (We advise that you use all lowercase letters when assigning an e-mail ID and security code, since they are easier to remember.)

III. If you make a mistake and exit or get disconnected during the registration process prematurely, simply click on "Create New Account." Do not click on "Edit Existing Account."

IV. When choosing your local access telephone number, you will be given several options. Please choose the one nearest to you. Please note that calling a number within your area does not guarantee that the call is free.

Connecting to AT&T WorldNet Service

When you have finished installing and registering with AT&T WorldNet Service, you are ready to access the Internet. Make sure your modem and phone line are available before attempting to connect to the service.

For Windows 95 users:
- Double-click on the ***Connect to AT&T WorldNet Service*** icon on your desktop.
  OR
- Select ***Start, Programs, AT&T WorldNet Software, Connect to AT&T WorldNet Service.***

For Windows 3.x users:
- Double-click on the ***Connect to AT&T WorldNet Service*** icon located in the AT&T WorldNet Service group.

For Macintosh users:
- Double-click on the ***AT&T WorldNet Service*** icon in the AT&T WorldNet Service folder.

Choose the Plan That's Right for You

The Internet is for everyone, whether at home or at work. In addition to making the time you spend online productive and fun, we're also committed to making it affordable. Choose one of two price plans: unlimited usage access or hourly usage access. The latest pricing information can be obtained during online registration. No matter which plan you use, we're confident that after you take advantage of everything AT&T WorldNet Service has to offer, you'll wonder how you got along without it.

©1997 AT&T Corp. All Rights Reserved. AT&T WorldNet is a service name of AT&T Corp., Microsoft and Windows are registered trademarks of Microsoft Corp., Macintosh is a trademark of Apple Computer.

AT&T

Explore our AT&T WorldNet Service site at http://www.att.com/worldnet.

IDG Books Worldwide, Inc.
End-User License Agreement

<u>READ THIS</u>. You should carefully read these terms and conditions before opening the software packet(s) included with this book ("Book"). This is a license agreement ("Agreement") between you and IDG Books Worldwide, Inc. ("IDGB"). By opening the accompanying software packet(s), you acknowledge that you have read and accept the following terms and conditions. If you do not agree and do not want to be bound by such terms and conditions, promptly return the Book and the unopened software packet(s) to the place you obtained them for a full refund.

1. **License Grant.** IDGB grants to you (either an individual or entity) a nonexclusive license to use one copy of the enclosed software program(s) (collectively, the "Software") solely for your own personal or business purposes on a single computer (whether a standard computer or a workstation component of a multiuser network). The Software is in use on a computer when it is loaded into temporary memory (RAM) or installed into permanent memory (hard disk, CD-ROM, or other storage device). IDGB reserves all rights not expressly granted herein.

2. **Ownership.** IDGB is the owner of all right, title, and interest, including copyright, in and to the compilation of the Software recorded on the disk(s) or CD-ROM ("Software Media"). Copyright to the individual programs recorded on the Software Media is owned by the author or other authorized copyright owner of each program. Ownership of the Software and all proprietary rights relating thereto remain with IDGB and its licensers.

3. **Restrictions on Use and Transfer.**

   (a) You may only (i) make one copy of the Software for backup or archival purposes, or (ii) transfer the Software to a single hard disk, provided that you keep the original for backup or archival purposes. You may not (i) rent or lease the Software, (ii) copy or reproduce the Software through a LAN or other network system or through any computer subscriber system or bulletin-board system, or (iii) modify, adapt, or create derivative works based on the Software.

   (b) You may not reverse engineer, decompile, or disassemble the Software. You may transfer the Software and user documentation on a permanent basis, provided that the transferee agrees to accept the terms and conditions of this Agreement and you retain no copies. If the Software is an update or has been updated, any transfer must include the most recent update and all prior versions.

4. **Restrictions on Use of Individual Programs.** You must follow the individual requirements and restrictions detailed for each individual program in Appendix C, "About the CD," of this Book. These limitations are also contained in the individual license agreements recorded on the Software Media. These limitations may include a requirement that after using the program for a specified period of time, the user must pay a registration fee or discontinue use. By opening the Software packet(s), you will be agreeing to abide by the licenses and restrictions for these individual programs that are detailed in Appendix C, "About the CD," and on the Software Media. None of the material on this Software Media or listed in this Book may ever be redistributed, in original or modified form, for commercial purposes.

5. **Limited Warranty**.

    (a) IDGB warrants that the Software and Software Media are free from defects in materials and workmanship under normal use for a period of sixty (60) days from the date of purchase of this Book. If IDGB receives notification within the warranty period of defects in materials or workmanship, IDGB will replace the defective Software Media.

    (b) **IDGB AND THE AUTHOR OF THE BOOK DISCLAIM ALL OTHER WARRANTIES, EXPRESS OR IMPLIED, INCLUDING WITHOUT LIMITATION IMPLIED WARRANTIES OF MERCHANTABILITY AND FITNESS FOR A PARTICULAR PURPOSE, WITH RESPECT TO THE SOFTWARE, THE PROGRAMS, THE SOURCE CODE CONTAINED THEREIN, AND/OR THE TECHNIQUES DESCRIBED IN THIS BOOK. IDGB DOES NOT WARRANT THAT THE FUNCTIONS CONTAINED IN THE SOFTWARE WILL MEET YOUR REQUIREMENTS OR THAT THE OPERATION OF THE SOFTWARE WILL BE ERROR FREE.**

    (c) This limited warranty gives you specific legal rights, and you may have other rights that vary from jurisdiction to jurisdiction.

6. **Remedies**.

    (a) IDGB's entire liability and your exclusive remedy for defects in materials and workmanship shall be limited to replacement of the Software Media, which may be returned to IDGB with a copy of your receipt at the following address: Software Media Fulfillment Department, Attn.: *Dummies 101: Creating Web Pages*, IDG Books Worldwide, Inc., 7260 Shadeland Station, Ste. 100, Indianapolis, IN 46256, or call 800-762-2974. Please allow three to four weeks for delivery. This Limited Warranty is void if failure of the Software Media has resulted from accident, abuse, or misapplication. Any replacement Software Media will be warranted for the remainder of the original warranty period or thirty (30) days, whichever is longer.

    (b) In no event shall IDGB or the author be liable for any damages whatsoever (including without limitation damages for loss of business profits, business interruption, loss of business information, or any other pecuniary loss) arising from the use of or inability to use the Book or the Software, even if IDGB has been advised of the possibility of such damages.

    (c) Because some jurisdictions do not allow the exclusion or limitation of liability for consequential or incidental damages, the above limitation or exclusion may not apply to you.

7. **U.S. Government Restricted Rights**. Use, duplication, or disclosure of the Software by the U.S. Government is subject to restrictions stated in paragraph (c)(1)(ii) of the Rights in Technical Data and Computer Software clause of DFARS 252.227-7013, and in subparagraphs (a) through (d) of the Commercial Computer–Restricted Rights clause at FAR 52.227-19, and in similar clauses in the NASA FAR supplement, when applicable.

8. **General**. This Agreement constitutes the entire understanding of the parties and revokes and supersedes all prior agreements, oral or written, between them and may not be modified or amended except in a writing signed by both parties hereto that specifically refers to this Agreement. This Agreement shall take precedence over any other documents that may be in conflict herewith. If any one or more provisions contained in this Agreement are held by any court or tribunal to be invalid, illegal, or otherwise unenforceable, each and every other provision shall remain in full force and effect.

Installation Instructions

The CD at the back of this book contains both exercise files and software programs. The exercise files are sample documents that you use while following along with the lessons in the book or that show you what your documents should look like after the lessons. You need to put these files on your hard drive. After you're done with the book, you can remove the files easily.

Some of the extra programs are integrated with the lessons in the book; other programs are just cool stuff that you'll find useful in creating Web Pages.

Here's how to install the exercise files in Windows. If you are using a Mac OS computer, see Appendix C, "About the CD," for more details. Also see Appendix C regardless of your operating system to install the extra software on the CD.

1. **Insert the Dummies 101 CD (label side up) into your computer's CD drive.**

   If you use Windows 95, the installation program should begin in a few moments. If the program does not start after 30 seconds, go to Step 2. If the program does, go to Step 4.

2. **If the installation program doesn't start automatically, click on the Start button and click on Run in Windows 95, or click File⇨Run in Windows 3.1 Program Manager.**

3. **In the dialog box that appears, type** d:\seticon.exe **(if your CD drive is not drive D, substitute the appropriate letter for** d**) and click on OK.**

4. **Click on OK in the message window.**

   After a moment, a program group called Dummies 101 is installed in Windows. Then another message appears, asking whether you want to use the CD now.

5. **Click on Yes to use the CD now.**

6. **Read the End-User License Agreement and click on Agree.**

   If you don't agree to the terms of the license agreement, you can't continue with the installation. After you click on Agree, the Dummies 101: Creating Web Pages For Windows installation window appears.

7. **Click on Install Exercise Files and follow the on-screen instructions.**

   After the exercise files install, you return to the installation screen.

8. **Click on the Exit button in the lower-right corner of the window.**

   The program asks whether you really, really want to exit.

9. **Click on Yes to exit, and you're done.**

IDG BOOKS WORLDWIDE REGISTRATION CARD

RETURN THIS REGISTRATION CARD FOR FREE CATALOG

Title of this book: **Dummies 101®: Creating Web Pages**

My overall rating of this book: ❏ Very good [1] ❏ Good [2] ❏ Satisfactory [3] ❏ Fair [4] ❏ Poor [5]

How I first heard about this book:

❏ Found in bookstore; name: [6] _____ ❏ Book review: [7]

❏ Advertisement: [8] _____ ❏ Catalog: [9]

❏ Word of mouth; heard about book from friend, co-worker, etc.: [10] _____ ❏ Other: [11]

What I liked most about this book:

_____

_____

What I would change, add, delete, etc., in future editions of this book:

_____

_____

Other comments: _____

_____

Number of computer books I purchase in a year: ❏ 1 [12] ❏ 2-5 [13] ❏ 6-10 [14] ❏ More than 10 [15]

I would characterize my computer skills as: ❏ Beginner [16] ❏ Intermediate [17] ❏ Advanced [18] ❏ Professional [19]

I use ❏ DOS [20] ❏ Windows [21] ❏ OS/2 [22] ❏ Unix [23] ❏ Macintosh [24] ❏ Other: [25]_____

(please specify)

I would be interested in new books on the following subjects:

(please check all that apply, and use the spaces provided to identify specific software)

❏ Word processing: [26] _____ ❏ Spreadsheets: [27] _____

❏ Data bases: [28] _____ ❏ Desktop publishing: [29] _____

❏ File Utilities: [30] _____ ❏ Money management: [31] _____

❏ Networking: [32] _____ ❏ Programming languages: [33] _____

❏ Other: [34] _____

I use a PC at (please check all that apply): ❏ home [35] ❏ work [36] ❏ school [37] ❏ other: [38] _____

The disks I prefer to use are ❏ 5.25 [39] ❏ 3.5 [40] ❏ other: [41]_____

I have a CD ROM: ❏ yes [42] ❏ no [43]

I plan to buy or upgrade computer hardware this year: ❏ yes [44] ❏ no [45]

I plan to buy or upgrade computer software this year: ❏ yes [46] ❏ no [47]

Name: _____ Business title: [48] _____ Type of Business: [49] _____

Address (❏ home [50] ❏ work [51]/Company name: _____)

Street/Suite# _____

City [52]/State [53]/Zipcode [54]: _____ Country [55] _____

❏ **I liked this book!** You may quote me by name in future
IDG Books Worldwide promotional materials.

My daytime phone number is _____

IDG BOOKS

THE WORLD OF
COMPUTER
KNOWLEDGE

 # YES!

Please keep me informed about IDG's World of Computer Knowledge.
Send me the latest IDG Books catalog.

NO POSTAGE
NECESSARY
IF MAILED
IN THE
UNITED STATES

BUSINESS REPLY MAIL

FIRST CLASS MAIL   PERMIT NO. 2605   FOSTER CITY, CALIFORNIA

IDG Books Worldwide
919 E Hillsdale Blvd, STE 400
Foster City, CA 94404-9691